Critical Muslim 32

Music

T0333882

Critical Muslim is published quarterly by C. Hurst & Co. (Publishers) Ltd. on behalf of and in conjunction with Critical Muslim Ltd. and the Muslim Institute, London.

All editorial correspondence to Muslim Institute, CAN Mezzanine, 49–51 East Road, London N1 6AH, United Kingdom.
E-mail: editorial@criticalmuslim.com

C. Hurst & Co (Publishers) Ltd., 41 Great Russell Street, London WC1B 3PL

ISBN: 978-1-78738-219-0 ISSN: 2048-8475

To subscribe or place an order by credit/debit card or cheque (pounds sterling only) please contact Kathleen May at the Hurst address above or e-mail kathleen@hurstpub.co.uk

Tel: 020 7255 2201

A one-year subscription, inclusive of postage (four issues), costs £50 (UK), £65 (Europe) and £75 (rest of the world), this includes full access to the *Critical Muslim* series and archive online. Digital only subscription is £3.30 per month.

Critical Muslim

Subscribe to Critical Muslim

Now in its eighth year in print, *Critical Muslim* is also available online. Users can access the site for just £3.30 per month – or for those with a print subscription it is included as part of the package. In return, you'll get access to everything in the series (including our entire archive), and a clean, accessible reading experience for desktop computers and handheld devices — entirely free of advertising.

Full subscription

The print edition of *Critical Muslim* is published quarterly in January, April, July and October. As a subscriber to the print edition, you'll receive new issues directly to your door, as well as full access to our digital archive.

United Kingdom £50/year
Europe £65/year
Rest of the World £75/year

Digital Only

Immediate online access to *Critical Muslim*

Browse the full *Critical Muslim* archive

Cancel any time

£3.30 per month

www.criticalmuslim.io

CONTENTS

MUSIC

ARTS AND LETTERS

REVIEWS

ET CETERA

Sahad and the Nataal Patchwork during the 7th Festival Coeur en Or.
Photo: Estrella Sendra (2019)

MUSIC

INTRODUCTION: PLAY ON

Samia Rahman

I could feel the sweat trickling down the back of my neck. The air was rarefied, and as I breathed in it seemed inexplicably cold. I was wearing an above-the-knee strappy dress with opaque tights. It was too hot to wear tights but I hadn't been out in public with bare legs since I was eleven years old and I was not about to start now. Plumes of dry ice periodically wafted over the crowd, reducing all vision so I could barely see my hand in front of my face. In those moments I could have been anywhere, set adrift by the hypnotic, rhythmic beats of the tracks as they pounded from the makeshift sound system with Josh Wink's *Higher. State. Of. Consciousness.* Agitated by an enthusiastic smoke machine, I asked someone whether the fog was toxic. Apparently not. It was just vaporised carbon dioxide, or was it liquid nitrogen. What certainly was toxic, however, was the sea of lit cigarettes lighting up the cavernous room like fireflies. Also lit up were everyone's eyes. Wide.

I had been to a club before, with school friends to celebrate finishing our A levels. The type of place which would refuse you entry if you were wearing trainers. Where the music was cheesy but dance-able. Where everyone was dressed smart/casual and would get drunk and obnoxious, and the atmosphere was heavy with aggression and misogyny. Resolutely sober I felt awkward and a bit revolted. It was not my kind of place at all. This, however, was an entirely different experience. We had trekked through a faceless industrial estate in London's Docklands, functional and un-pretty buildings forming our landscape deep in urbanity but far from all things residential. We only knew we were getting close to our destination as the heavy thump of the bass, suddenly discernible, became gradually louder and eventually deafening. The derelict warehouse was like a huge void, and once inside you had no choice, actually no other desire, than to surrender to the music. There was a bar selling alcohol and many people had taken recreational drugs, but I detected no air of menace. What I did feel was the unifying effect of the trance beats culminating in a simultaneous feeling of collective purpose, and internal expansion. The music captivated every single being, sending them into a state of seamless, unadulterated ecstasy. In Raving Iran, Jasmin Irscheid mentions the impossibility of drawing neat parallels between raves in Europe, like the ones I have attended, and those in Iran, where the stakes are far higher. Organising and attending techno raves are criminal acts in the Islamic Republic, whereas all we feared was the arrival of the police to shut everything down. But ultimately, escape through pleasure, a pride in the purity and quality of the music, the bonding and highly intimate collective experience of dancing with abandon in the company of equally ecstatic revellers, is a universal tumult.

It is not a solely universal emotional response that music elicits. Academics researching cognitive psychology recently discovered the way in which listening to music you love, impacts the brain. When hearing a favourite piece of music, particularly one that has a 'drop', having built up to a momentous crescendo, the listener's heart rate increases, pupils dilate and dopamine, a common neurotransmitter in the brain, is released. Dopamine has been associated with activities that humans depend upon in order to survive, such as eating and sex. Listening to music has never before been considered a pleasure vital to our existence. However, the fact that two distinct parts of the brain are activated, releasing dopamine at the exact moment of peak pleasure when listening to a much cherished passage of music, and also the moment just before it, when we feel the anticipation of our favourite part of the song, indicates that music is far more biologically significant than we previously assumed. We all know that listening to music can be relaxing, invigorating, and calming, and it is the release of tension combined with emotional catharsis that bestows so much pleasure. In his Last Word on Recycled Muslim, C Scott Jordan delves further into the intricacies of neuroscience to explain why some songs, with their irritatingly catchy use of repetition, manage to get into our heads, and play out our internal audio system on an incessant loop whether we like it or not.

Whether in Iran or in London, once you step out from the linguistic templates that confine and contract what it means to listen to and enjoy tunes, what opens up is endless possibilities of escape. As the music takes over, the listener is invited to clamber into the empty chambers that exist between the lyrics and devour those feelings that are inspired, that rise up within our complicated, contradictory selves, and shake off those states that have made-to-measure labels, or expected outcomes. Instead, hidden depths can be accessed by feeling around in the non-illuminated spaces for the non-conformity that is out there, and by using enlightenment to cast light where previously only dark chasms stretch out. In his review of *Blinded By The Light*, based on the book by Sarfraz Manzoor, Shaizir Aly relates to Manzoor's deeply profound connection with the lyrics of Bruce Springsteen's songs. The words he sang spoke to him, they articulated his pent up teenage angst, those songs made sense of everything he was feeling, hoping, dreaming and fearing. And to share this sublime connection with strangers at a gig or at a club or at a classical concert, as Jeremy Henzell-Thomas movingly reminisces in his essay, is a musical frisson for the soul that can be compared to very few other collective experiences. Henzell-Thomas laments the reductive 'music is haram' narrative, pointing out the healing potential of music. He cites the research undertaken by the neurologist Oliver Sacks who has spoken of the way in which sufferers of dementia and Alzheimers can be 'reached' through the playing of pieces of music they are known to have once cherished.

Whether it is techno or another genre of music drawn from anywhere in the world, the ability to be catapulted into an unexpected mental space, either in the form of collective, shared experience with others or as part of a deeply introspective, inner journey, reigniting almost-forgotten memories and being transported to the past, the potential for untold pleasure, self-knowledge, healing and escape, exists. In times of crisis, illness or difficulty, the lyrics of a song suddenly speak to us or the melody melts away our worries. We all know the song, 'Last Night The DJ Saved my Life', and this is how Leyla Jagiella describes her relationship with the late, great Meena Kumari's art. 'Meena Kumari is somewhat of a patron saint of the broken hearted. And I do actually often invoke her, like an actual patron saint. I have done so often in my own times of heartbreak. But also in far more mundane moments. In moments when I need the strength of a woman who has never stopped giving beauty to the world even though the world broke her. A woman who continues to offer her allure to the world even beyond her death, through her heartfelt and exquisite songs that offer comfort to those of us who have ever longed for a love that society seeks to deny.' Forbidden love, unrequited love, disappointed love, love that society chooses not to understand; fractured love suddenly coheres and is given the kiss of life in song, in the iconic vision of a woman who embodies the tragedy of the heart through her enchanting voice and sublime elegance.

Music can be a balm on a world so fraught that it is easy to feel disconnected. We are encouraged to put the best versions of ourselves out there by posting on Facebook and curating the Instagram superficiality that is the airbrushed story of our lives. We project an image in an attempt to feel better, craving virtual validation and acceptance from external sources. What we are not encouraged to do is to draw resilience from within. Music can provide the soundtrack to our lives and offer a medium that aids every effort to express our response to all that is going on in the maelstrom of our inner and outer realities. Notes can be immeasurably moving, lyrics breathtakingly familiar. A piece of music has the inexplicable capacity to capture our emotional anarchy as if the songwriter was a fly on the wall, lurking in the deepest recesses of our minds. This fast-paced, distracted era in which we live throws up so much background noise, but what if we took a moment to stop and listen and allow ourselves to be swept away by the sounds, the words and the feelings they evoke. To consciously and deliberately feel the poetry of both pain and euphoria, each with our own Meena Kumari or Bruce Springsteen.

But to be a true poet, is it enough to be an avid and passionate consumer of music? Sometimes I feel as if I should immerse myself even further, upskilling my musical persona to create, not only consume. Anyway, the time is nearing when I will need to rest this tired body and leave the raving to the young. So it was that I recently decided to learn to play the electric guitar, a long-held ambition despite long ago burying all hopes of joining a band and becoming a rock star. Anyway, as Shanon Shah testifies in *My Pop Star Life*, the transience of celebrity is surely confirmation that fame is not all it is cracked up to be. I logged on to the local buy-and-sell FB page. Someone in my area, living on a far more salubrious street than mine, was selling a black and white Encore electric guitar for £40. I immediately consulted a musical friend who agreed it was an excellent investment and deigned to give me my first guitar lesson in exchange for dinner, oblivious to my lack of culinary prowess. I excitedly informed my husband. He shook his head, muttered something about a mid-life crisis and put his headphones back on. Clutching two £20 notes I went to get my guitar at the pre-arranged time, picking up a friend on the way who was up for tagging along and we set off on our adventure as if enacting a scene from an episode of *Seinfeld*. I knocked on the door and a kind, matronly-looking woman answered. 'My son is just changing one of the strings, let me call him down'. A tween bounded down the stairs clasping the guitar that evidently held great sentimental value. 'He's loathe to sell it but he's grown out of it now that he's almost thirteen. Are you buying it for someone?'. My friend and I looked at each other. He asked to handle the guitar in a show of faux inspection and to buy me some time to come up with a back story. 'Oh yes, it's for my niece. She's so looking forward to learn.' My niece was five years old and not party to this charade. 'Yes it looks fine. We'll take it. She's going to be thrilled' my friend humoured, enjoying the ride. 'I hope she has as much fun learning to play as I did' said the twelve-year-old boy as I handed over £40 for the guitar he had grown out of. 'Did you bring a case for it?' 'Er... no'. 'Oh.' 'Don't worry, we'll just carry it like this.'

My first lesson was not a success, despite the patience and enthusiasm of my friend as he tried to teach me 'Seven Nation Army' by The White Stripes. I ordered a take-away from the local Indian restaurant and it went downhill from there. My fingers seemed too small and lacking in dexterity to make the moves I had seen carried out so effortlessly by PJ Harvey when I saw her play with Nick Cave and the Bad Seeds. It was tricky and technical and not fun at all. I decided I would give the guitar to my niece and my nephew who is three years younger, when they're a little older. Until then it continues to live in the corner of my living room, a 'talking point' and reminder of my need to persevere against adversity. Every now and then I pick it up and put the 'Lesson One: How to Play the Guitar' YouTube video on. Quickly frustrated as my fingers start to hurt I regretfully put it back.

I am now contemplating piano lessons, conscious that I may be coming across as a fickle child who begs their caregiver for a particular toy, only to tire of it within days and hanker after the next shiny must-have item advertised on kids' TV. Not that I wish for the single mindedness of the protagonist of Nadira Babayev's short story, dedicating his young life to the accomplished playing of a particular instrument. Hot-housed in music schools, the prodigy from the East practises for hours every single day and is encouraged to view escape from his post-communist homeland to the West as vital to pursuing a successful career as a classical musician. Escape, not through pleasure as experienced by Rim Jasmin Irscheid's ravers in Iran, but escape through music as toil. Music becomes his ticket to a new life away from the economic hardship and state oppression of the society into which he was born. Talented and precocious he is exactly the type of good immigrant we are told we want. That is until the UK's 'hostile environment' towards foreign nationals means he is forced to survive on his wits, living on the margins and leaving him dependent on the kindness of strangers who attach expectations to their generosity, which he inevitably disappoints. Escape to the West, because he is led to believe the monopoly on high culture lies here. From a young age, music dominates his life, the only respite from incessant practising comes five times a day when he flees to the mosque to pray. His mother, who is herself constantly struggling with the 'music is haram' conundrum, cannot conscionably, after all, curtail her son's newly discovered piety even if they both know that it is just to escape the monotonous routine of his practice schedule.

Escape through music need not always be a ride of pleasure, although who am I to define what constitutes pleasure? Years ago I watched the spoof rockumentary *Spinal Tap* and was fascinated by Nigel Tufnel's assertion that D Minor is the saddest key on a piano. The entire scene was hugely amusing but it did make me think about the pathos we feel upon hearing songs which carry great personal resonance for us, while leaving others utterly unmoved. The response is unique to those experiences only we have had, which is precisely why we have our own highly select soundtrack to our lives. Bruce Springsteen fans may feel convinced The Boss is speaking directly to them because the sadness evoked by the music already resides within us, it is not the music that creates the sadness. Just as D Minor may well be the harmonic match for a version of melancholy, those who create music seek to articulate the infinite realities of the human experience through the language of sound.

The sounds we hear, the notes that are created and fused together in rhythms and melodies to make music, speak to us in a transformative language of wonder and discovery, about the universe and ourselves, our inner worlds and the abstract world around us. I yearn to learn to play an instrument because I wish to grasp the mechanics of music, and make sense of the mathematical shapes and geometric patterns that are forged from this language that sings out our innermost fears and desires. Music is often described as a succession of sonic waves and patterns but the secret is to be able to place patterns within these sequences through our subjective thoughts and emotions. Music will project the meaning we are searching for within but only we can unlock the answers we think we need. Within bountiful sequences there will be an opportunity to place our own pattern in the right place at the right time. Whether it is the rapture of techno beats or the guitar riff of a Led Zeppelin song, we superimpose our own personal history to the music and pack it away in the treasure trove of our secrets.

We attempt to possess our personal history through our favourite songs, denoting the highlights, the lowlights, the joys and successes we have witnessed, because songs are a witness to our world(s). Aural tracks experienced by Estrella Sendra in Senegal communicate social justice and the blue-collar experience, while, as one of few Muslims active on the punk scene of the 1970s, Hassan Mahamdallie details the anti-establishment message of that era's music. Music offered escape through resistance, and endless live gig experiences that were similar yet dissimilar to the 'extreme' intimacy of the rave experience. He describes seeing Eddie & The Hot Rods play 'Do Anything You Wanna Do' at the Marquee in London in 1977 and tells us the song 'still rings in my ears – the '77 anthem for all the bored, angst-ridden, pissed off teenagers who were attracted to punk:

I'm gonna break out of the city
Leave the people here behind
Searching for adventure
It's the type of life to find
Tired of doing day jobs
With no thanks for what I do
I know I must be someone
Now I'm gonna find out who'

Songs of revolution that rail against the system and descry the status quo, not only offer escape from harsh realities but hope for the future, a rousing call to action to aspire to a new social order. Escape from the frustrations of youth, but also escape from this life, placing hope in the next. Songs of revolution are rather like songs of devotion, a belief in the possibility of something better, an escape to a. Higher. State. of. Consciousness.

Devotional music from Nasheed to the Sufi-inspired murid music of Senegal has sent the faithful into raptures of meditative observance for centuries. I went through my own Nasheed phase, and, in a move that went against all my better instincts, opted at the last moment to have a Nasheed band play at my wedding, instead of the wonderful klezmer ensemble She'Koyokh who I had initially approached. She'Koyokh play an extensive repertoire of Jewish wedding and Eastern European folk music. I had met Jim Marcovitch, co-founder and leader of the band years earlier, at a backpacker hostel in Kathamndu in Nepal and we had hit it off immediately and kept in touch.

He and the band had been very excited at the prospect of playing a Muslim wedding and disappointed when I inexplicably cancelled. I was deputy editor of the Muslim lifestyle magazine *emel* at the time of my wedding and can only imagine that my tastes had temporarily turned a little vanilla as a result, perhaps brought on by a fit of piety. I had just attended my first ever Living Islam Festival, organised by the Islamic Society of Britain and had enjoyed it. It wasn't like any festival I had attended before and although sleeping in a damp sleeping bag in a non-waterproof tent was a somewhat familiar feeling, I knew I was a fish out of water when I woke up in the women-only marquee at around midday to find I was literally the only person still asleep. Mine was the only occupied sleeping bag where there had previously been around a hundred women and girls jostling for room to lay down their head for the night. The majority had woken at *fajr*. Anyway, Jim forgave me and when I learned of his untimely death just a few years later, I was particularly pained that I had missed a beautiful opportunity.

At my wedding I got my dear university friend Tony to put together a playlist that was the soundtrack of my life. Another close friend, Andy, mixed one of my favourite songs of all time – 'Angel' by Massive Attack with the intro of 'Anokha' by Talvin Singh to create the song I would 'walk down the aisle' to. My husband was incredibly underwhelmed and lamented the lack of heavy metal and guitar-based rock but as he had offered zero input in the wedding planning, choosing to be as passive as can be humanly possible in all things nuptials-related (a sign of things to come) he had no one to blame but himself.

I went to see Massive Attack perform the entire Mezzanine album live at the O2 in early 2019. The show was an Adam Curtis-inspired, politically-charged, anti-nostalgia work of art. At the end of the evening, the musicians implored devotees of their music to move on. I don't know if I can obey their command for unsentimentality because I feel so incredibly sentimental about their sound. After all, they remixed Nusrat Fateh Ali Khan's mesmerising Qawwali song 'Mustt Mustt' into the moody trip hop track that spoke to my postmodern teenage angst. It was a song that, for me, settled the 'music is haram' debate. How can music be dismissed as ungodly when it is a medium through which faith can be celebrated. As Ziauddin Sardar writes in his essay on Qawwali: 'This world, the old Sufi mystics used to teach, is a mirage. There is a higher Reality that exists by its own essence. The purpose of existence is to love the higher Reality more than this mundane world of illusions. Like the (oblivious?) selfless moth immolating itself in the candle flame, Sufis direct their passion towards *fana*, or the annihilation of self in the higher Reality of the One. In the particular form of Sufi devotional music practised in the Indian subcontinent, Qawwali, the function of the performance is to enable the self-annihilation of the listener.'

Music is food for the soul. The angel Gabriel emitted sound when he met with the Prophet and sound is music, and it is therefore through music that the soul entered the human form. The power of music is to help us to transcend to something beyond the surface. Listening to music in a club and hearing the recitation of the Qur'an are part of the same experience. Whether it is a spiritual experience at a rave or being swept away by emotions at a gig, music can be as meditative as prayer. We can choose to respond with congregational dance or the solitude of inner appreciation. However we choose to consume, create or fathom the music we hear, we are another step closer to escape to a. Higher. State. of. Consciousness.

HIDDEN WINDOWS

Jeremy Henzell-Thomas

I need to begin with a confession. I approach music not as a disengaged academic or critical exercise but from an experiential perspective as a keen amateur pianist, music lover and unashamed advocate of the power of music to move, inspire and heal the soul. My first piano lessons at the age of six initiated an immersion in music as a lifelong inspiration. At school, I studied music to an advanced level, and for a while I wanted to become a professional musician or a scholar of musicology.

Brought up as an Anglican Christian, attending chapel at boarding school every day of the school term for five years, I was also steeped in the beautiful choral tradition of the Anglican liturgy, and was privileged as a teenager to stand in for the organist at the parish church in my home town for Sunday services and for weddings during the summer holidays. I revered the canon of sacred choral music in the broader Christian tradition, from Gregorian chant, through the works of Thomas Tallis and William Byrd, to the devout masses, passions and cantatas of JS Bach, the dramatic oratorios of Handel, the great requiem masses of Mozart, Brahms and Verdi, and later twentieth century works such as Benjamin Britten's War Requiem and Edward Elgar's Dream of Gerontius. And that sense of the sacred permeates not only music that is explicitly religious. In discussing with me the music of Anton Bruckner, a friend remarked on how 'utterly overwhelming and elusive' and 'impossible to capture' was 'the effect of the sacred on the soul' so deeply felt and perceived by this composer. Although Bruckner wrote a series of masses, nowhere perhaps is the sense of serenity and awe evoked by the transcendent more movingly expressed in his music than in the ninth symphony, dedicated by him to 'dem lieben Gott' ('beloved God'). The same transcendent spirit can be heard in such works as the Second Symphony ('The Resurrection') of Gustav Mahler, and the opera *Parsifal* by Richard Wagner. I hear it too in the majestic natural landscapes painted by Sibelius in his symphonies.

Later, as a young man extending my cultural and spiritual boundaries, practising yoga and immersed in the Hindu tradition of Advaita Vedanta, I discovered Indian music and attended concerts featuring Ravi Shankar, the celebrated Bengali sitar player. Only much later did I become aware of the major influence of Muslim Mughal musical culture on the historical development of Hindustani classical music, including the creation of new ragas and the development of instruments such as the sitar and sarod. Musicians occupied a prominent place in Mughal paintings depicting daily life, ceremonial occasions, and hunting and battle scenes, emphasising that no part of the life of the Mughal court was without the enjoyment of music and dance.

In 1998, the year that I entered Islam, my love of music and my belief in its educational and cultural importance found very concrete realisation in a charitable project that culminated in one of the most rewarding and moving experiences of my life, one which affirmed unequivocally for me the healing power of both art and music. This was something I observed for myself in my own inspirational encounters in Sarajevo in that year.

Sarajevo had been under siege for almost four years from April 1992 to February 1996, during which an estimated 10,000 people were killed or went missing, including over 1,500 children. The inspirational spirit of Bosnian musicians had been most famously exemplified by Vedran Smailovic, known as the Cellist of Sarajevo, who regularly played his 'cello in ruined buildings during the siege. A striking picture of him playing amidst the ruins of Sarajevo's National Library in 1992 caught the imagination of people around the world. He also played at funerals during the siege, even though funerals were often targeted by snipers. The same spirit was captured by Ivana Velican, a fourteen-year-old piano student during the siege at the Sarajevo Conservatory, who said, 'I play to defend myself. I mean, I am not – I cannot be – free. But I can sit at the piano. And I can hope that everyone learns to feel the love that I feel.'

I first went to Sarajevo in 1998 for the opening of the exhibition of artworks by Ahmed Moustafa at the Umjetnicka galerija. The exhibition was titled 'Where the Two Oceans Meet' (*gdje se dva moral srecu*) and had originally been held earlier in the year at the Pontifical Gregorian University in Rome, the first exhibition by a Muslim artist in the precincts of the Vatican. It honoured the theme of art as a means of fostering mutual respect and understanding between different cultures and peoples. It was particularly appropriate that the Sarajevo exhibition was opened by President Alija Izetbegovic, who did so much to underline the common heritage of Islam and the West.

During my stay I was introduced to the Director of the Primary Music School in Ilidza, a municipality in the Canton of Sarajevo, and saw for myself the damage inflicted on the school by Serbian forces during the siege of Sarajevo. Inspired by his story, and realising the tremendous importance of cultural reconstruction as a means of raising the spirits and expressing the soul and unique identity of the Bosnian people, I resolved that when I returned to England I would initiate an appeal for charitable donations to replace some of the musical instruments which had all been pillaged or destroyed during the occupation of the school. The only vestige of the former resources of the school was a charred grand piano, set on fire and left behind as a symbol of cultural destruction and the demoralisation it brings.

Starting as the special focus of the charitable work of the school in the south west of England where I worked as Director of Studies, the appeal rapidly developed into a national project, the core of which was a nationwide 'Scaleathon' initiated by Topwind, a leading music shop in London, involving 7,000 children playing sponsored scales during music lessons. With the substantial funds raised from this exercise (highly popular, as you can imagine, with music teachers!) and other events, including concerts, we were able to purchase over forty new musical instruments, including pianos, drum kits, accordions, clarinets, flutes, recorders, guitars, violins and cellos. More were kindly donated by children and parents of the school. We were able to arrange for all the instruments to be flown free of charge to Split in Croatia by RAF Brize Norton, and collected by a contingent from British (SFOR) forces based in Sarajevo. A complete PA system was also included. Most symbolically, a new grand piano was purchased and transported to the school from Germany.

In the autumn of 1999, the project reached its climax with a televised presentation and concert at the music school in the presence of the Bosnian Minister of Education and Culture, the British Ambassador, the Commander of British forces in Sarajevo, and a large audience. But just as the heart of the project was the work of British children in amassing thousands of individual donations, so the heart of the presentation event was the presence of 400 children, all pupils or former pupils of the school (with war orphans amongst them) who came from across Bosnia and stood along the ruined walls of the gutted concert hall in the evening twilight. They touched our hearts most deeply as they sang *na rata ne bude* ('let there be no war'). We made a special presentation of a new accordion to a talented young orphan musician, and we were also able to announce that there were sufficient funds left over to begin the reconstruction of the gutted concert hall. It was, all in all, the most moving event I have ever been privileged to attend.

It was deeply symbolic, too, that I was presented with an artillery shell casing most beautifully engraved with pictures of a mosque, a church and a synagogue, delicately interwoven with engraved flowers, to take back to my school. To this day, it is exhibited at the entrance of the recital hall, and is a reminder not only of the remarkable way in which young musicians in one country helped to heal the wounds of those in another, but also of the peaceful co-existence of different faith communities for which Sarajevo was historically celebrated. How fitting it is that young musicians in one country stretch out a helping hand to young musicians in another, for music is a universal language, which knows no boundaries, just as the natural openness, friendliness and generosity of children is a lesson to us all.

As a model of peaceful co-existence, I turn my attention also to the legendary West-Eastern Divan Orchestra which evolved out of the West-Eastern Divan workshop for Israeli, Palestinian and other Arab musicians founded in 1999 by Daniel Barenboim and Edward Said. This materialised the hope 'to replace ignorance with education, knowledge and understanding; to humanize the other; to imagine a better future.' In the workshop, 'individuals who had only interacted with each other through the prism of war found themselves living and working together as equals.' Three years after it was established, the orchestra was given a home in Seville by the regional Spanish government of Andalusia. The area's historical importance as a hub of peaceful coexistence (convivencia) between Muslims, Christians and Jews in Europe continues in the West-Eastern Divan's rehearsals and discussions, in which the musicians listen carefully to each other, 'traversing the deep political and ideological divides of the Middle East.' This is one of the special gifts bestowed by music, because in playing in an orchestra, each player learns to improve his or her musicianship by playing in ensemble with others, by listening to the other. The orchestral musician is not in a bubble hearing only the notes that he or she plays, and deaf to all else, and this applies just as much to a soloist accompanied by an orchestra. I learnt this from my own experience at the age of 17 when I played the piano in Beethoven's first piano concerto with the town orchestra at my last school concert. The review of this performance in the school magazine said it all: 'Henzell-Thomas took the final movement at a reckless speed, getting faster and faster and seemingly oblivious to the struggles of the orchestra to keep up with him and to the baton of the conductor trying to impose a manageable tempo.' So I learned that even the soloist in a concerto is not a law unto himself, a self-centred maverick, but has to be part of bigger picture under the coherent direction of the conductor, and always alert to the other players.

In 2005, the West-Eastern Divan performed in Ramallah, marking the orchestra's first event in the Occupied Territories. For many Palestinians in the audience, this was the first time they had encountered Israelis in a non-military setting. One young girl remarked to Daniel Barenboim, 'You are the first thing I've seen from Israel that is not a soldier or a tank.'

Also worthy of approbation is Zohra, a unique all-female orchestra named after a Persian goddess of music, formed five years ago in Afghanistan, where not so long ago music had been outlawed and women barred from education under Taliban rule, despite the fact that music has always traditionally been a thriving and rich part of Afghan culture. The BBC website showcased the orchestra in March of this year when Zohra was visiting the UK for the first time and mentioned the work of the Afghanistan National Institute of Music (ANIM), founded in 2008, with international support, to bring music education to young Afghans. Today in Kabul, ANIM teaches music skills to some 250 young people, both male and female. 'Above all it sends a message of gender equality to other Afghans,' Ahmad Sarmast, the founder of ANIM, explained. 'Zohra is a symbol of the freedom of Afghan women. This is the message we take around the world.'

Given my perception of music as a perfectly natural human activity, and the special place in my heart for sacred music, whether vocal, choral or instrumental, it came as a shock to me to discover that most of the ways in which I participated in music, as a performer, listener, and supporter were regarded as *haram* (forbidden) within certain Muslim circles. I had never been aware of this in Bosnia, but it came home to me when I travelled to the Gustav-Stresemann Institut in Bonn, Germany, four years later in 2002 as a relatively 'new Muslim' to speak at a conference organised by the Association of Muslim Social Scientists (AMSS) on Islamic education in Europe. My topic was Citizenship, but I was looking forward to attending a workshop on music education that the conference organisers had set up. I knew this was a controversial subject likely to polarise the participants between those who believed that education in music was *haram* (or at least suspect enough to be avoided) and those who recognised its value. I wanted to count myself with the latter. To that end, I had arranged with the organisers of the conference for a lecturer in Music from London University to attend and speak on the transferable cognitive and social benefits of music education that had been brought to light by reputable research – or, in other words, how music education had a significant effect in enhancing a range of cognitive and social skills. In my own presentation I expressed my support for the broad range of research evidence verifying the benefits of music training and education. After the session, I was approached by one of the attendees, a practitioner in Islamic education, who pronounced emphatically, 'Jeremy, music is haram!'

I will return to the vexed question of the status of music in Islam in due course, but first let me briefly summarise the extensive body of research that music education is one of the most powerful tools for realising a child's intellectual, social and creative potential. Learning a musical instrument, including learning to sing, and other forms of participation in formal musical training, speed up the development of language skills, including speaking, reading and listening, vocabulary acquisition, verbal and non-verbal reasoning, general intelligence, memory (including verbal recall proficiency), attention, social awareness, empathy and emotional resilience. The virtue of perseverance, so essential for deep learning, is also nurtured through long hours, months and even years of sustained practice. (A detailed survey of such research by Sharon Bryant can be accessed on the website of the National Association of Music Merchants (NAMM) Foundation, which promotes the benefits of making music, while other surveys by John Rampton and Laura Lewis Brown, amongst many others, also come to mind). Study after study prove that regardless of socioeconomic background, music-making students do better in school than those not involved in music, showing an increase in academic performance at multiple educational levels and across many subjects. Music education not only enhances sound discrimination and fine motor tasks, but can also help students develop spatial intelligence, the ability to visualise elements that go together, a crucial skill in solving maths, art, architecture, engineering and computer problems. Many educationalists also strongly believe that music education can help to build the innovation, communication, problem-solving and critical thinking skills more than ever needed in the twentieth century. Neuroscientific research has revealed that children involved in music have larger growth of neural activity than those not in music training. Most notably, the corpus callosum, a massive bundle of nerve fibres connecting the two sides of the brain, is larger in musicians. Quite simply, when you're a musician and you're playing an instrument, you have to be using more of your brain.

And we should not forget the well-documented evidence of the positive effects of music therapy on patients suffering from dementia and Alzheimer's. When used appropriately, music can shift mood, manage stress-induced agitation, stimulate positive interactions, facilitate cognitive function and coordinate motor movements. The neurologist Oliver Sacks, whose work has featured in a stream of best-selling case histories (including those related in his book *Musicophilia: Tales of Music and the Brain*, as well as the Oscar-nominated 1990 film *Awakenings*), discussed the healing power of music in a panel at Columbia University in 2012 titled 'Reawakening the Brain Through Music'. The discussion focused on 'the ability of music to heal patients afflicted with severe neurological and physical problems. During the session a clip from a documentary called 'Alive Inside' by Michael Rossato-Bennett showed how an elderly man suffering from dementia 'would break out of his catatonic-like state when his favourite music was played for him.' After he finished listening to the music, he could 'respond to questions about the songs' and 'interact with other people.' Music has been a part of Sacks' life since he was a little boy, when he fell in love with the music of Bach. Underscoring Sacks' lifelong passion, panellist and Grammy-nominated jazz guitarist Stanley Jordan came on stage to play one of Bach's Two-Part Inventions. After the performance, a video clip from the PBS series Nova was played showing how Sacks' brain responded during an MRI to hearing Bach compositions – 'it lit up all over'. Petr Janata, a cognitive neuroscientist at the University of California, who studies the psychology of music, noted that 'our responses to music are widely distributed throughout the brain.'

Some of my close friends have also related to me their personal experience of the healing power of music. One of them, a medical doctor, told me: 'I am fascinated by the healing properties of vibration and frequency of music and spoken words such as recitations and songs and poetry in various languages. I know in my heart that the future of medicine will include music for healing as medicine and therapy just as it is still done in some small villages across Asia and Africa and was once done in the tekkes in Ottoman times.' Another described how her experience of learning to play the ney flute was 'incredibly important to my own journey in healing the wounds that are blocking me from my essential self', and she offered this poem to express the essence of that process:

> The ney meets you where you are
> Like a true spiritual lover.
> That's how music is made.

The Qur'an (2:31) tells us that God '*imparted to Adam the names of all things*'. Muhammad Asad interprets the knowledge of the names to mean the faculty of logical definition which gives us the ability to arrive at precise and distinct concepts. He adds that it is in this ability to think conceptually through the medium of 'the letter' that humankind is privileged to be superior even to the angels. Yet my own experience of the power of music, like that of so many others, has convinced me that we should certainly not conceive of music merely as a primitive precursor to the communication of concepts through language.

And neither should we limit it to what modern research has revealed about its role in social bonding or enhancing cognitive skills and healing neurological and physical disorders, important as all those benefits are. Just because of the evidence that music can increase intelligence, we should not restrict its impact to the single unitary or 'g' factor for 'general intelligence' as measured by IQ tests. Rather we should see musical/rhythmic intelligence as one of the innate 'multiple intelligences' identified by Howard Gardner, along with visual-spatial, verbal-linguistic, logical-mathematical, bodily-kinesthetic, interpersonal, intrapersonal, and naturalistic intelligence, with existential and moral intelligence later added to his list.

I want to go further and affirm the power of music to move, inspire and heal the soul. In speaking of the practice of *zhikr* (remembrance of God) Suleyman Dede, the Mevlevi Sufi shaykh, taught that it opens the heart and makes 'the intelligence more refined and expansive', such that 'a beautiful condition comes about – similar to the one that is brought about by good music.' And it is no surprise that Jalaluddin Rumi, who inspired the founding of the Mevlevi order by his followers, advised that 'today, like every other day, we wake up empty and frightened. Don't open the door to the study and begin reading. Take down a musical instrument.'

In preparing for the Bonn conference, my own early inquiries into the status of music in Islam had extended to what is probably well-known to most of us: that the Qur'an nowhere prohibits music, and the belief that it does is entirely unfounded. This false belief stems from a totally unjustified interpretation of the phrase 'idle tales' (*lahwal hadith*) as meaning 'listening to songs or instrumental music' – a belief strengthened by certain hadith which proscribe this kind of music as unlawful. Muhammad Asad makes it clear in his note to the verse in question (31:6) that this phrase has nothing to do with music but refers to those who rely on idle talk instead of divine guidance and indulge in a 'pseudo-philosophical play with words and metaphysical speculations without any real meaning behind them.' I mentioned this to the man at the Bonn conference who was insisting that music was haram, and also suggested to him that the copious instances of hadith purporting to forbid music were of doubtful authenticity. His response distilled for me what I have come to see as one of the main reasons for intellectual stagnation, lack of creativity and spiritual paralysis in Muslim societies. 'If there is any doubt', he said, 'even a speck, avoid it!' That way, 'innovation' and 'deviation' can be avoided at all costs.

This attitude is evident in the many lengthy articles expounding why music should be condemned as haram, often without making any clear distinction between different types of music, such that a sacred mass by J.S. Bach and a profane pop song played at a disco are implicitly put in the same boat because they both involve instrumental music and singing! One such article is 'The Status of Music in Islam' by Shaykh Saleem Bhimji on the al-Islam website. This states that, according to various sources, notably the collection of hadith entitled *Wasa'il ash-Shi'a* compiled by Shaykh Hurr al-Amuli (as specified in Ayatullah Sayyid Dastghaib ash-Shirazi's book *The Major Sins*) playing musical instruments, including all stringed instruments (guitar, sitar, violin, piano, etc.), tambourine, cymbals, drums, and flute, as well as singing, is haram and a 'great sin'. 'Divine bounties' are denied to 'the occupants of any house where there are musical instruments. Angels do not even enter such a house and even the prayers of the inhabitants of this house are not accepted'. One reported hadith warns in graphic language that 'A person who possesses a sitar will be raised on the Day of Judgement with a black face. His hands will be holding a sitar of fire. Seventy thousand angels with maces of fire will hit him on the face and the head. The singer will arise from his grave – blind, deaf and dumb, as will the adulterer.' (I hasten to add that I am not an authority on the authenticity of hadith, but I do know that the sitar made its first appearance in the sixteenth century, some 900 years after the death of the Prophet!)

Listening to music as well as teaching it is also held to be a great sin in Bhimji's article. He maintains that all the Mujtahids are also unanimous in their opinion that the manufacturing, selling and purchasing of musical instruments is haram, as is any income derived from musical activity. It is even haram 'to keep instruments of music in one's possession and is obligatory to destroy them'. He refers to various hadith reported by Imam Ja'far ibn Muhammad as-Sadiq, including one in which the Prophet Muhammad is reported to have said, 'I prohibit for you dancing and playing flute and drums', and another in which it is claimed that the Prophet said that he was ordered by Almighty Allah 'to eradicate the playing of flute, other instruments of music, all games of vice, idol worship and all practices of the days of ignorance'.

Amongst the catalogue of vices held to be promoted by music, these stand out:

Music stokes carnal desires and promotes shamelessness and hypocrisy, 'Playing the violin,' for instance, 'promotes the growth of hypocrisy in the heart' in the same way as algae is promoted by water, and the playing of drums and cymbals in one's house causes Allah 'to impose satans to infiltrate every cell of the body. With the spread of this evil, the person loses all sense of dignity and self-esteem,' so much so that 'he will not be concerned or affected even if his women are dishonoured.' Music also 'creates vibrations which are conveyed to all parts of the body through the nervous system' resulting in various maladies ranging from indigestion, high blood pressure and heart disease, as well as mental illness and even insanity.

The 'Hadith of the Day' website agrees that 'there are numerous physical, mental and spiritual harms associated to music' and maintains that 'Those close to Allah will not listen, associate or occupy themselves with music', attributing this blanket injunction to 'the pious predecessors and classical Muslim scholars' who 'regarded music as prohibited'. This is held to be 'the jurisprudence ruling of music, even if the lyrics are not questionable'.

Such strictures tend to be applied indiscriminately to all genres of music defined as being geared to 'vain and futile entertainment', but even music that is 'permitted according to the Fiqh of Islam' should be refrained from 'if one wants to reach to that station of proximity to Allah in this world, and one of closeness to the Prophet and his Ahl al-Bait in the hereafter'.

It is important to point out that reservations about the effect of music in promoting vice have not been codified only by strict Muslim jurists, but have seen historical expression within Western civilisation even if there has been a progressive relaxation over time in the scope of disapproval. Plato was in no doubt that music is a force for good or evil, and an extraordinarily powerful influence in ruling people's lives. 'Rhythm and harmony', he taught, 'permeate the inner part of the soul more than anything else.' Because he saw music as potentially dangerous, he wanted to limit its expressiveness and its capacity for innovation. Different modes, or musical scales, express and stoke different sentiments in people, and the majority were seen by Plato as destructive to the status quo.

In Kallipolis, the ideal city founded on the rule of justice, in which everything is proportionate and has its proper place in the natural order, Plato allowed only two modes or scales, the Dorian, imitative of the person who is courageous under stress, and the Phrygian, which expresses self-control, temperance and moderation. The aulos, a reed instrument capable of extensive modulation and range of expression, was banned from Kallipolis, partly because it can have an exciting and orgiastic effect, and partly because it is an instrument used in solo performances and can therefore encourage the radical individualism which Plato so despised. The use of rhythm was also under strict control in the ideal city.

For similar reasons, during the Middle Ages, only certain austerely 'pure' musical intervals such as the perfect fourth and fifth were allowed in sacred music performed in Christian churches and it was only in the Renaissance that 'dangerous' intervals, including the major third which had previously been shunned as too 'sweet' and was associated with profane secular music, began to be tolerated. Until the Baroque period in the eighteenth century, the dissonant tritone or augmented fourth (three adjacent whole tones), referred to as *diabolus in musica*, or 'the devil in music', was avoided, and it was only in the Romantic period that composers started to use it freely in an expressive way to exploit the 'evil' connotations culturally associated with it, as in Wagner's use of timpani tuned to C and F♯ to convey a brooding atmosphere at the start of the second act of the opera *Siegfried*.

We might well be wary of the way in which people's emotions are so easily manipulated by music, as in advertising and movies, as well as nationalistic and political propaganda, and certain styles of music criticised for encouraging misogyny, but even if we agree with Plato that music can be misused, we are not likely to agree that in today's world such dangers can be directly controlled or eliminated by theocratic or other kinds of totalitarian government. We are not likely to see Platonic-style censorship of music in our culture.

In the democratic society in which we live, responsibility shifts from government to the individual citizen to make personal choices and exercise discrimination. The Qur'an advises us that we should 'listen closely to all that is said, and follow the best of it' (39:17), and such discernment in the face of words can surely also be taken to apply to music, as well as art and film. Even if there will never be consensus (*ijma*) on all the criteria that distinguish what is of benefit from what is not. Just as the suppression of forms of art is against the spirit of the times and can only lead to artistic illiteracy, so too is the current trend of marginalising the performing arts in a narrowly prescriptive school curriculum that increasingly reflects not a broad and rich educational experience but a robotic schooling regime geared to turning children into cogs in an economic machine. Children who are, in the words of John Taylor Gatto, 'dependent, conforming, materialistic, and lacking in curiosity, imagination, self-knowledge and powers of reflection'. With the explosion of technology and the advent of

Artificial Intelligence (AI) with its potential to replace many of those employed in mechanical, utilitarian tasks, we will surely need fewer workers of this kind and more of those who have the human skills nurtured by an education rich in the humanities and the creative arts. Without them, the risk of dehumanisation imposed by the emergence of AI will be all the greater, perhaps even, as warned by the late Stephen Hawking, 'the worst event in the history of our civilization.'

Rather than bow to the strongly prescriptive view that imposes a blanket ban on music, we might well ask what there is in Islamic teachings that might help us to find reasonable criteria for discriminating between music that is beneficent, uplifting the soul and polishing the heart, and music that is corrosive, with the power to rust it. To resolve this, Abdal Hakim Murad states that the 'never-ending debate' over instrumental music 'can be short-circuited quite simply by remembering that the human voice is the most beautiful of instruments, and that by cultivating its correct harmonies we can produce genuinely spiritual sounds that are superior to anything that an instrument could generate'.

While I concur about the potential beauty of vocal music (without attempting to prescribe the 'correct harmonies' involved), and greatly respect his intention to resolve the debate, I steer away from such a categorical distinction between instrumental music and the human voice because it does not accord with my own experience. As I write this, I am listening to 'The Lark Ascending', a much-loved work for solo violin and orchestra by the English composer Vaughan-Williams, and hear in the soaring notes of the violin the 'genuinely spiritual sounds' that Abdal Hakim Murad attributes to the human voice. The composer's use of the pentatonic scale (five notes per octave instead of the more usual seven notes in the heptatonic scale), conveys impressionistic feelings because it frees the violin from being anchored in the strong tonal centre that marks the diatonic system of mainstream Western classical music. Pentatonic scales were integral to the music of many ancient civilisations and are still used in Chinese traditional music and US country music and blues, as well as many other musical genres worldwide, suggesting that they are rooted in our essential nature.

Another attempt to set out clear criteria can be found in an article by Oludamini Ogunnaike in the Journal of Zaytuna College. As he writes, 'Many who know little about music or Islam confidently proclaim that "there is no such thing as Islamic music" due to the lack of consensus about the status of music in Islamic law.' He distinguishes the English term 'music' from the Arabic *musiqa*, pointing out that 'although both are derived from the same Greek word meaning "the art of the muses," they have slightly different meanings and connotations. Whereas a native English speaker would classify the religious chanting of poetry, prayers, the *adhan*, or the Qur'an as music or musical, these arts would not be considered *musiqa,* which has the connotation of involving instruments and being non-religious. Similarly, the instrumental and vocal music (in the English sense) that accompanies some Sufi ceremonies is seldom considered *musiqa;* rather, it is called *sama* (audition) or *dhikr* (remembrance).'

Nevertheless, for the same reasons as advanced by Plato, instrumental music, whether musiqa or sama, remains controversial in Islamic jurisprudence precisely because of its tremendous power to elevate or debase the soul. Ogunnaike draws a stark distinction between 'the behaviour of an audience at a heavy metal concert with that at a concert of Andalusian music', and doubts that 'when criminals or soldiers pump themselves up to commit acts of violence' they have been listening to 'the Indian classical music of Ali Akbar Khan'. Ogunnaike goes on to describe how Muslim philosophers developed elaborate musical theories based on the principles of Pythagorean harmony, and how court musicians produced 'a refined and refining art that served as the acoustic equivalent and accompaniment of adab'. Affirming the 'remarkable power' of traditional Islamic music power 'to induce states of remembrance, peace, contentment, joy, courage, harmony, balance, and most especially love and longing for the divine'. He describes how the Sufi orders in particular developed elevated and ecstatic traditions of spiritual music 'capable of transporting the soul into the divine presence'. Martin Lings tells us that the great Algerian Shaykh Ahmad al-'Alawi, whom he describes as 'an unsurpassable mover to tears', is recorded as having said: 'Music is not crippled by the dry bones of words. Liquid and flowing like a stream, it carries us into the presence of God'. Ogunnaike concludes that 'for the skilled musician in an Islamic tradition, playing music is like praying with one's instrument, and for the prepared listener, it is like listening to the wordless praise of the angels and the cosmos'. As Seyyed Hossein Nasr notes, 'Islamic civilization has not preserved and developed several great musical traditions in spite of Islam, but because of it.'

To conclude, I would like to return to my authentic personal experience of music and relate an event that distils for me the essence of what great music means to me. Driving on the M4 on my way to Heathrow to catch my flight to Bonn for the conference on Islamic education, I was listening to a CD of one of the last piano sonatas of Beethoven, a composer intimately associated with the city of Bonn. I was listening to the closing bars of the last movement of one of those sonatas, a climax that I have always found intensely moving, expressing with unparalleled beauty the inner serenity attainable by one given the grace to transcend hardship after heroic struggles. For me, the music audibly distils the essence of the Qur'anic promise that 'after hardship comes ease'. We need to remember that Beethoven had struggled with deafness for most of his life, and at the time he wrote the last piano sonatas he was stone deaf. He could hear his own music only in his head.

As I listened, overcome with the beauty of the music, my eyes filled with tears, and I said audibly, 'Beautiful! Beautiful!' And I thought, how on earth could this music, so deeply human and so essentially spiritual, be haram? How could a work of art that uplifts the human soul be forbidden to us?

And at the very moment that I said and thought these words, a sleek and gleaming black limousine, perhaps a Mercedes, suddenly appeared on the slip road to the left and joined the motorway just ahead of me. It had the distinctive presence of something out of the ordinary, something of special excellence. I had the feeling that it too was bound for the airport. Then my eyes caught its rear number-plate. It was a personalised number plate of only five capital letters which leapt out at me and made the hair on the back of my neck stand up. And the letters? J A M I L. Beautiful. The very word I had just spontaneously uttered in response to the sublimity of the music. Immediately I had spoken the word, the word itself in Arabic had appeared out of the blue in front of me.

Of course, sceptics who seek to deny the existence of the *ghayb* (that which is beyond the reach of human perception) would say that this was a mere coincidence. The same kind of people argue that the development of complex proteins from basic molecules came about through random events, even though statisticians tell us that the degree of probability of this happening is equivalent to the likelihood that a hurricane sweeping through a junkyard could randomly assemble a complete jumbo jet.

No, this was not a coincidence. It was what the Swiss psychologist Carl Jung would have called an example of 'synchronicity', a coming together of two events which are apparently unrelated but which are connected on a deeper level. Our existence is governed by *tawhid*, and everything is ultimately interconnected. At moments of inspiration or exaltation, the authenticity of what we are experiencing can be affirmed by just such a moment of synchronicity when a window opens into the *ghayb*, and something 'out of the blue', from the inner, hidden world (*batin*) enters the outer, apparent world (*zahir*). When it happens, it has the force of revelation, and there is complete certainty (*yaqin*) about its authenticity.

Such is the window opened by the best music in any tradition.

QAWWALI

Ziauddin Sardar

This world, the old Sufi mystics used to teach, is a mirage. There is a higher Reality that exists by its own essence. The purpose of existence is to love the higher Reality more than this mundane world of illusions. Like the (oblivious?) selfless moth immolating itself in the candle flame, Sufis direct their passion towards 'fana', or the annihilation of self in the higher Reality of the One. In the particular form of Sufi devotional music practised in the Indian subcontinent, Qawwali, the function of the performance is to enable the self-annihilation of the listener.

In recent times western audiences have been alerted to Qawwali through the work of one of its great exponents: Nusrat Fatah Ali Khan. How Nusrat became a chic cult figure in the West is, however, only part of my tale. Appropriately, since our subject is Qawwali, mine is a story of annihilation, involving considerable self immolation. It is the amazing adventure of the one Qawwali most people in the western world are likely to have heard: Nusrat's '*Dum mustt qualander*', or 'Mustt Mustt' for short. The story of 'Mustt Mustt', how it came about, how it evolved, changed and transmogrified, is a revealing narrative of our postmodern times.

To set the scene, I must begin at the beginning, with the origins of Qawwali, a compendium of the Indian Subcontinent's musical traditions, itself. Its invention is attributed to Amir Khusrau, an immensely colourful and influential character in Indian music and literature. A court poet of Ala-ad-Din Muhammad Khilji, Sultan of Delhi (1296–1316), Khusrau is credited as the first Urdu poet in history. Sufi tradition also credits him with introducing such musical instruments as the sitar and tabla to the Subcontinent. There is an apocryphal account of how in a spate of invention he cut the *pakhavaja* (a drum with twin striking surfaces) in half, thus creating the two small drums of the tabla, one to be played by the right hand the other by the left of the drummer. Khusrau also innovated new vocal forms, as well as *rags* and *tals*.

Rags are central to Indian music, yet they have no counterpart in western musical theory. Loosely, *rag* is equivalent to melody, which in Indian classical music exists in free rhythmic form. The concept of *rag* is that certain characteristic patterns of notes evoke heightened states of emotion. Each *rag* can be described according to its ascending and descending lines (which may involve turns) as well as its characteristic melodic figures. Indian melody can also be presented in its metric form, its tempo governed by the *tal*, a particular time measure. *Tal* is a cycle with both quantitative and qualitative aspects: the quantitative concern the duration of a cycle measured in terms of time units or beats which can be slow, medium or fast; the qualitative concern the distribution of stresses or accents within the cycle at different levels of intensity. In a *raga*, a composed piece, the character is derived from the specific deployment of the *rag* and *tal*. There are over two hundred extent *rags,* each a melodic basis for composition and improvisation, each performed at a different time of day or season to enhance particular emotions.

Qawwali is a fusion of the emotive power of Indian music with the emotional content of Sufi mystical poetry. The work of poets such as the Arab Sufi ibn Arabi or Turkish mystic Jalaluddin Rumi, is difficult to fathom for rationalist minds. In a society where one has to 'freak out' or 'drop out' to pursue mystical leanings, the idea of infinite emotion that is both unbridled passion and controlled, purposeful, spiritual endeavour is difficult to grasp. For Sufis, poetry is not just a vehicle, it is a transport of direct mystical experience. It represents and perpetuates the legacy of Sufi saints and teachers. This is why Sufi poetry provides such a vast range of aesthetic expression for mystical love, often utilising stylised imagery of human love as a metaphor for the manifestation of spiritual passion:

> O wondrous amorous teasing, o wondrous beguiling
> O wondrous tilted cap, o wondrous tormentor
> In the spasm of being killed my eyes beheld your face:
> O wondrous benevolence, o wondrous guidance and protection.

Amir Khusrau wanted to combine the passion of Sufi poetry with the heightened emotions of a *rag*. However, since Sufi poetry often incorporated a verse from the Qur'an or a saying of the Prophet Muhammad, it was important that the texts remained intact and their meaning was not distorted. A tricky situation to which Khusrau provided an ingenious solution. He was also the originator of the *tarana* style of vocal music, a type of singing in fast tempo using syllables. To an ordinary listener, the syllables appear meaningless but when they are pieced together they form recognisable Persian words with mystical symbolism. Khusrau introduced a few syllables of *tarana* to add balance to the *rag* in which the piece was composed (called *shudh kalyan*) and Qawwali was born.

The word Qawwali itself is derived from the Arabic word Qaulah, meaning to speak or give an opinion. As an artistic form, it is strong on opinion: the Urdu or Persian couplets, that form the invocation and mystical text of the Qawwali, are all important. This distinguishes Qawwali from a classical *raga* where music has primacy over text. The *tals* used in Qawwali are also distinct, being of a type seldom used in classical music. But the real difference between Qawwali and all other musical idioms of the Indian Subcontinent is its specific mystical function and context of use. Qawwali is designed to perform three specific functions: generate spiritual arousal, convey the mystical message of the poetry and react to the listeners' diverse and changing spiritual requirements.

Sufis consider a rhythmic framework and an emphatic stress pattern or pulse, reflecting the heartbeat, to be essential for stirring the soul. The reoccurring beat suggests the continuous repetition of God's name and guides the Sufi towards ecstasy. The rhythmic framework itself is characterised by two techniques. The first is handclapping; the second is a particular drumming technique that uses mainly open-hand or flat-hand strokes. With the downbeat of the drum, the listener's head moves in silent repetition of God's name; indeed, the drum beat alone may cause ecstasy. By the time the Sufi utters the word '*Allahu*', that is, 'God Is', he is already on the way to another realm. It is said that the thirteenth century mystic Sheikh Qutbudding Bakhtiar Kaki was so overwhelmed by ecstasy that he died while listening to Qawwali. Many Sufi saints, like the Indian mystic Sheikh Nizamuddin Chishti, have been known to go into a deep trance during Qawwali and remain oblivious to the world for days on end.

So, Qawwali is basically a form of mystical worship. Subcontinental Sufis often describe it as *zikr*, remembrance of Allah, which is the basic pillar of Sufism. Therefore, the music must serve to clarify the text, both acoustically, by making it clearly audible, and structurally, by placing emphasis on the salient formal features of the poem. Acoustic clarification of the text is sought by volume, singing at a high dynamic level, often with strong and exaggerated enunciation of consonants. Group singing reinforces the solo voice; the solo performer picks out the pertinent units of text that are repeated by the group.

As a form of spiritual communication, Qawwali is not a one-way exercise; singer and musicians must themselves react to the listeners, respond to their changing requirements, adjust their performance to their audience's state of being and ecstasy. The interaction requires the Qawwali to isolate both musical and textual units and repeat them as necessary, amplifying or cutting short any unit of the text, rearranging or even omitting an element, going forward, backwards or proceeding in an infinite loop. Or, it may require the creation of additional musical units as setting for portions of text that may need to be inserted out of the blue! I have heard the same poem presented in two minutes and performed for over two hours. The audience and musicians are mutual participants locked in a mystical encounter. The listeners' ecstasy can impose a particular structure upon the music and take the musicians for an unplanned ride.

This incredibly versatile and rich musical tradition has been sustained since the time of Amir Khusrau by the Sufi communities of the Indian subcontinent in the *mahfil-e-sama*, or the 'Assembly for Listening'. Through the act of listening – *sama* – the Sufi seeks to activate his personal link with his living spiritual guide, with saints departed, with Ali, fourth Caliph of Islam who was the cousin and son-in-law of Prophet Muhammad, with Prophet Muhammad himself and ultimately with God. By opening himself to the Qawwali, the listener means to transcend his mundane, materialist and conscious existence by kindling the spiritual flame of mystical love. Once ecstasy has been reached, the goal of both Qawwali and the listener is to sustain the intensity of the experience and, well, go *Mustt, Mustt*, or totally lose oneself in the love of God.

One cannot have a more profound or vivid Qawwali experience than at an *urs* – the commemoration of a noted saint's own final union with God, held at the saint's shrine on the anniversary of his death. Throughout the Indian Subcontinent, shrines continue to be the centres for mystical teaching and tradition, and therefore prime focii for Qawwalis. At any time of the year one can find an *urs* in progress somewhere on the

Subcontinent. I have attended Qawwali *mahfils* in Lahore and Pakpattan, two important centres of *urs* in Pakistan. But the *urs* to beat all *urs*, where the Qawwali reaches unparalleled heights, is the *urs* of the great saint Nizamuddin Auliya and of his favourite disciple, Amir Khusrau himself, that takes place in Delhi.

The Qawwals, the performers of Qawwalis, not surprisingly, tend to be both the followers of the Sufi path as well as highly versatile musicians. The ideal voice for a Qawwal is considered to be loud and full, a voice with life and strength, rather than one that is melodious or modulated. As Qawwals have to project their voice in huge assemblies that gather at shrines, they tend, like operatic tenors, to be rather large. Enter the subject of our story: the late Nusrat Fatah Ali Khan.

Nusrat was not just a big man with a big voice; he was big in every way. And as befits big men, he is shrouded in myths and legends, much like Amir Khusrau and Sufi Saints of yesteryear. The popular story of Nusrat's life that circulates in towns and villages of Pakistan is an enchanting narrative of dreams, remote viewing, and mystical encounters. These begin at the beginning: with his name itself. Apparently, his original name was Parvez, meaning 'conqueror', 'lucky', 'happy', a common enough and perfectly acceptable designation amongst Muslims of the Subcontinent. Yet, one day a mystic by the name of Pir Ghulam Ghaus Samadani came to see Nusrat's father, Ustad Fateh Ali Khan, himself a noted Qawwal. Our hero entered the room and when his father introduced him as 'Parvez'. Samadani was startled and enraged. 'Change his name at once', he thundered. 'Do you know who was Parvez? He was the king of Persia who tore up the letter sent to him by Prophet Muhammad. This name does not augur well for a boy destined to be a global Qawwal. It should not be the name of someone who will sing the rosary of Allah'. There and then, the fat boy's name was changed to Nusrat.

The word 'Nusrat' means 'God's grace' and 'success with His help'. So the young Qawwal was only too conscious of his prospects. On the way to his global triumph he is said to have performed several musical miracles. Take, for instance, the occasion when he was called upon to accompany the Indian classical singer Pandit Dina Nath on the tabla. The good Pandit had declared himself disappointed by all the tabla players in Pakistan - none of them could keep sufficient tempo to enable him to express himself fully.

But the youthful Nusrat and his nimble fingers did such a brilliant job that the Pundit had to declare 'I am defeated. Nusrat is highly talented'.

It was at the Amir Khusrau Festival in Islamabad in 1975, marking the poet's 700th anniversary, that Nusrat performed his breakthrough musical miracle. All the great Qawwali singers of Pakistan were invited to the Festival, which was broadcast live on radio. However, Nusrat, as yet an unrecognised Qawwal, was the last to be invited. So, by the time he and his party arrived the other Qawwals had already picked all the more popular poems and songs of Amir Khusrau for their own performances. It seemed there was nothing left from the Khusrau heritage for Nusrat. But the up-and-coming artist astonished them all by singing a rare and hardly ever performed poem:

> *Mein to pia sey nainan mila aayi rey*
> *Par nari ganwari kahey so kahey*
> *Mien to pia sey nainan mila aayi rey*
> I am not thirsty, I have met my beloved
> Whatever the ignorant girls of my village might say
> I am not thirsty, I have met my beloved.

After that, Nusrat went on to perform one of Amir Khusrau's most difficult compositions in a particular style of Qawwali known as the Qaul Qalbana. Divided into five tals, Qaul Qalbana is only attempted by the most accomplished artists, those confident in their total mastery of their art. This was Nusrat's way of telling the other Qawwals and everyone listening not only that he had arrived but also that he was on his way to higher places.

So far our tale has been of the world of tradition, Sufi tradition that continues to circulate and whirl around its own concerns. Clearly, Nusrat was established, so much within his proper ambit that his own life took on the form and character of popular Sufi narratives, replete as they are with the little miracles of daily life. But we live in one world, and eventually even the unworldly are tracked to their assemblies and whirled by centripetal forces onto the global stage. And so it was that Nusrat was propelled on a trajectory no other Qawwal had ever taken, or even dreamed might exist: to the recording studio of Peter Gabriel.

Gabriel is the unquestioned doyen of world music, the eclectic genre of chic that merchandises the illusion we are real aesthetes, full members of a pluralist global culture. The great achievement of World of Music, Arts and Dance (WOMAD) and 'RealWorld', the organisation and record label founded by Gabriel, has been to purloin, appropriate and commodify traditional genres of music from distant corners of the world and thereby make fortunes for recording companies, but few if any of the traditional musicians involved. The world, as the Sufis say, is a mirage, a distorted flickering image of reality. Or as a western poet once noted: the world is too much with us, late and soon, getting and spending. I merely note that what world music commodifies is the lure of other worldliness, in easy, though contextually incomprehensible form. For the West, spirituality, mystical power is the continuing domain of non-Western, natural man. The three fifths of the world who remain bereft of the worldly goods of modernity have only ethereal consolation in other worldliness to warm their hands and stir their mess of porridge by, it has become a natural order in quite a different sense of the word.

World music summons an assembly of listening for the global mirage based on the assumption that by being fascinated by what we do not understand we actually belong to one world. It is a delusion, because it lacks exactly those defining criteria that make Qawwali: mutual endeavour for a common higher purpose. Yet, if world music fails to transport us beyond the dynamics of the mundane natural order, at least it sounds nice.

And so it was that Nusrat was drawn to participate in that most bizarrely eclectic and truly postmodern exercise of adding a Qawwali to the sound track of Martin Scorsese's *The Last Temptation of Christ*. What better accompaniment to the deconstruction of Christology could there be than decontexualising another spiritual tradition? Postmodernism is nothing, if not the vehicle to transport us all beyond the meaningful content of grand narratives of belief. In the studio, goes the story, Nusrat performed a number of ragas and Gabriel kept on recording the recital. Then Nusrat did something unusual. He sang the tunes of Darbari ragas in higher tones, rather than his characteristic falsetto. Gabriel liked it and it ended up on the track of the film.

When the recording was complete Gabriel said: 'I wish you could do something with western musical instruments.' Again the postmodern refrain, the quest for fulfilment by losing all meaning in hybrid fusion form. Decontextualised, uprooted and free floating postmodernism would have us absorbed in genuine meaningless pastiche. Nusrat started to hum and play on his harmonium in an absent minded way. After a little while, he rendered the scale:

sa re sa: ni sa pa ni ma pama ni ga re ga.

Nusrat immediately realised the significance of what he had done. Peter Gabriel so liked what he heard he proceeded immediately to record it. Thus was born Nusrat Fatah Ali Khan's masterpiece, 'Mustt Mustt.' When cinema audiences heard the intriguing sounds of Qawwali they asked for more. They too wanted to go 'Mustt Mustt', and lose themselves in dreams of postmodern inclusiveness. Nusrat became a must on radio and in record shops far and wide.

Irony is a special delight of postmodernism. The first incarnation of 'Mustt Mustt', was released on the Real World label. Although guitar and other western instruments are there, the Qawwali is sung in the traditional way largely to the accompaniment of tabla. The text is a mixture of Urdu and Punjabi and its subject is Caliph Ali:

Dum Mustt Qualander, Mustt Mustt
My remembrance moment by moment
Ali in my every breath

The text is not all together original. Rather, it's a variation on the old Punjabi Qawwali *'Dama dum mustt Qualadar'* which I have heard many a fakir sing in the streets of the Pakistani province of Sindh. As Qawwali, 'Mustt Mustt' exists within the traditional orbit of improvisation, with a new element added out of the blue. It includes some enchanting *tarana*, Nusrat presents the whole performance as a showcase of virtuosity and talent. A passive assembly for listening among the uninitiated can be transported by fascination without commitment, yet it works within the terms of a committed assembly for listening.

The opening words of the Qawwali are very significant. The word 'Dum' has the double meaning of 'life' and 'breath'. 'Mustt' is the state of being lost to this world, or being located in another realm, or intoxicated in the love of God. Qualander is a mystic. So, collectively *'Dum Mustt Qualander, Mustt Mustt'* signifies a mystic lost to this life and breathing the very love of

God. The Qawwali is both an expression of mystical experience as well as an invitation to abandon worldly life and adopt the mystical way, the way of the Qualander. The nod towards western music and tastes is quite marginal, as a global recording phenomenon this Qawwali speaks its own language as it ever has.

And now our story takes another turn, ascending cadence becomes descending. The infinite loop of improvisation cuts short, backtracks, goes forward, amplifies and lays its stress on something quite unexpected. It is the responsibility of the Qawwal to react to the listeners. Nusrat himself now proceeds to produced two further versions of 'Mustt Mustt'. In its second incarnation, the Massive Attack Remix, Nusrat seeks to engage with that assembly for listening that is his new western audience. As all Qawwals must he searches for a means to keep in step with the spiritual capacity of his audience. So at the second turning of this story he brings instrumental music to the fore and renders the text, the words that are anyway incomprehensible to his listeners, secondary. Some of the conventional Qawwali vocal features disappear altogether. But, for all that, the subject of the Qawwali is still Ali, a refrain simple enough to be repeated emphatically and picked out by the most untrained ear.

The third turning of our tale describes a loop back to the ground on which Qawwali was first born. 'Mustt Mustt' returns home, this time to know its birthplace as it has become. In its third incarnation it is released largely for audiences in the Indian subcontinent. It is the function of the Qawwal to attend to the changed spiritual requirements of the assembly for listening, a Subcontinental audience that can both understand and know the tradition and engage with path presented. So what is one to make of 'Mustt Mustt' mark three, released in the Subcontinent under the title 'Mastt Qalander'? To what realm does it transport? It is a fast paced affair with Nusrat joined by female vocalists. The synthesised music drowns everything and all is lost in funky *tal*. Although Ali is still there, he is no longer the subject of the song. What was meant to be listened to in devotion and ecstatic contemplation now becomes disco dancing music – ecstasy of quite another kind.

It was at this point, with just three versions in hand that I determined to make 'Mustt Mustt' a subject of a diatribe on the awful assaults of global postmodern popular culture on my heritage. My assembly for listening was to be, appropriately enough, in Delhi. Listen to this anti-progression, this heedless descent into meaninglessness, I began. I played the three incarnations only to become aware of a certain lack of reaction in my audience. Were they not concerned at how our tradition was being debased by the pernicious influences from the West? They had news for me. Never mind three versions, now there are four: "but you chaps living in the West would have no idea about that," they noted. Feeling like some innocent abroad I listened as they brought me up to date.

The fourth incarnation of 'Mustt Mustt' appears in the 1994 Bollywood film, 'Mohra'. Here the original subject disappears totally and becomes an *object*: an object of material and sexual desire. The lyrics are changed slightly so the original idea of loosing oneself in the love of God evaporates and objectified sex comes into play:

Tu Cheese Bari Hay, Mustt Mustt

The word 'cheese' translates as 'things', 'commodities' and 'material'. In the original version the word 'bari' refers to higher Saints. Here, wordplay is used to connote the idea that a purely sexual object of love can also be divine and you can get 'high' on material things too! The changed spiritual requirements could not be more explicit. This is a world turned upside down, but, as my audience in Delhi clearly pointed out the turning was a home grown revolution. There was more to come. You should get yourself a copy of the new compendium edition, I was told with a certain impish glee by my audience that had now become my teachers. They sent me in search of the appropriately named, 'The New Massacre' version of 'Mustt Mustt' by Boota and Master G. Here, a number of different versions of the Qawwali – including the original and the Indian film version – are brought together in a postmodern blend. But instead of *tarana*, we have Rap. The entire amalgam is defined by absolute meaninglessness. The *object* now becomes a pure extravaganza, a fusion of sounds that is 'with it', a commodity that is only a commodity.

Like a moth, irresistibly drawn to the flame, I followed the path of 'Mustt Mustt' to the final immolation, the *coup d'grace.* It was delivered during the 1996 Cricket World Cup. Where once the Subcontinent had spiritual passion it now has unbridled devotion for cricket, and, incidentally, leads the world in betting syndicates that corrupt that erstwhile gentlemanly path as well. The sponsors of the game broadcast a special advertisement on numerous satellite channels throughout Asia and selected countries in Europe. The advertisement features a group of young children playing cricket in a Pakistani village. On the soundtrack 'Mustt Mustt' is just about audible. It's a joyous occasion with much colour and excitement around the game. Then a child hits the ball, which flies towards the sky, spins as if catching fire and revolves into the symbol for 'Coke'. The soundtrack swells with the unmistakable sound of 'Mustt Mustt' at full volume. What became a commodity now promotes another commodity, one with rather imperial tendencies. Nusrat Fatah Ali Khan's crowning achievement, the Qawwali that brought him the accolade of 'Shahen-Shah-e-Qawwali', the King of Kings of Qawwali, is finally drained of all its original meaning. Its real essence, intoxication in the love of God, is reduced to the desire for Coke: 'the *real* thing'.

I remember asking Nusrat, shortly after 'Mustt Mustt' took, whether it was a good idea to westernise the Qawwali. 'I cherish the tradition of classical music more than my life', he said. 'I consider its protection and preservation as my spiritual duty. As an experiment I do not mind the use of western musical instruments. But it will be great injustice to introduce any change in classical music. I use western musical instruments because I believe that you can dress up a pretty child in any clothes and it will stay pretty. But the more important thing is that the child should not get injured while putting on those clothes'.

In the case of 'Mustt Mustt', the clothes did much more than injure the child. Innocence, as the Sufis are quick to point out, is not barrier to annihilation. But the story of 'Mustt Mustt' has a strong moral. We live on one planet, in multiple worlds, we are different assemblies of listeners for we have not yet the wit to learn how to communicate across and through our differences. I am that traveller that returns to tell we have more problems than we know. There is not only one postmodernism out there. There is not merely one global popular culture that proliferates the meaningless mundane cause of pure commodity – the world is busy building many and different postmodernisms, we are all rushing headlong to meet each other on the common ground of nothingness. The flames are dying out all over the world.

PUNK DAYS

Hassan Mahamdallie

We can't choose where and when we are born and grow up, or how we spend those teenage years where we are told everything should be possible, but rarely turns out to be so.

I was born in the old St George's Hospital, Hyde Park Corner in 1961, into a 'mixed race' family, which was then a fairly rare home set-up. My father, an Indian Muslim from Trinidad, had arrived six years earlier aboard the SS Colombie, a former World War Two troop carrier. His forebears had been indentured labourers, transported by the British empire from Calcutta to the Caribbean to work the sugar cane fields in the period following the abolition of slavery. My mother was white working class, but like many 'white' Londoners, had foreign ancestors, in her case Jewish and Greek.

My parents met, courted, got married and got a mortgage on a house in Earlsfield, south-west London, before moving to suburban Worcester Park, near Kingston-Upon-Thames, to raise their family. They had twelve children, of whom I am the second eldest. I was taught Qur'an by the Pakistani family up the road, and one of my earliest memories is going with my father to the Shah Jahan mosque in Woking, Surrey. In those days, it didn't matter if you were Sunni or Ahmadiyya, you prayed in the same mosque.

For white women to marry 'a coloured' and produce 'half-caste' kids was widely viewed as an unforgivable crossing of the race-line, with the offspring regarded as cursed and pitied for 'not being neither one nor the other'. Growing up we had to cope with, or resist if were able to, a certain level of racism on the streets and at school. This uneasy, but not unhappy, existence was twisted into something darker in the late 1960s and 1970s with the rise of Enoch Powell to the level of a national political figure and the revival of Britain's fascists in the wake of his race-baiting speeches.

Powellism quickly manifested itself on the streets in violent gangs of National Front (NF) skinheads out 'Paki bashing'. The rise of the NF coincided with the Punk Rock explosion. My taste in music shifted from David Bowie and Stevie Wonder to The Clash, The Damned, The Adverts and The Vibrators. I laughed my head off when patriarchal belligerent drunk ITV presenter Reg Grundy got trashed by The Sex Pistols in a foul-mouthed encounter on the live 'Today' show in December 1976, instantly terminating his career. I took to walking up and down the Kings Road on a Saturday afternoon with other punks, purchasing my first pair of bondage trousers (pink) and going to gigs at the Marquee club in Soho, where, along with the punk and pub-rock bands, I first saw reggae poet Linton Kwesi Johnson perform, his low, melodious tones perfectly complemented by a backing dub band fronted by the amazing musician/producer Dennis Bovell. Punk and reggae – the 1970s' musical bastard twins.

My punk teenage rebellion is best chronicled through the sounds of the city, beginning in a less than fashionable part of suburbia. In the 1970s Croydon was the destination of choice for cut-price shoppers from across south London. They would travel there either by public transport or in their clapped-out Ford or Vauxhall cars that chugged round the one-way system, over the flyover and into the maw of the monstrous Whitgift Centre, a concrete wind-tunnel of shops that squatted the middle of town.

During the week and on Saturdays the Whitgift was engorged with bored and boring families looking for bargain clothes and electrical goods – fidgety men looking for the nearest pub or bookies, cajoled into shops by their wives, prams and pushchairs in front and screaming brats behind. When the shops shut at 5.30pm, Croydon would empty completely of humans, who would be replaced by obese rats out to scavenge in the vast amounts of rubbish left swirling around.

But on a Sunday night Croydon drew a different species of mammal altogether – a stream of oddly-dressed misfit teenagers could be observed getting off buses and trains and making their way to a pub in the centre of town where they would spend the evening drinking weak beer out of plastic glasses, jumping up and down to weird tuneless bands before staggering out completely deafened and sweat-soaked to catch the last bus or train home. I was one of them.

The Greyhound pub on Park Lane, Croydon, billed itself as 'Surrey's Premier New Wave Venue'. It was an unpleasant dump, but it was the place to be if you were into punk. (In a previous incarnation it had been a rock venue). You flashed your members' card, paid your quid, made your way past the beer-bellied bouncers (in those days all bouncers were white, drunk and quick to violence), up some stairs and into what must have once been a ballroom. It reeked of stale beer, cigarettes and body odour even at the start of the night. There would be two or three bands on the bill and, between the sets, the floor and chandeliers would vibrate with the heavy bass of a reggae sound-system.

Every punk, new wave and pub-rock band around at the time, except the Sex Pistols and maybe The Clash, squeezed onto the tiny stage at the Greyhound at some point, to be spat on by the pogo-ing crowd. The Jam, the Buzzcocks, The Lurkers, X-Ray Spex, Generation X, The Ramones, Tom Robinson, Motorhead, The Vibrators, Talking Heads, The Stranglers, Ian Dury, Lene Lovich, Penetration, The Fall, The Heartbreakers, and a long list of other bands now forgotten all played there.

The first female punk musician I saw at the Greyhound was Gaye Advert (Gaye Black), The Adverts' bass player. The Adverts' first single 'One Chord Wonder' remains one of the best ever punk anthems:

> I wonder what we'll play for you tonight.
> Something heavy or something light.
> Something to set your soul alight.
> I wonder how we'll answer when you say.
> 'We don't like you – go away'
> 'Come back when you've learned to play'

The follow up record – the gothic fantasy 'Gary Gilmore's Eyes', about an executed US murderer who apparently donated his eyes to science – was just as good. Gaye Advert did come in for a lot of sexist comment. The misogynistic music press couldn't get past her appearance – leathers, dog-collar, black clothes and eye make-up. That she didn't seem to acknowledge the crowd gave her some kind of silent allure in the eyes of the journalists. Then the story went around that she chalked the chords on her bass – in other words she couldn't play. But then who could? Wasn't that the point? Anyway, how could you even see chalk marks playing a gig in some dingy hole like the Greyhound.

It was also at the Greyhound that I first saw X-Ray Spex perform, fronted by the magnetic Poly Styrene. It is good to today see that the late Poly Styrene is right up there in people's consciousness of what punk sounded like and stood for. This remarkable figure was born in Bromley, Kent, in 1957, of a Scottish-Irish mother and Somali father. She is described as a dispossessed aristocrat, which I assume means being descended from one of that country's pre-colonial sultans. Her name is recorded as Marianne Joan Elliott-Said (the similar Maryam is a common female Somali name). Poly recorded her first demo album when she was eighteen, and then formed X-Ray Spex after seeing the Pistols in Hastings in July 1976. The timeless single 'Oh Bondage Up Yours!' was released in September 1977 on Virgin records. First we hear Poly Styrene's faux-girly voice: 'Some people think little girls should be seen and not heard, but I think...' before she yells: 'Oh bondage, up yours!...one, two, three, four...' and then we are into the anti-consumerist, anti-sexist song proper.

However, without doubt the best live band I saw at the Greyhound was local group The Damned. For me, they truly embodied the spirit of punk (London version). Vampirish lead singer Dave Vanian would dart about the stage (his sallow undead Bella Lugosi persona only surpassed by the vintage pub-rocker Screaming Lord Sutch, whose act always began with him being carried onstage in a coffin). The Damned's bass player was Captain Sensible, a cartoon character with peroxide hair, outsized plastic sunglasses, tutu and Doc Martens. Popeye-tempered Rat Scabies destroyed the drum-kit, contrasting with the only remotely 'normal' member, lead guitarist and songwriter Brian James (who had previously been in proto-punk band London SS with future members of The Clash and Generation X). The Damned were amphetamine-fuelled vaudeville, fun to watch and jump around to.

The songs were great as well. James was a talented writer. His tunes were well crafted and exquisitely short. The Damned were also quick off the mark – 'New Rose', just 2 minutes and 40 seconds of pop perfection, was the first proper punk single to be released. A dark love song, it starts with the classic pop line: 'Is she really going out with him?' before pitching headlong into Scabies's thumping beats, James's sharp guitar riffs and Vanian's vocals.

'New Rose' was the third 7" single put out by Stiff Records, the radical independent London label. It hit the record shops in October 1976, a month before the Pistols' debut *Anarchy in the UK* (published by the multinational EMI label) was released. 'New Rose' was unlike anything I had ever heard. The track was pleasingly miles shorter in length than a Deep Purple guitar-break and unlike Purple didn't send you to sleep. The lyrics were brief and simple and free of references to hotels in California or elves and all that obscure hippy shit. The B-side was a madly speeded up, though recognisable, version of the Beatles' 'Help'.

The second single The Damned put out was the equally memorable 'Neat Neat Neat', with its great cover of the band members with paper bags on their heads.

> No crime if there ain't no law
> No more cops left to mess you around
> No more dreams of mystery chords
> No more sight to bring you down
> I got a crazy, got a thought in my mind
> My mind's on when she falls asleep
> Feelin' fine in her restless time
> Then these words upon me creep, I said
>
> Neat neat neat
> She can't afford a cannon
> Neat neat neat, she can't afford a gun at all

The Damned were also the first punk band to release an album: *Damned Damned Damned*. I must have seen The Damned live seven or eight times, mostly at the Greyhound entertaining their loyal home crowd. And a very eclectic, suburban crowd it was – mostly young men dressed in DIY punk gear – home-ripped and hand-sloganned t-shirts, flares, Doc Martens, fake leather or denim jackets, longish hair gelled up. We working class discontents out for a high-energy anarchic evening looked askance at the lifeless Bromley contingent of middle-class posers with their expensive Vivienne Westwood fetish outfits and swastika armbands.

It was a friendly crowd most times. I don't recall many fights at the Greyhound, although the boozy bouncers, who clearly regarded the punters as some kind of two-legged disease, were fond of grabbing over-enthusiastic punters and giving them a punch or two before throwing them out onto the grimy Croydon concrete.

The Black nationalist leader Marcus Garvey had predicted that when the two sevens clashed, Armageddon Time would descend. The summer of '77 may have not been apocalyptic, but they were certainly strange days. The Provisional IRA was bombing London, the Yorkshire Ripper was striking terror in the North, the National Front was still on the rise, the Miners arrived in West London to support the Asian women strikers at Grunwick and ended up in a punch up with the Met Police, and the Queen's Silver Jubilee celebrations were rudely undermined when the Sex Pistols' 'God Save the Queen' went to Number One in the charts, and was promptly banned by the BBC.

> God save the queen
> The fascist regime
> They made you a moron
> Potential H-bomb

But the youth anthem that summer was undoubtedly 'Do Anything You Wanna Do', by Eddie and the Hot Rods. One of my best memories of that long summer was going to see the band live at the Marquee club in Soho. The Rods were one of those many bands that anticipated punk proper; part of the pub rock scene that included bands like The Feelgoods, Kilburn and the High Roads (featuring Ian Dury), Roogalator, Motorhead, Graham Parker and the Rumour, Wreckless Eric, Dave Edmunds and a load more.

The pub rock bands were the seedbed for punk. Punk didn't really come out of nowhere. Not only did the London pub circuit that the bands established provide venues for the proto-punk bands such as the 101ers (Joe Strummer of The Clash's first band) their back-to-basics, rhythm n' blues temperament foreshadowed the punk attitude. And once the punky reggae party got going, the pub rockers were (mostly) happy to join in. Geezers from Canvey Island were over-represented on the pub rock circuit. The reclaimed marshland on the Thames Estuary in Essex, dominated by oil refineries – hence the nickname Oil City – is still literally the end of the road for those who, for whatever reason, flee London town.

As well as the Feelgoods' stable of musicians, you had the Kursaal Flyers from nearby Southend (of hit single 'Little Does She Know'), and the demon harmonic player Lew Lewis (whose 'Caravan Man' is an utter classic). And Eddie and the Hot Rods. The Rods had already had a successful residency at the Marquee in 1976, out of which came a sizzling EP (Extended Play) single 'Live At The Marquee', with its great live rendition of Van Morrison's 'Gloria' that slid into the Stones 'Satisfaction'. One of their support bands in 1976 had been the Sex Pistols, apparently ending with the Pistols trashing the Hot Rods' gear – which sounds par for the course.

'Do Anything You Wanna Do', one of those perfect pop songs, was released on Island Records as a 12" 45rpm vinyl. It was a cracking single, belted out by lead singer Barrie Masters; permanently up and down the stage on his toes, who would start his gigs wearing his trademark white denim jacket, soon discarded as the heat began to rise. And did it rise. I saw The Rods on their return to the Marquee Club in August 1977 (a few days after a provocative march by the NF, who were smashed off the streets by an anti-fascist mobilisation at The Battle of Lewisham). Good times. It was my first visit to the dingy Wardour Street venue. The Marquee was little more than a shopfront, through which you entered, and via a corridor into the venue proper – a very dark, very basic and very hot cavern. It had a long history, going back to when it opened in Oxford Street in the late 1950s. It relocated to Soho in 1964, and had hosted every rock legend, from Jimi Hendrix to The Who and Genesis. In the late seventies it became one of the go-to punk/new wave venues. It was a licensed club, so you had to buy a membership card at the booth before you shelled out one quid for your ticket for the night.

To this bookish sixteen-year-old South London boy, Soho was a very strange, slightly dangerous and exciting place to walk through. You have to remember that in the late 1970s Soho was still ridding itself of its gangster reputation. In fact in 1977 there was a major trial of coppers in the Obscene Publications Squad, all of whom had been in the pocket of The Syndicate who ran Soho's red-light district.

'Do Anything You Wanna Do' was in the charts at the time, and the Marquee was rammed for the band's triumphant return. The week before

Bob Geldof's Boomtown Rats had played one night, but The Rods were booked for five straight. Their set was white working-class rhythm and blues, with some classic pop numbers thrown in. I cannot remember the supporting acts, but The Rods were superb. Somehow, I managed to get myself wedged at the front, next to the speakers, and so managed to get crushed and deafened. I passed out at one point.

I must have looked a right state later on, swaying down Wardour Street, through Piccadilly with people sitting round the statue of Eros, on my way across the Thames to catch the last train home. 'Do Anything You Wanna Do' still rings in my ears – the '77 anthem for all the bored, angst-ridden, pissed off teenagers who were attracted to punk.

> I'm gonna break out of the city
> Leave the people here behind
> Searching for adventure
> It's the type of life to find
> Tired of doing day jobs
> With no thanks for what I do
> I know I must be someone
> Now I'm gonna find out who

My father, was – among other things – a compulsive gambler. He was also a charmer, with a hint of Clarke Gable about him, I always thought. Even after the family bank account was made out in my mother's name to stop him cleaning out his wages on payday to hit the bookies, he managed to cash cheques at the bank by sweet-talking the cashier. Eventually, during my teenage years, my mother was forced to hide the cheque book in the one place in the family home he would never dare look – under a vivarium in my bedroom that housed my pet snake. My father had an utter phobia of snakes ever since his youth, when he snapped his wrist falling out of a palm tree after being surprised by a serpent hiding among the coconuts. At least that's the story he told me.

You would have thought he would steer his kids away from gambling, but when I left school at eighteen he got me a job in Mecca Bookmakers – a firm in which he had over the years 'invested' a substantial portion of the family budget. I guessed he thought they owed him something. I went to work in a bookies in the horse-racing town of Epsom and fed back to my father the tips the diminutive stable-lads brought into the shop. The betting-shop manager was a lovable rogue called Bob who became my early mentor in life. He owned a couple of greyhounds and every Tuesday morning he would send me off to Wimbledon dogs with a stopwatch to clock the trials before the Thursday evening race meeting.

There I rubbed shoulders with the urchins, chancers and mouthy fly-boys who worked in the kennels for thirty quid a week. So when Jimmy Pursey, the lead singer of punk band Sham 69, burst on the music scene with the band's first single 'I Don't Wanna' in 1977, I clocked him immediately. Pursey and his mates from Hersham, Surrey, (a couple of miles from Epsom) had formed Sham 69 the year before, while he was working at Wimbledon dogs.

Although most people think of Surrey as posh stockbroker-belt territory, it was (and is) a patchwork of towns and villages divided between the haves and have-nots. In the 1970s the have-nots, like Pursey and his crew (and me) lived in mainly white working-class areas and scratched around to make a living. So although music journalist Julie Burchill in typically sniffy fashion wrote, 'It must have been a bloody strong wind the day the sound of Bow Bells reached Hersham', Sham 69 might not have been cockneys, but they were certainly working class. They didn't come out of the art school scene that created London punk bands like the Clash, the Sex Pistols and Generation X. Crudely speaking Sham's reference points were more likely to be Wimbledon dogs, the bookies, the pub and family life than the ICA, the student union bar and cultural networks.

Coming from south of the river, Surrey 'geezers' would likely be Chelsea or Fulham supporters, in the days when the fascist National Front had a strong grip on the terraces. I do remember going to the Shed – the home end of Chelsea's ground – in the mid 1970s: it was stuffed full of racist skinheads and NFers, the exception being a mixed race hooligan – the infamous 'One-Armed Babs' – who was deemed 'alright' because he was a psychopath, and despite his physical impairment had a fearsome reputation for wanton violence.

So when Sham 69 emerged, it was inevitable that they would attract a racist fan-base as well as young pissed-off kids like me. It tore them apart in the end, as punk became a battleground between its anti-racist element organised around Rock Against Racism (RAR), and the racist skinhead contingent, who confusingly would dance to Jamaican ska before going out for a spot of Paki-bashing. I know people will say there were 'Redskins' as well, but it took me a very long time – decades in fact – before I supressed my learned instinct to expect imminent danger whenever I found myself walking towards a group of white men with cropped hair.

Despite all this, I was very fond of Sham 69 and their music. I bought their first single 'I Don't Wanna'. For me it was what a punk single should be – under two minutes long, guitar intro, then drums, then vocals. Simple rebellious lyrics with a bit of 'eff you all' nihilism thrown in.

> I don't wanna work in no factory
> And I don't want no strike
> And I don't want no dole queue
> No I don't wanna
> No I don't wanna
> No I don't wanna be
> I don't wanna work to sixty five
> And I don't want no gold watch
> And I don't want no pension book

'I Don't Wanna' was produced by John Cale of the Velvet Underground (of Lou Reed and Nico fame) and put out on the punk purists' label Step-Forward Records, founded by Mark Perry who created *Sniffin' Glue* – the original punk fanzine. Sham 69 were then signed to mainstream Polydor, and produced a slew of top-selling top-of-the-pops singles: ('There's Gonna be a Borstal Breakout', 'Angels With Dirty Faces', 'If The Kids Are United', 'Hurry Up Harry' and 'Hersham Boys'. The cover of 'Borstal Breakout' was a photograph of the band members 'breaking out' of the prison gates in what was a deliberate echo of Thin Lizzy's inside gatefold cover for their hit 1976 album *Jailbreak*.

Sham 69 were continually touring throughout 1977–79, but their gigs were increasingly dogged by violence as their racist NF and British Movement skinhead following literally fought a rearguard action to claim the band as 'their own'. They eventually failed and had to go off and invent the stupid talentless racist Oi! movement instead + left-wing turned right-wing journalist Gary Bushell's very own musical goldfish bowl.

The violence and Nazi politics repelled Jimmy Pursey and eventually forced him to side with the anti-fascists – his big public stand being his brief stage appearance at the Rock Against Racism Carnival in Victoria Park in April 1978 (a life-changing event for me personally). Radical journalist Dave Widgery in his account of RAR, *Beating Time*, recalled the scene:

> It was the arrival at the microphone of a haggard-looking Jimmy Pursey that brought the crowd of 150,000 to their toes. In a voice hoarse with emotion he bellowed, 'All this week you've probably read a lot of things about me and Sham 69. We've been dictated to. Last night I wasn't going to come. Then this little kid said to me, "You're not doing it because all your fans are NF". They said I ain't got no bottle. But I'm here. Nobody's going to tell me what I should or should not do. I'm here because I support Rock Against Racism.'

It was actually a very brave and principled thing to do. Standing in Vicky Park that day I remember being very surprised by Pursey's appearance and what he said. By 'coming out' at the carnival Pursey was signing Sham's death warrant and an end to what had been up to that point a very successful few years. The band's gigs were already being disrupted by massive fights, and they intensified through 1978 as their Nazi followers realised that they had lost the war and would rather see Sham 69 destroyed than see them go over to the anti-fascist camp. Later that year Sham 69 went on tour with seminal UK reggae band The Cimarrons, who were RAR stalwarts – that must have really pissed off the NFers.

I had my own little taste of the battleground Sham concerts had become when, later in 1978, I went to see them at Kingston's Coronation Halls in south west London, a 213 bus-ride away from home. I must have been mad – when I got to Kingston the town centre was crawling with NF skins getting drunk and aggressive, and of course all of them, plus me, then made our way to the venue. So there I was, waiting for the band to come on, trying to will myself into invisibility, surrounded by hundreds of half-pissed Sieg-Heiling skins, all of whom seemed, in my mind at least, twice my size. Many of them didn't have tickets and had barged their way in past the bouncers the venue had hired supposedly to keep order.

Eventually the band leapt on stage, the stiff-arm salutes reached a frenzy, completely drowning out the opening song. Then behind me there was an almighty crash, as the thuggish bouncers threw a skin through the entrance-hall's plate glass doors. And then all hell broke loose. I remember looking towards the stage at Jimmy Pursey, who was pleading and weeping, attempting in vain to get the fighting stopped. But it was too late – the entire hall seemed to be one mass brawl, which soon spilled out into Kingston town centre. The final image I have in my mind is of Pursey leaping off the stage and running through the hall and out the (broken) front doors. The gig had lasted maybe ten minutes.

I followed the crowd out onto the street, where gangs of skins were now busy throwing bins and bricks through the windows of Bentalls, the town's main department store and taking advantage of the chaos to do a spot of looting. After watching them for a while disporting themselves, I made my way to the bus station, got on the top deck of the 213, and watched as the police cars arrived and the skins melted away.

Within a year Sham 69 had split up.

In the 1970s there was a thriving independent record shop on Worcester Park's high street. (Hard in these days to believe, but true.) It was a bit of a lifeline to the outside world for a teenager from a hard-up family, painfully aware that we were looked down on by the town's 'polite society', the consensus being that our mother was a depraved woman for shacking up with a 'darkie' (my Indo-Caribbean father) and then shamelessly producing twelve 'half-caste' urchins ('How could she? They'll all grow up confused about what they are…')

Every week, after scouring *Sounds* music newspaper for the latest punk releases and upcoming London gigs, I would head straight for this record shop. It stocked a wide spectrum of music to suit its suburban London clientele: Gary Glitter or Bay City Rollers singles for the kids, Pink Floyd and Genesis albums for the long-haired grammar school boys acting out polite rebellion before becoming career civil servants, and under-the-counter punk and new wave 7" and 12" records for rejects like myself.

In November 1977 as punk hit its peak, the shop assistant – who kept new stuff aside for me – reached under the counter. There was a flash of yellow as he slipped a single into a brown paper bag. 'You'll like this one.' I handed over my 70p, grabbed the bag and was off home to play it. The single was called 'Orgasm Addict'. Its picture sleeve, that I concealed deep in my record collection, was a collage of the upper half of a nude woman with an iron for a head (designed by radical feminist visual artist Linder Sterling).

'Orgasm Addict' was of course banned on the BBC, with workers at the vinyl pressing plant refusing to handle it. Unsurprisingly, it didn't sell very well, but I was thankful a copy had been thrust into my hands by my mate at the record shop. It was Bolton band the Buzzcocks' first single, with Pete Shelley on vocals. The founder and original front man Howard Devoto had just left, despite the success of the band's first release, the EP 'Spiral Scratch', which included the iconic track 'Boredom'. Glasgow new wave band Orange Juice later paid homage to it when they sampled it in their exquisite upbeat hit tune 'Rip it Up'. Devoto went off to form his own band Magazine, which had a string of hits, including the outstanding song 'Shot by Both Sides'.

I had never travelled outside of London, so I had no idea where Bolton was, or Manchester, or Lancashire for that matter. But I liked the sound. So when the Buzzcocks were set to play the Greyhound a week or so later, I made sure I was there. It was a great gig, as the band tore through their set, fronted by diminutive Pete Shelley whose reward for turning in an excellent performance was to be gobbed at relentlessly, regardless of his soft-spoken, Lancashire-accented objections. I even bought an Orgasm Addict badge – although I can't remember ever wearing it.

From then on I began to seek out records from punk bands from the Greater Manchester area. Soon I was picking up and getting into singles by Slaughter and the Dogs, Ed Banger and the Nosebleeds, the Drones, Magazine, John Cooper Clarke, The Fall and later Joy Division. One of my all-time favourite singles has to be Ed Banger and the Nosebleeds' 1977 track 'Ain't Bin to No Music School'. Like all the best punk tunes produced at the time it had the feel of a Music Hall turn about it – larger than life, speaking straight to its audience, brassy, raucous and giving it to the top-hats. The front cover of the single has the Nosebleeds plonked in a secondary-modern pre-fab school classroom with their feet on the desks like something out of that awful racist seventies sitcom *Please Sir!* The back cover has a sketch of the boarded-up door of 'Wythenshawe Royal Music School' (presumably a reference to the Royal Northern College of Music in Manchester's Oxford Road) with the warning KEEP OUT! The message that working class oiks were not welcome in the conservatoires may have come from band-leader Vincent Reilly, a working-class Mancunian whose precocious musical abilities weren't nurtured by the RNCM but through

after-school sessions by classical music tutors paid for by his mum. As
befits Reilly's formal training 'Music School' starts with a snatch of grand
orchestral violins interrupted by a spiralling sonic guitar riff by Reilly, cut
across by choppy punk chords and drums and then we're into the lyrics –
the bellowed chorus of which is:

> I ain't been to no music school,
> I ain't nobody's fool.

So what attracted a south London teenager to Manchester punk? In a
Melody Maker article in 1977, titled 'New Wave Devolution: Manchester
Waits for the World to Listen', local record label owner Tosh Ryan credited
the city's distinctive punk sound, outlook and energy as a particular
response to the final tortured stages in the industrial decline of the city and
life on the working class estates in areas like Wythenshawe, Salford and
Moss Side. This was even before Thatcher laid waste to what little
remained. Ryan argued: 'The area is so neglected, so economically
deprived and full of massive housing complexes, that the mood of the place
was right and ready for a new movement in music with markedly different
criteria of success. What has developed is peculiar to Manchester.'

Maybe I somehow identified with this 'different criteria of success', and
its working-class sensibility. The London punk scene in 1977 could
certainly feel very middle-class, individualistic and overtly controlled by
Thatcherite precursors like Malcolm Maclaren. Maybe I sniffed a hint of
proletarian pride and solidarity in the Manchester scene. I don't know.
Later in life I would end up working in theatre in Manchester and
Lancashire, living in Rochdale and then St Helens. It was only then that I
came to appreciate the region's rich socialist traditions, culture and
historical memory. But let's give the last word to the Buzzcocks' 'Boredom'
– from the *Spiral Scratch* EP, all four tracks laid down in three hours and
mixed in two:

> I've taken this extravagant journey
> so it seems to me
> I just came from nowhere
> and I'm going straight back there

Out of the nihilism of punk finally emerged something much more radical and unifying. The Clash really did 'seize the time'. Yet, it's quite something, when you think about it, that the debut single of the most successful punk band of all, clocked in at just one minute fifty-eight seconds and was widely misinterpreted at the time as having racist overtones.

The Sex Pistols' 'Anarchy in the UK' had exploded in November 1976 like a random depth-charge, blowing all the accepted musical rules out of the water, but instant converts like myself had to wait another six months until we had something else to compare it to. So we could begin to join the dots: 'that song is punk, and this one is also punk, so this must be what punk is. This is what it sounds like and this is what it is all about'. All we could do in the intervening period was tune in to the BBC Radio One John Peel show in the evenings to hear what new bands he was raving about.

If 'Anarchy in the UK' had slashed a big X in the centre of a new soundscape, The Clash's debut single 'White Riot', released in March 1977, would be an arrow pointing us in a particular direction. But what direction? What exactly was a White Riot I asked myself? Wasn't that something that the razor-wielding Teddy Boys had been up to in Notting Hill in 1958 when they had attempted to pogrom the local West Indian population? Or what the Enoch brigade and the NF thugs would like to do to 'pakis' given half a chance? It wasn't until The Clash included their interpretation of one of my all-time favourites, Junior Murvin's reggae masterpiece 'Police and Thieves' on the first album, that I realised where The Clash stood.

I came to understand that 'White Riot' was in fact a song of praise for the Black youth who had bravely fought the Met police to a standstill during the 1976 Notting Hill Carnival, and an admonishment to white youth who had yet to find their own route to confrontation with the state. Indeed 'White Riot' was composed out of the first-hand experience of Clash singer Joe Strummer, bass player Paul Simonon and manager Bernie Rhodes, who had been caught up in, and participated in the insurrection against state repression and racism that flared in Notting Hill in the August of that searing long hot summer of '76.

White riot – I wanna riot
White riot – a riot of my own
White riot – I wanna riot
White riot – a riot of my own

Black man gotta lot a problems
But they don't mind throwing a brick
White people go to school
Where they teach you how to be thick

…All the power's in the hands
Of people rich enough to buy it
While we walk the street
Too chicken to even try it

'…Are you taking over or are you taking orders? Are you going backwards, Or are you going forwards?' the song concludes, echoing Trinidadian revolutionary CLR James's eloquent insight:

> Times would pass, old empires would fall and new ones take their place. The relations of countries and the relations of classes had to change before I discovered that it is not the quality of goods and utility which matters, but movement, not where you are, or what you have, but where you have come from, where you are going and the rate at which you are getting there.

The Clash were as much an expression of the UK reggae scene and Caribbean culture and rebel politics as they were of the pub rock and art-school scene. Joe Strummer had lived in a communal squat in Maida Vale, just north of Notting Hill. Mick Jones had been a south London schoolboy in multi-racial Tulse Hill. Paul Simonon had been raised in Brixton and Ladbroke Grove, growing up in and around London's Black community, and was a huge reggae fan – clearly manifested in his loping ska/reggae bass-playing style. Before going on to manage The Clash, Bernie Rhodes had run a record shop in Kilburn specialising in reggae imports. Apart from using photo imagery from the '76 Notting Hill riot as backdrops to their gigs and on their record sleeves, The Clash were visually inspired by artwork they came across adorning Jamaican reggae album covers.

In 1977 the journalist, cultural activist and maybe best chronicler of punk, Vivien Goldman, wrote an insightful article in *Sounds* magazine that traced out the punky-reggae conversation that was going on at the time. Goldman wrote that, setting aside Don Letts' famed reggae DJ sets at punk gigs:

> The main impetus for punk enthusiasm for reggae is down to the musicians. The Clash definitely lead the way – their cover of 'Police And Thieves' is the strongest vinyl evidence to date of new wave sympathy for their black peer group. Even down to the shot of the rioting under the Westway at the '76 Notting Hill Carnival on their album sleeve, The Clash have always laid their souls on the red, green and gold line. Bernie Rhodes was right when he described them as 'a roots band'.

In June 1978 The Clash were to return to the inspiration of 'Police and Thieves' with the distinctive single '(White Man) In Hammersmith Palais':

> White youth, black youth
> Better find another solution
> Why not phone up Robin Hood
> And ask him for some wealth distribution.

Between 1977 and 1979 The Clash never stopped evolving their sound and subject material, and widening their political reach into areas I could appreciate and agree with, the opposite of their early rivals, the Sex Pistols, who, for whatever reason you like to give, never moved forward musically, rapidly descending into both tragedy and farce. In the same month as '(White Man) In Hammersmith Palais' was released, what was left of the Pistols messily exited musical history with the charmless 12" single 'No One Is Innocent' – a seedy karaoke sing-a-long with sad-sack train-robber in exile Ronnie Biggs:

> God save Martin Boorman and Nazis on the run
> God save Myra Hindley God save Ian Brady
> Even though he's horrible and she ain't what you call a lady

The Clash were the most exciting live band I have ever experienced – even beating my old favourites The Damned. I saw The Clash perform at The Rainbow, Finsbury Park in December 1977, at the Victoria Park Rock Against Racism gig in April 1978, Harlesden Roxy in October 1978 and at the Mecca Lyceum Ballroom on the corner of The Strand, central London, in December 1978.

In those days you had to rush to the venue ticket office as soon as the weekly music press announced that tickets had been released, queue up for hours, put up with passers-by stopping to gawp at the assorted rabble slumped untidily in the road (me and my fellow Clash fans), and hopefully make it to the box-office grill before the gig sold out, passing over some greasy bank notes to the rude ticket lady who had drawn the short straw that day. I remember going up to the Strand and queuing up outside the Lyceum to buy two tickets for a fiver each – and thinking at the time that was a bit steep and it had better be worth it.

It proved to be a phenomenal gig – Joe Strummer spitting out lyrics through his crooked teeth, his left leg furiously pumping up and down to the beat, Mick Jones fronting up to his left, Paul Simonon, low slung bass across his hip to the right and Topper Headon hard at it on the drum kit at the back. Tune after tune rocketed out from the stage like fireworks into the auditorium one after the other in feverish bursts of hot energy – 'White Riot', 'City of the Dead', 'Remote Control', 'Janie Jones', 'What's My Name?', 'Garageland', 'Tommy Gun', 'Drug-Stabbing Time', 'Capital Radio', 'Police and Thieves', 'I Fought The Law', 'Stay Free'.

Then out into the West End night, drenched with sweat, my ears ringing (as they would continue to do so for days after), completely numbed, on autopilot I crossed the Strand and over the river towards Waterloo Station and home. Whatever individual thoughts and emotions that had been with me that day had been burned clean out of my skull.

Joe Strummer later remarked that those were the nights 'when it burns. When you cease to be even anybody at all. You're just part of something. You don't know what you're doing or saying. It burns and that is what the audience want to be part of, that burn'.

AZIZ BALOUCH

Stefan Williamson Fa

The exploration of connections between flamenco, the main musical and dance tradition of Andalusia and the Romani people of Spain, and the music of the 'Islamic world' has been in vogue in recent years. Countless collaborative and 'fusion' projects have brought together artists and musicians from across the Strait of Gibraltar and beyond. Some of these projects, including Tony Gatlif's 1993 film, *Latcho Drom,* have attempted to trace Romani routes from South Asia to the Iberian Peninsula. Others, such as Faiz Ali Faiz's *Qawwali-Flamenco*, have focussed on the genre's perceived 'Islamic roots' in Al Andalus. Having been born and brought up in Gibraltar with family on both sides of the Strait, I have long been interested in music from across the Mediterranean. My own interest in the Islamic history of Andalusia developed over time and eventually led to my decision to train as an anthropologist specialising in music and sound in Islamic contexts. Although I have been drawn to these attempts to 'uncover' lost connections or 'bridge' cultural gaps between the place I was born and the music I love, many of these projects have unfortunately failed to impress me. While some productions achieve popular, commercial and critical success they have often represented a fairly superficial and unequal engagement across musical boundaries geared towards particular audiences of 'world music' consumers.

This changed in late 2009. Whilst listening to a weekly flamenco radio programme on Spanish national radio, I came across a voice which made a huge impact on me. The radio presenter said little before playing a recording announcing the name of the performer as 'Abdul Aziz Balouch' and mentioning he was a Pakistani singer who had travelled to Spain in the early twentieth century. The recording was an immaculate rendition of a *Malagueña* – one of the traditional styles of flamenco song. Balouch's voice was moving and though there was little to tell that the singer was not from

Spain, the idea of a singer travelling from Pakistan to Spain to study flamenco almost a century ago completely took hold of my imagination.

Years passed and I was unable to find much more information about this singer or any of his recordings. The radio presenter's announcement gave me little to search with on Google or in libraries. I had given up all hope of listening to this voice again until one day I managed to find, by chance, an online bookseller in England with a lot for sale containing books by an author called Azizullah Balouch. Amongst the various books – with titles like *What is a Sufi?*, *Mystic Songs of Islam*, *Selections from the Poems of Shah Latif* – was one titled *Spanish Cante Jondo and Its Origin in Sindhi Music*. I realised that this must be the same singer I had heard years ago, purchased the books immediately and waited impatiently for them to arrive at my door. Upon delivery I opened the first page and was struck by an image of Balouch wearing a karakul hat with Spanish guitar in hand. I was sure I had found the man behind the voice I had heard years ago. As I read through the pages, I slowly began to piece together a rich and fascinating life of a fellow soul who had a similar passion for music, flamenco and Islamic history and culture. A life which intersected with mine in multiple ways – not only did we share these interests but Gibraltar, my home town had been a central part of his life journey. While my attempts to learn about this extraordinary life have since been extensive, taking me in the opposite direction, from Gibraltar to Sindh, there are still many gaps in his story.

I began by tracing the path of Aziz Balouch as he travelled first from modern-day Pakistan to Gibraltar, where he began training as a flamenco singer and later between London and Madrid, where he propagated Sufi philosophy, poetry and practice and proposed a hypothesis of the South Asian and Islamic origins of flamenco. Although his work may not have been conclusive in proving the Islamic or South Asian roots of the genre, his life reveals a complex and lesser told story of music, movement and Islam across continents in the twentieth century.

Azizullah Abdurahman Balouch was born into a Buledi family in Baluchistan (under British colonial rule) on the 5 March 1909. Shortly after his father's death his family moved to Sindh where they settled in the town of Pir-jo-Goth, the centre of the Hur Sufi community headed by the Pir Pagaro who had led several armed insurgencies against British rule. It was here that he began his studies at the madrasa of the Pir Pagaro's Dargah, learning Sindhi, Arabic and Persian and studying the Qur'an alongside the lyrics of Maulana Jalaluddin Rumi and the seventeenth century Sindhi Sufi-poet Shah Abdul Latif Bhittai amongst others. At the shrine, he was also exposed to Sindhi devotional song through the chants of devotees who came to the *dargah* from across the province during festivals. Later on, at secondary school in Hyderabad, he developed his early interest in song learning to recite Sindhi folk verses and melodies, and he performed regularly at various social functions across the town. It was here in Hyderabad, while simultaneously working and studying for his entrance exams for Aligarh University, that he had his first encounter with flamenco when he listened to the record collection of a successful Hyderabadi Hindu businessman Hotu-Khemchand, who had established a business and house in Gibraltar. Balouch was so enamoured and 'spiritually uplifted' by the voices of the singers he heard that he did not have to think twice when he eventually received a job offer by the said businessman to go and work in Gibraltar.

In the latter part of the nineteenth century, the Western Mediterranean port city of Gibraltar became a hub for Sindhi merchants who travelled across new routes opened up by the creation of the Suez Canal and who settled along what was referred to as 'the lifeline of the British Empire', Karachi to Aden, Cairo, Malta and Gibraltar. As a result of this movement, the Sindhi community of Gibraltar had been in existence since 1870 when the first business was established selling cotton textiles. The expansion of businesses based on patron and client relationships between families meant that a relatively steady flow of, mostly male, merchants and workers came to the colony. Some stayed for short periods while others decided to remain longer, eventually making a home for themselves there. As the Hotu-Khemchand family still own a number of shops in Gibraltar's Main Street, I managed to track down the daughter of the businessman who had first invited Balouch to work with him. She remembered that her father and Balouch had worked and lived together in Hyderabad, Karachi and Gibraltar and were so close that they referred to each other as brothers. Her grandfather Khemchand Mahtani was also so fond of Balouch that he used to say he had adopted him as his son. The Hindu family's close relation with Balouch, a Muslim, is said to have been quite unusual. However, they had been heavily involved in the founding of the Theosophical Society in Karachi, something which clearly must have appealed to Balouch and had a profound influence on him.

For Aziz Balouch, moving from Sindh to Gibraltar was more than just an opportunity to make a living – it was a chance to pursue a spiritual and musical path. Other than his love for the flamenco records, he had read and heard much about the history of Al-Andalus, the wonders of Cordoba and Granada and the great Andalusi mystic, Ibn-Arabi. It was a joyful Balouch who arrived in Gibraltar by boat in July 1932. In his memoirs he writes: 'we arrived at Gibraltar, the historical *Jabal al-Tariq*; when I beheld the *peñón* and the Castle of Tariq, the frontiers and the first vistas of Southern Spain, I felt like one returning to his own land.' Despite this romantic arrival his first year was spent working long hours in a shop and it was not until the following year that he would have his first live experience of flamenco. For much of Gibraltar's history the land border with Spain has been relatively fluid with people living, working and socialising across the frontier in the neighbouring town of La Linea de La Concepcion. One evening Balouch had the chance to attend a live performance in La Linea by the most renowned flamenco artists of the time, including Pepe Marchena. Ecstatic about the performance, Balouch insisted his friends invite the artists to their house in Main Street Gibraltar the next day as he wished to sing for them. Accepting this odd request, the artists visited the business premises in town where Balouch performed a number of flamenco pieces and Sindhi songs accompanying himself on a harmonium he had brought from Sindh. Astonished by the short recital Marchena invited him to perform on stage with him the following evening at the Teatro Cómico de La Linea. Balouch gave a rendition of Marchena's own song 'La Rosa' which proved so popular he was called back seven times before the curtain fell.

This event, reported in the newspapers of Gibraltar at the time as, 'an extraordinary event in the history of flamenco', was the beginning of Aziz Balouch's fascinating, though now rather forgotten, career in music. Marchena agreed to take on the young Balouch as his student and he soon took on the nickname *Marchenita* – 'Little Marchena'. Balouch became an established singer in Gibraltar, eventually travelling on to Madrid. His reception there was mixed. It is clear that some, including Marchena himself, were truly impressed and inspired by Balouch's talent and passion for the genre while others saw him only as a curiosity. In concert posters he was often billed as such – 'THE INDIAN who sings flamenco, disciple of Marchena, with his MAGICAL INSTRUMENT'. On several occasions he was also confronted by journalists requesting to see his passport, believing he was really just a Spaniard masquerading as a foreigner. Along with Marchena he also established a group of musician and artist friends in Madrid, who facilitated opportunities for him.

Balouch made various concert appearances in Madrid, which led to an invitation from the director of Parlophone Records in Barcelona for him to record a number of his songs. The short four track EP, his only catalogued release, was a first on many levels. It was not only unprecedented for a young man from South Asia to record an album in Spain, but it was also the first example of experimentation and 'fusion' in flamenco music. The release was titled *Sufi Hispano Pakistani* as Balouch blended Persian, Sindhi, Arabic and Hindi poetry with the melodies and Spanish lyrics of *Cante Jondo*.

In one track, Aziz Balouch transitions from the poetry of eleventh/ twelfth century Persian poet Sanai to the expressive mood of the *seguiriya*.

Malikā zikr-i tu goyam ki tu pākī-yu khudāyī
Naravam juz ba hamān rah ki tu'am rāh nu(a)māyī'
Oh King, I sing your *dhikr*, for you are pure and regal
I shall not fare except on the path that you have pointed out to me
Ahora tú vienes hincá de rodillas pidiendo perdón,
te apartaste de mi vera y te fuiste sin apelación.
Now you come to me on your knees begging forgiveness,
You left my side ignoring my appeals.

Despite his love for flamenco, Balouch was critical of the licentious behaviour of the musicians and their audiences. His insistence on avoiding the 'excesses of physical pleasures' for the benefit of singing was not taken seriously and was even ridiculed by some. Early on in his engagement with flamenco he felt that there was a spiritual and mystical heritage of flamenco which had largely disappeared but remained hidden in a few modes of *Cante Jondo*, such as the more sorrowful melodies and themes of *soleares*, *seguiriyas*, *serranas*, *fandanguillos* and the Holy Week laments of *saeta*.

During his first period in Madrid, Balouch founded the Sufi Society whose aim, in his own words, was 'to propagate the ideas of Sufism, a soul-purifying philosophy of the East in which music also plays an important part'. In Madrid he gave several lectures on the 'intellectual, mystical and practical side of Sufi philosophy'. In his own writing he claims there was sufficient interest amongst musicians and intellectuals there, but the outbreak of the Civil War quickly disrupted his activities. As the fighting intensified Balouch was injured during a bombing in Madrid and had to flee the country in order to receive treatment in the United Kingdom. He was hospitalised for a year in Southampton before moving to London.

Once recovered, Aziz Balouch continued his musical development undertaking vocal tuition at the London College of Music and performing flamenco at social gatherings as well as making a few appearances on BBC radio. Now settled in London, Aziz sought to continue his promotion of Sufism, founding the 'Sindh Sufi Society' in 1948. Compared with Madrid, London provided perhaps a more fertile ground for the propagation of his ideas. The Theosophical Society, with its interest in 'non-Western religions' had already been established in the city and 'Sufism' was known amongst certain social circles. The imperial connection between Britain and South Asia meant that there were already scholars from the subcontinent present in the capital. The Theosophical Society had published a book in 1924 by Jethmal Parsram Gulrajani titled *Sind and its Sufis* with short biographies of saints from the region along with some extracts from their lyrics translated for English readers. Furthermore, Inayat Khan had already established the idea of Universalist Sufism in London over two decades before Aziz Balouch's arrival in the 1940s. Though Aziz makes no mention of these predecessors in his writing, they no doubt provided a substrate for him to carry out his own activities, organising regular events, writing and publishing from his small home in Notting Hill, West London.

The inaugural meeting of the society was held on 12 December 1948 at the premises of a Mr. C. Ramchand where Balouch gave an introductory lecture on Sufism and a performance of the songs of Shah Abdul Latif attended by friends from Spain, Morocco, Bombay and Trinidad. The following meeting was held in a private venue again and attracted a large number of both Europeans and Sindhis before the meetings were moved to Alliance Hall on Palmer Street, SW1, a venue belonging to the Temperance movement, a social movement against the consumption of alcohol, and thereon known as 'Sufi Hall' to regular attendees. The Fifth Meeting on 16 December 1949 at this new location was a lecture on 'The

Sufis of Persia and their influence over the spiritual and literary world', with half the programme given over once more to a performance of Sufi music by M. Minovi, an Iranian critic and writer. This was followed by a performance by Prince F. Farhard of songs by Hafiz and Rumi accompanied on the *tar*.

The topics of the society's sessions over the following years ranged from lectures on other Sufi poets from Sindh (such as Sachal Sarmast), the Sufi influence on European authors and medicine, music and spirituality. Of course, Balouch's passion for music meant these events were always complemented with a musical programme, with live recitals of Persian and Indian Classical music; Balouch gave renditions of Sindhi lyrics, accompanying himself on guitar or harmonium, and even of Spanish Andalusian folk songs for a celebration of a 'Sufi interpretation of Christmas'. From the breadth of these events and available correspondence it is clear that Balouch managed to grasp the attention and interest of a wide range of personalities from European musicians to established intellectuals from the Subcontinent living in the city. Balouch used the society's publication as a means of elaborating on his own interpretation of Sufism. The ideas he presented resonated strongly with the Universal Sufism of Inayat Khan or the Theosophical Society, who were some of the main distributors of his works, and often downplayed the centrality of the sharia in Sufism to open aspects of Sufi thought and practice to others of different faith backgrounds, the majority of those interested in the society. His insistence on the idea that God was to be found everywhere was clearly drawn from the thoughts of Mansur Al-Hallaj and Ibn Arabi who he repeatedly quoted and referenced in these works, alongside the lyrics and tales of Persian language Sufis such as Hafiz, Rumi, Saadi Shirazi and Sanai, whom he must have come to know through his Persian language education in Sindh.

The popularity of the Sufi Society was significant enough to catch the attention of the British magazine *Tatler*. In December 1959, the magazine published a feature on the society with the terrible title 'Oriental Religions Among Us'. The piece, covering a range of non-Christian religions present in London at the time, includes an image of Balouch playing the guitar with a young English man standing behind him. Next to the image the commentary reads: 'Sufi teacher Aziz Balouch plays the guitar for his followers. Smallest of the eastern religious sects in London, Sufism preaches

the pursuit of spiritual experience by bodily restraint and mystical intuition.'
Balouch did consider himself to be a teacher and was clearly trying to gain a
following in London. His text *The Sufi*, first published in 1958, was his
clearest attempt to lay out a practical guide for the members of his society.
The volume deals with what he considered a number of important aspects of
Sufism, including 'Important Hints for the development of Spiritual
Powers', 'Care of the Body', and 'Music in Sufism', which he related to the
disciples passing through four stages: right physical conduct, correct moral
feeling, clear mental vision and spiritual realisation. Reading the work today
it appears in places to be little more than a New Age self-help guide, with its
discussions on 'Mental and Emotional Development', postures for
meditation and insistence on vegetarianism. Balouch's perspective on Sufism
may seem somewhat outdated, deeply entrenched in the context of early
twentieth century spiritual movements rather than in the works of eternal
Sufi thinkers. Yet through a careful reading of his texts it is clear that Aziz
Balouch had a deep knowledge and respect for the great Sufi philosophers
whom he passionately desired to promote everywhere he went. Balouch's
devotion to the saints of Sindh – in particular to Shah Abdul Latif, whose
lyrics he first sang to the flamenco artists that night in Gibraltar – can be seen
throughout his life. His publications referred to and cited these figures more
than anyone else. He put together a collection of translated lyrics from Sindh
called *Mystic Sufi Songs of Islam* illustrated, transcribed and arranged though
never released. While the poetry of the saints of Sindh had been brought to
the attention of European audiences by Gulrajani, mentioned above, and
early translations of Shah Latif's *Shah Jo Risalo* and later the work of
Annemarie Schimmel, Aziz Balouch brought these lyrics to life in his
performances in their original language and attempted to demonstrate their
relevance to his audiences' own lives far from Sindh.

After his first stint in London, Balouch was invited to return to Madrid
in 1952 at the request of the newly appointed Pakistani Ambassador to
Spain, Syed Miran Mohammad Shah, who shared 'a love of art and music,
and devotion to Shah Abdul Latif of Sindh' with Balouch. In Madrid, he
was given the role of Cultural Attaché at the new Embassy of Pakistan.
Here his intention was to serve his 'two beloved countries', as he called
them – 'the newly formed country of Pakistan – the land of his birth [and
Spain] the land of his adoption through its music'. With the support of the

embassy he founded an association called *Amigos de Pakistan* and continued to perform solo and alongside Pepe Marchena across Spain. However, this time his performances had the particular aim of demonstrating the similarity between *Cante Jondo* and the profound singing of Sindhi Sufi songs of Pakistan. Press reports attest to the general acceptance and appreciation of Aziz Balouch's theory and work, all the more impressive given the context of the insular nationalist dictatorship of General Franco in Spain at the time. His tenure at the embassy ended following the departure of Syed Miran Mohammad Shah, but he continued his promotion of the connections between Spain and Pakistan in a personal capacity, writing his book in Spanish *Cante Jondo su Origen y Evolucion – Cante Jondo Its Origin and Evolution* (1955) — and even organising a recital for Pepe Marchena in Karachi in 1962.

In 1968 an English version of the book was published by the Mehran Arts Council in Hyderabad, Pakistan, under the title *Spanish Cante Jondo and its Origin in Sindhi Music*. With this publication he aimed to promote Flamenco in Pakistan as well as putting forward his theory of the Sindhi and Sufi origins of Flamenco. The book gives several examples of parallels between the two musical traditions and compares certain forms of these in depth. Balouch compares, for instance, the *saeta,* a lament sung in Andalusia during Holy Week, with the *marsiya* recited in Pakistan to commemorate the martyrdom of Imam Husayn. He writes:

> Just as in Spain, the songs in the Holy Week are sung in processions without instrumental accompaniment except the drum, so are the *Marthiyyas* in Sind as well as in other parts of Pakistan sung only to the accompaniment of *Ghazzi* and drum. The most typical of these songs, falling within the general category of the *Marthiyyas* sung exclusively in the Lower Indus Valley of Sindh, are known as *Osara*. The semblance between the *Osara* of Sind and the *Saeta* religious songs of *Cante Jondo* is typical.

He offers several different possibilities for the connections between Spanish and Sindhi music. Balouch makes the claim that the influential medieval composer Ziryab (789–857) was actually of Sindhi origin, something that he provides little valid evidence for. His suggestion that Romani in Spain originate in South Asia, therefore bringing elements of their musical culture with them, is slightly more credible given recent research on the topic. Despite the weak evidence for his claims, the book marks a first in the history of flamenco, in which a concrete connection between the current tradition and Islamic past was not only highlighted but celebrated. In Pakistan the work reached a limited audience but the idea that a musical tradition in a country far away had its roots in Sindh was popularly received. When I travelled to Karachi in 2018 to present a paper on Aziz Balouch's life and work I was surprised to find that Balouch had a cult status amongst Sindhi intellectuals and nationalists. Though little was known about the man, he was proudly remembered as an individual who had proven the Sindhi origins of Spanish music.

Despite his deep-rooted love for Sindh and his homeland, Aziz's life, work and efforts were characterised by an incredible openness to the worlds, cultures and love of others. In a lifetime riddled with struggle, strife and oppression – living through world war, Partition in his homeland, civil war in his adopted home of Spain followed by fascist dictatorship, and life in London, which was plagued by institutional and everyday racism – he stuck by what he believed to be a key principle of Sufism: love and equality for all. One of the stated aims of the 'Sindh Sufi Society' was 'To fight against ignorance, starvation, disease and cruelty and to develop the intellectual and spiritual side of life'. Balouch stressed that the first requirement before any spiritual development can take place is that one be 'Free of Caste, Colour and Creed'. Of course, his ability to travel and spread his ideas was partly due to his middle-class background and education but it is undeniable that he was uniquely driven on his path by his love and passion for Sufism and the arts. Unfortunately, the figure of Aziz Balouch and the values of cross-cultural collaboration, respect, love and dialogue he embodied and stood for, remain relatively unknown. Within Spain, Aziz Balouch's legacy is that of a curious figure and episode in the history of flamenco. Other than an appearance in the 1963 Cordoba Arab Poetry Festival there is little trace of the final decade of his life. Records show that he married an English singer, Margaret Manella, and returned to England, where he spent the final years of his life. Aziz Balouch died in Surrey, outside London, in 1978 where he is buried in an unmarked grave. Five miles away from where I now live. How our lives continue to intersect.

MY POP STAR LIFE

Shanon Shah

I never know what to say when people ask if I was a pop star in Malaysia. I did win Best Male Vocal for my debut album, *Dilanda Cinta* (*Love-swept*), at the thirteenth annual Malaysian Music Industry Awards in 2006. In Britain, I explain that these are the Malaysian version of the BRIT or Grammy awards. While this description sounds semi-impressive, it doesn't quite capture what really happened the night I won.

My category was presented by Erra Fazira, the last Muslim contestant to win the Miss Malaysia crown (before Muslims were banned from entering beauty pageants) and who went on to carve out a successful music and acting career – Malaysia's answer to Bollywood royalty Aishwarya Rai! – and Juliana Banos, another fairly famous actress-cum-singer. My fellow nominees consisted of industry veterans and impressive up-and-comers whose names were read out in alphabetical order, with audible applause accompanying each announcement. Mine came last and was greeted by pin-drop silence. When Erra and Juliana opened the envelope, they both raised their eyebrows in bemusement and could barely pronounce my name properly. Maybe three people cheered – my sister (as my plus one), the late Toni Kasim (my mentor and best friend), and another mutual friend who got Toni in as his plus one.

I've tried my best to flush this memory out of my system. Against my will, I still recall the embarrassing silence, hugging my sister to near suffocation (the Malay-language paparazzi were a bit confused – was that my wife? 'friend'? *mother*?), and the first thing I said in Malay in my acceptance speech: 'If you're all shocked, imagine how I feel.' I've resurrected these memories by consulting YouTube, which was itself instructive. The search terms 'Shanon Shah' and 'Anugerah Industri Muzik' ('Music Industry Awards') or 'AIM' returned zilch results. It's only after I typed something like 'AIM' 'Vokal Lelaki Terbaik' ('Best Male

Vocal') and '2006' that I found a grainy video transfer – and I had to scroll pretty far down to get to it. It has had barely 900 views and four 'Likes' at the time of writing. That's how much of a 'pop star' I was in Malaysia.

I'm relieved this particular clip doesn't get viewed very much. I mean, those mutton-chop sideburns and that Michael Jackson-esque facial foundation – what on earth was I thinking? I am proud of one thing, though. I had a red ribbon pinned to my jacket, and not just any old red ribbon. It was one that was specially made by volunteers for the Malaysian AIDS Council (MAC), and I was wearing it because I worked with and supported not only MAC but several other social justice non-governmental organisations (NGOs), including Sisters in Islam, Amnesty International Malaysia, the Centre for Independent Journalism and Suaram (Voice of the Malaysian People). But this was still the early 2000s, when Malaysia was a semi-dictatorship (or fledgling semi-democracy, if you want to be glass-half-full), and so the MAC ribbon seemed like the least likely to get my record label into trouble. It was also probably the only symbol that more than a handful of people watching would recognise – even that's being optimistic.

I delivered my acceptance speech in bookish, soft-spoken Malay and English, an unconscious affectation that probably didn't help endear me to the mainstream music industry. The biggest cheer came when I kind of laughed at myself and said, 'Thanks to my fans – there's probably only a handful of you but I hope this award changes things.'

It didn't, really. My album sales remained dismal and it would take another five years before I released my sophomore recording which was even less commercially successful than my debut.

Sure, there were glimmers of hope after my win, but I was too insecure to recognise them. The next morning, for example, I got invited onto an English-language morning talk show. I felt way more comfortable chatting with the two hosts, Daphne Iking and Naz Rahman, than I had in a long time, awkwardly trying to promote my album to the Malay-language media. ('You're Malay? Really?') Daphne and I started giggling when she said the trophy looked like a *batang* (literally, 'log', but a euphemism for penis). Naz kept a straight face when I asked, 'Can she say that on air?' and Daphne replied, feigning innocence, 'Say what? What's wrong?' To my most pleasant shock, there was also a caller – a young Malay-speaking man who said I reminded him of Antony and the Johnsons. This was a huge compliment, since I was also at that point discovering their second album, *I Am a Bird Now*, and more significantly because Antony (now Anohni) is a trans activist. I checked with all my friends afterwards – was it one of them doing me a favour by 'spontaneously' calling in? Nope, it was a *bona fide* fan. Hello Erra Fazira and Juliana Banos – did you guys see that? My AIM award did mean something and wearing my MAC ribbon really was a good idea!

I look back and wonder what would have happened if I had just hung in there and responded to these moments with grace, generosity and good humour. But I was already being weighed down by the potent mix of Malay nationalism, soft Islamism, homophobia and class hypocrisy that infused the mainstream music scene.

My first brush with mini fame came five years before that, in 2001. I had just returned to Malaysia after graduating in chemical engineering. I was trying to inveigle my way out of working with PETRONAS, the state-owned oil and gas company that had paid for my degree. I had landed a job as a junior reporter at *Radiq Radio*, a now-defunct independent web news project of the Centre for Independent Journalism (CIJ), a media watchdog. I did not know the first thing about journalism, but I knew I simply could not bear working for an oil company – even one that was ostensibly committed to nation-building.

When I accepted the PETRONAS scholarship to study chemical engineering in Australia, I knew I was going to be bored. No disrespect to all the cool and fashionable engineers out there, but it just wasn't for me. I was a classically trained pianist and wanted to make music, not monitor valves or whatever else happened in an oil refinery. But the list of university degrees and professions that my parents found acceptable was very short – it was either become a doctor, lawyer or engineer (or *maybe* an accountant). My siblings were already in medical school and managed to persuade my father to let me 'rebel' by going overseas to study engineering. Notwithstanding the bad-boy appeal of chemical engineering, I still sought different creative outlets during my degree. I learnt very basic Hindi, won a full scholarship to study stage acting for a year (at the St Martins Youth Arts Centre in South Yarra), became an open mic regular at a Melbourne pub, and enrolled in an optional gender studies module offered by the social sciences faculty in my penultimate year.

Getting exposed to feminism – especially the postcolonial variety I was taught – helped me make sense of the political turmoil back in Malaysia, triggered by the sacking of former deputy prime minister Anwar Ibrahim on charges of sodomy. Malaysia has gone through other political crises in the past two decades and is arguably in democratic transition, with Anwar a free man again, but back then this was simply too traumatic for me.

My extra-curricular activities were helping to join several other dots as well. Most notably, I was traumatised in a different way when I learnt about the execution of the Nigerian writer Ken Saro-Wiwa in 1995 by a special military tribunal, allegedly supported by Royal Dutch Shell, for his environmental activism against the oil industry. One piece of research led to another, and I simply did not want anything to do with the oil and gas industry for the rest of my life. Along with the political crisis in Malaysia, this is what led me to seek out more independent sources of news and activism in Malaysia and, on the eve of my departure from Australia, I spotted the journalism vacancy and emailed an expression of interest. The fifth track on my debut album, 'Jurutera' ('Engineer') is a jazzy, Billy Joel-esque number that summarises this period of my life. The refrain basically repeats, *ad nauseum*, the line: 'because I don't want to be an engineer'.

My family – and PETRONAS – had other ideas. After graduating in late 2000, I returned to Malaysia and could not stop moping in my parents' house. My father, excited about my potentially prestigious job at the PETRONAS Twin Towers, bullied me into learning golf to help me schmooze with my potential managers. I then quietly wrote a short story about a young man who breaks both his feet with a golf club to spite his father. (I still don't care for golf.) Curiously, however, my mother left a newspaper clipping on my desk one day – it was a call for entries for a patriotic songwriting competition, organised by the Kuala Lumpur-based International College of Music (ICOM). I locked myself up in my room for a couple of weeks and wrote five different numbers – some in English, some in Malay. I recorded myself singing them to my own piano accompaniment in our living room when no one was around, on my fuzzy-sounding cassette player, and posted the tapes and lyric sheets, not daring to think about my chances.

Soon afterwards, I was interviewed for the *Radiq Radio* post and started work as a naïve reporter – in one of my first assignments of a political protest, I decided to interview a few bystanders for 'colour'. They said they couldn't talk to the press. 'It's OK, we're an independent news outfit, we won't censor you,' I tried to reassure them. 'We're police,' they replied, curtly. 'Police? But you're not wearing uniforms!'

Yes, indeed – on one of my first major reporting assignments, I tried to get the Special Branch to tell me what they thought about political repression in Malaysia. Thankfully, my idiocy saved me from being put on any police surveillance. (I think.) Some days after that incident, my mother screeched over the phone that I had been shortlisted for the songwriting contest for my Malay-language song, 'Kisahmu Belum Berakhir' ('Your Story is Not Over').

I was surprised that the selection panel chose this number. Not that I wasn't proud of it – musically, it was inspired by a little bit of Shawn Colvin and Sheryl Crow (although it sounds like nothing either of them have ever written or sung). Lyrically, I wanted to write a song that, as I later put it to a friend, a secularist or an Islamist could sing about Malaysia and mean it. I wanted to write a song that would transcend the bitterness and violence between then (and present) prime minister Mahathir Mohamad and Anwar, his protégé-turned-nemesis (turned-somewhat-ally again). The chorus, translated into English, is:

Your episodes of renown will one day reappear
Inspiration has not run dry – your story is not over

I wondered if the panel knew what my song was really about – truth-telling about the country's political crisis and ideological bridge-building as interconnected forms of patriotism. Worse, I wondered if I hadn't made my analysis sharp enough such that they missed it. In hindsight, I think they knew exactly what the song was about – and that was its appeal, besides its piano hook and pop-rock peppiness. The event was shown live on RTM, the national broadcaster, and I won first prize – RM50,000 (approximately £5,000) in cash. My giant mock cheque was presented by none other than Mahathir – I was so awestruck that I only managed to stammer, 'Thank you, PM,' when he handed it to me.

My colleagues and supervisors at *Radiq* were thrilled, my new friends within the activist and independent arts scene in Kuala Lumpur and Petaling Jaya (KL's satellite city) were thrilled, and I was thrilled. One month later,

I still had to quit my job as a reporter and to begin working as a Marketing Executive in the Crude Oil Group at PETRONAS. I had received The Call and I was not allowed to refuse. I might have been RM50,000 richer, but defying the summons to start work would have meant forking out more than RM350,000 to repay PETRONAS. Choking back sobs in the middle of the night, I did the maths. Repeatedly. And gave in.

My first six months at PETRONAS were miserable. I got bullied by colleagues who joined the company the same time I did or slightly earlier and got ignored or yelled at by different managers and supervisors. The rest of the days I would spend mostly reading through the Reuters and Bloomberg newswires on my desktop and eyeing the CNN ticker tape on the massive TV screens in the office. I started work in October 2001, weeks after the 9/11 attacks, and witnessed crude oil prices dramatically spiral upwards, especially amid the jingoism of US president George W Bush's administration. One day, when all the senior executives and managers were crowded round a CNN news report about impending military action in Afghanistan, one of the managers blurted at the TV screen, 'Just bloody bomb it already!' She wasn't pro-Bush by any means, but his sabre rattling about Al Qaeda and Osama bin Laden was wreaking utter havoc on crude oil trading. In these interminable months, I did what I always do when I'm bored, stressed or desperate – I ate away my pain and put on a ton of weight. I was renting a barely furnished room, with no bed (just a thin mattress), and went home after work, night after night to stare out of my window, read a bit, and go to sleep. I owned a crappy CD/ cassette player, so I would listen to quite a bit of music every night, too.

A curious thing happened, though – RTM started playing clips of me singing my prize-winning song in the gaps just before the evening news. My colleagues, many of whom would be surprised to see me pop up on television, would comment favourably the next day. I never knew what they were referring to because at that point I still couldn't afford a TV. I'll never know what those clips looked like because no audio or visual recording of this song exists anymore – it did not survive the analogue-to-digital transition.

Things started looking up after six months. I saved up enough to get myself a bed, a television and, most importantly for me, an electronic keyboard, a guitar, and a music stand. Now I would go to work, stare at the prices of Brent, Tapis and other crude oil varieties all day when my boss was around, and browse Trotskyite critiques of the War on Terror when nobody was looking, then rush home so that I could wolf down my dinner, listen to my favourite music and then make music. I was happy for a while, even though I was still bored out of my brains at PETRONAS. I joined a gym and went early every morning before work and spent my evenings holed up in my room writing, on average, one song per week.

Soon, my *Radiq* friends and new friends I had made through them took pity on me and started inviting me out to dinner, gigs, movies, nightclubs, public lectures and other wonderful things that invigorated the KL literati. One thing led to another, and months later, I found myself performing my Malay song, 'Dilanda Cinta', at the open mic segment of Songwriters' Round, organised by the envelope-pushing Sabahan musician and filmmaker Pete Teo, at the smoky, classy No Black Tie pub, to rapturous applause. Pete loved my stuff so much that he invited me back several times to be part of the main line-up for subsequent editions of Songwriters' Round. And that's how I was discovered by my record label, Pony Canyon, which later changed its name to InterGlobal Music. At the same time, I was getting acquainted with some truly remarkable women from Sisters in Islam – some of whom would hang out at No Black Tie when I was performing – and became enticed by their mixture of postcolonial feminism, progressive Muslim piety, creativity and unforced kindness. In other words, I started leading a double life. I was a drab, closeted Credit Risk Analyst in the oil-and-gas industry by day, but a flamboyant, rising musician-cum-activist by night, thriving on the combined powers of indie music and Islamic feminism.

The songs that would make it into *Dilanda Cinta* were all written in my rented room in Petaling Jaya, and several of them were premiered at No Black Tie. When Cheah Mun Kit, the boss of InterGlobal/Pony Canyon, approached me, he was unfussed about my progressive politics and budding activism. One of our more interesting discussions was about whether I would cut an album solely in English or Malay, or if it would be bilingual. I opted for Malay, because I wanted to contribute my own voice and sensibility to the Malay music scene and Cheah agreed. It was, as one of my PJ-intellectual friends succinctly put it, my brand of 'cultural activism'.

The consequences of that choice have been nothing short of humbling. After I released my album – but, pointedly, before I won Best Male Vocal – a heavyweight Malay producer and songwriter (or 'composer', as people like him are more likely to be labelled in Malaysia) pulled me aside after we bumped into each other at a television studio taping. Before I could express my admiration for his work, he said, 'I don't like your album – do you want to know why?' Taken aback, I asked him to continue. 'The Malays want fancy crockery and cutlery when they dine – they like drinking from crystal goblets and hearing the tinkling of silver forks and knives on delicate porcelain plates. But they still want to be served *nasi lemak* and rose syrup. You – you are force feeding them gourmet French cuisine. You're arrogant.'

He turned around triumphantly and left – I was speechless. It is the strangest analysis of my work that I've ever come across. I'm still trying to decipher it after all these years. Initially I wondered if he was accusing me of being a cultural impostor. Was I a westernised, anglophone coconut – brown on the outside and white on the inside – trying to deracinate my listeners just as I had been deracinated, with my Western classical piano training and overseas education?

He was right, in a way. My musical references have always been Western – Anglo-American, to be exact. Every single track I wrote on *Dilanda Cinta* is modelled after some British or North American songwriter I have idolised or wanted to plagiarise. The title track was inspired by Rufus Wainwright's 'Poses'. The closing track, *'Angkasawan'* ('Astronaut'), was partly a tribute to the space-themed classics of 1970s glam rock – Lou Reed's 'Satellite of Love', David Bowie's 'Starman', and even Elton John's 'Rocket Man'. *'Kunci'* ('Locked') was an ambitious attempt to rip off Bonnie Tyler's 'Total Eclipse of the Heart'. I wasn't trying to be dishonest or uppity by referring to these models in my Malay songwriting. I was just playing around and trying to feel comfortable in my own bilingual, middle-class, multicultural skin.

Still, wasn't the bigshot composer's diatribe a double-edged sword, anyway? Was he not also accusing the Malays, *en masse*, of being cultural impostors? He was basically insinuating that they aspired to all the trappings of elite Western modernity without transforming their inner peasantry. That, I think, is a powerful if unintentional admission of self-Orientalism.

Ultimately, however, as viscerally powerful as his critique was, it short-circuited my brain because it just didn't make sense to me. I like French cuisine, but I'm the kind of guy who flavours my coq au vin with a splash of soy sauce and my boeuf bourguignon with a hint of chilli. And nothing beats scooping up mouthfuls of nasi lemak with my bare fingers, cutlery be damned. Whatever happened to enjoying variety, Western and non-Western, for the sake of it?

I can't say whether this cultural straitjacket is a defining feature of the Malaysian music industry. I never became as deeply embedded in it as I would have liked (and maybe, in hindsight, I am relieved about this) and I have not kept up with recent trends. I do know that I felt incredibly vindicated when I discovered recently that the Malay humour magazine, *Gila-Gila* (which Google Translate renders as *Crazy*) was directly inspired by the American satire magazine, *Mad*. *Gila* on its own means 'mad', but the doubling of the word could either mean that the magazine is absolutely batshit bonkers or that it is 'crazy about *Mad*'. Yes, that's right – the most successful Malay humour magazine by a mile was directly inspired by an American magazine. In other words, I am not alone in domesticating and localising creative inspirations of foreign origin. I just never had the cultural confidence to stand by my choices.

It is by turning to the academic, social scientific study of religion that I have finally made my peace with the bizarre exchange between me and the hotshot Malay composer. One of my interests is the impacts of British imperialism on Muslim politics, especially in multicultural, postcolonial nation-states like Malaysia. But I don't want to fall into the trap of opposing Western imperialism by championing the fantasy of some primordial and therefore 'superior' Islamic or Malay nationalism. That would be hypocritical, because as opposed as I am to political, economic and cultural exploitation of all kinds, I am also aware that the shaping of people's individual tastes, outlooks and identities is complex. So, for example, my Malayan-born Pakistani father and Malayan-born Chinese mother decided to raise all their children as Muslims who primarily spoke English and Malay. My siblings and I never picked up Urdu, Punjabi or Mandarin Chinese (although we speak the Penang Hokkien dialect of Chinese, albeit badly). We mostly devoured English fiction, listened to English music, and watched English television programmes. This made us language elites but political and cultural nothings in Malaysia and, as I'm discovering, here in the UK, too. This is why I sometimes cringe at the phrase 'cultural appropriation' – what or whose culture am I appropriating, exactly, as a brown-skinned, mixed-race, semi-practising Malaysian Muslim who speaks and writes primarily in English (and occasionally Malay), used to sing primarily in Malay (and occasionally English), and who learnt Bollywood classics and Chinese nursery rhymes phonetically, barely understanding a single word?

My recent reflections have been greatly inspired by the work of the Beninese philosopher Paulin J Houndtonji, especially his seminal book *African Philosophy: Myth and Reality*. Houndtonji certainly takes a bludgeon to European colonialism which, from a scholarly perspective, plundered Africa for exotic empirical data to be analysed and theorised back in Europe by white Europeans about Africa and Africans for the purposes of tutoring, stereotyping, exploiting and waging war against them, without ever engaging African peoples in dialogue as equals. More importantly, however, Houndtonji also strikes at the postcolonial responses of African cultural nationalists who, in order to fashion collective anti-colonial pride and self-esteem, conjured entire discourses of 'African philosophy', 'African science' and so on by appropriating and internalising colonial stereotypes of Africa and Africans. According to him, there is no such thing as an epistemologically separate, distinctive 'African' philosophy. Yes, there are African thinkers, and some are philosophers, but the label 'African philosophy' and its connotation of a bounded, organised epistemological tradition is an ideological invention that is devoid of empirical substance.

Besides, it is perfectly fine to acknowledge the advances and influence of Euro-American philosophy in the world as we know it. For Houndtonji, a truly African philosophy, if we want to call it that, can and should confidently draw upon the insights of continental European philosophy – critically engaging with Kant, Hegel and Marx, for example – without needing to subjugate these to a more 'authentic', 'indigenous' framework, as long as it disseminates these insights to fellow Africans for them all to debate, critique and utilise to build African societies. The nationalist 'ethnophilosophers', Houndtonji argues, are more interested in the reverse – they parade the virtues of a supposedly African philosophy to address and impress white European elites, not to empower Africans tangibly. Houndtonji argues that this is not only intellectually bankrupt and dishonest, it also perpetuates a kind of racism – does it mean that Africans can only ever excel within an ethno-philosophical ghetto? Why should Africans not learn and engage with the best of Western and other non-African varieties of philosophy, so long as they use these tools constructively to engage directly with their own communities?

In hindsight, my decision to cut a Malay album was very much inspired by the reasons that I can only now articulate with the help of thinkers like Houndtonji. I wasn't trying to serve 'gourmet French' cuisine to show off or act superior. I wasn't trying to replace or denigrate good old 'nasi lemak and rose syrup'. I was trying to express, with delight and joy, all the musical influences I had absorbed to communicate with other Malaysian music lovers of all ethnic, linguistic and religious backgrounds. True, I did stubbornly try to impose some conventions of Anglo-American song writing on my Malay efforts, but in doing so I was also learning what worked and what didn't in the context of Malay pop music. This is what happens when artists try to find their voice. And I was seeking an authentic voice that would work in Malay and eventually in English, too. I just wish I had stood my ground a bit more convincingly.

The mix of soft Islamism and homophobia that permeated the Malaysian entertainment industry probably also catalysed my musical undoing. From the moment my album was released, I was constantly harassed by my record label to 'man up'. Journalists from Malay entertainment circles – several of them closeted gay men – would ask pointed questions about what type of woman I wanted to pursue and whether being effeminate was going to affect my marital prospects. Once, a television entertainment host ambushed me at one of my gigs and demanded that I respond to allegations that I was *lembut* (literally 'soft', but a euphemism for effeminate gay man). 'Yes, I'm soft,' I said, deciding then and there to subvert the concept of 'soft'-ness. 'But people like me are the least of your problems,' I continued. 'The problem with the world now is too many "hard" men trying to run it. Who do you think invaded Afghanistan and Iraq? "Soft" men? Which idiots flew those planes into the Twin Towers? Who do you think is spearheading all the neo-colonial Islamophobia in the world?' The host and camera crew left, and the exposé of 'Shanon the Softie' that they had been teasing their viewers with during the week never aired.

After a while, I just got sick of everything. Despite this, I was trying to write songs for my sophomore effort, which I now sulkily thought should be in English after all. But the songs were coming out bitter and twisted – very not me – and alarmed my record label, friends and nascent fan base. Some choice titles from this period, which I've thankfully never recorded, include 'Lost', 'I Surrender', 'I Won't', 'What If' and 'It Doesn't Matter'. No wonder my record label refused to let me cut my English album. I sounded like a way less talented, more depressed version of Leonard Cohen. I sank into even deeper self-pity, though: 'So they're stifling my creative freedom now, just like Interscope did with Aimee Mann.' It was not until I suffered real grief that I snapped out of being a victim and got my musical mojo back.

Around the time that I started performing at No Black Tie and getting involved in the NGO scene, I formed a profound, intense bond with the late Toni Kasim, a legendary human rights activist and core member of Sisters in Islam. Toni was thirteen years older than me and, when we started getting to know each other, was at the beginning of a long, painful divorce from a man who was also her best friend. Toni and I became each other's angels – I sat and listened to her as she cried for hours, and she counselled me through my frustrations at PETRONAS. Most crucially, she mentored me, lovingly and generously, as a human rights advocate. I supported her in campaigns on Acehnese refugees in Malaysia, community projects with the Malaysian AIDS Council, and protests about the draconian and now-repealed Internal Security Act – a colonial relic which allowed for the detention of anyone, especially political dissenters, without trial. I was intrigued by her other work, including with rural Indian women plantation workers, indigenous communities in Sabah and Sarawak who were displaced by mega-projects to build hydroelectric dams, and her advocacy of disabled people's rights. It is within this tapestry of social justice concerns that she patiently guided me through her ideas about Islamic feminism, and this is how she and her friends introduced me to the work of Sisters in Islam. Eventually, when *Dilanda Cinta* was released, I gained the courage to quit PETRONAS and embark on a freelance portfolio career in music, human rights education, and independent journalism. I still had to fork out a lot of money to repay PETRONAS, but the amount had reduced significantly and, as I pleaded with my father, was a reasonable price to pay to salvage my sanity and conscience.

I make Toni sound like a saint – she had a silly sense of humour and a fierce temper, too. One of my most enduring memories of an initial outing we had was how I fell out of my chair laughing at her dead-on impression of an angry budgerigar. I thought of this constantly when *Angry Birds* first came out. Toni also became very lonely during her divorce and perhaps demanded much more from our friendship than I could humanly fulfil. But apart from my family, she was my number one music fan. She attended all my gigs, kept buying copies of my album to give as gifts to friends, and helped in countless other ways to promote my work. She also kept me real – it is through her that I eventually became the performer of choice for events organised by folks like the Socialist Party of Malaysia, Amnesty International, and other local rights-based NGOs like Aliran and Suaram. I even had my own Pete Seeger-esque moment when we were both protesting the forced eviction of the residents of Kampung Berembang, an urban village in Kuala Lumpur, by some rapacious developers, arm in arm with the state, and I spontaneously adapted the Indonesian star Kris Dayanti's megahit ballad *Menghitung Hari* ('Counting the Days') into a protest song.

Toni was going to run as an independent feminist candidate in the 2008 general election as part of the Women's Candidacy Initiative (WCI) and I had put myself forward as her campaign manager. Elections in Malaysia have historically involved bureaucratic hurdles designed to disenfranchise candidates not aligned with the incumbent Barisan Nasional (National Front) regime, including the requirement for an exorbitant candidacy deposit. The philosophy of WCI's involvement in the 2008 election (and the 1999 election, when WCI was born), as Toni put it, was therefore: 'We realise that this time we can't just sit and watch the elections go by with the excuse that politics is for politicians. Sometimes, to make a change or even drive home a point, you need to stand up and take part in the electoral process. That is the essence of our campaign – politics is for everyone. If you want to make changes, you need to get involved.'

Sadly, Toni became ill in the middle of the campaign and had to be hospitalised. I came up with the idea of running the campaign anyway as a media strategy by fielding a fictitious feminist candidate, Mak Bedah – a character created by a mutual close friend, the artist Norhayati Kaprawi (whose work was featured in *CM28: Narratives*). We got different volunteers and activists to play Mak Bedah and disrupt the hustings in different constituencies by asking the candidates if they supported WCI's ten-point manifesto on inclusion, diversity, social justice, and transparent and accountable governance. We ran a social media campaign, shooting videos of Mak Bedah and my musical alter-ego, Justin Timeforchange, adapting chart hits into protest songs. I'm particularly proud of my work on the Pussycat Dolls' 'Dontcha' (in which I changed the chorus to 'Dontcha wish your MP was real like me') and Fergie's 'Fergalicious' (where I rapped, y'all, changing will.i.am's original 'D to the E to the L-I-C-I-O-U-S' to 'D to the E to the M-O-C-R-A-C-Y). The campaign was a hoot and a hit with the English-language press – an indicator of its undeniably urban and middle-class origins. It nevertheless succeeded in putting gender equality on the agenda of what was to be a historic election, delighting Toni and the WCI team of volunteers. But the immediate aftermath of the election was devastating – Toni was diagnosed with advanced cancer of the gallbladder, and died barely three months afterwards, on 4 June 2008.

When Toni was diagnosed, I had just resigned – for several complex reasons – from a brief stint as Director of Amnesty International Malaysia. In hindsight, I am grateful that it gave me the opportunity to dedicate myself as one of Toni's primary caregivers. I spent several nights in hospital with her, terrified and anxious, reading her stories and singing Spice Girls and Bananarama anthems to distract her from her pain. Later, when she was discharged because the cancer was just too advanced and aggressive, our friends devised a rota in which we'd take turns spending the days and nights with her at home. My final memory of Toni was when her older sister Aminah, fondly known as Mindy, picked her up to spend a few nights with her family, including a severely disabled niece whom Toni loved dearly. Toni was so weak that she could barely step into the car, but once she got on board, she faced the window and blew me a kiss. She died the next dawn, just before Fajr prayers, in her sister's arms, surrounded by her brother-in-law, nieces and nephew. My world was shattered. I was beset by a grief that remains quite impossible to describe.

Toni made me promise to keep making music, but after she died, I could not listen to or write anything. As part of my healing process, however, I formed another profound friendship with a mutual friend and neighbour in Brickfields (the official name of Kuala Lumpur's 'Little India' neighbourhood, where I had moved from Petaling Jaya) – the Sabahan filmmaker and artist Chris Chong Chan Fui. Chris had already won several prizes at international festivals for his short films *Kolam* ('Pool') and *Block B*, but really wanted to make a feature film. Chris, too, loved Toni dearly and was devastated by her death. As part of our bereavement, he and I would meet for breakfast before I went to work – I had just started a new job as Columns and Comments Editor at *The Nut Graph*, a now-defunct independent Malaysian news site, a couple of days before Toni passed away – and hang out in the evenings. One day, he showed me a screenplay he had written, titled *Karaoke*, that he wasn't entirely satisfied with. He asked if I wanted to collaborate on it, and we ended up co-writing the script. Set in an oil palm plantation in the poorer outskirts of Kuala Lumpur, the film depicts the fortunes of a rural, working-class karaoke bar amid industry-induced anomie and predatory urbanisation. I wrote a few songs for the karaoke bar scenes, just for a laugh – they were supposed to be pastiches of Malay hits. I had so much fun that I ended up writing a few more songs that would make it into my second album, *Suara Yang Ku Dengar* (*The Voice I Hear*).

The film got financial funding and was shot in 2009. It then gained official entry to the Cannes Film Festival that same year, screening at the Directors' Fortnight – it remains the second of only three Malaysian films in history to achieve this accolade. Due to post-production delays, however, my album was only released in 2010, after I had arrived in London on a scholarship to pursue my Master of Arts in Religion in Contemporary Society at King's College London. I learnt later that Toni had bequeathed a small amount of money for me to pursue a musical career. I begged for her forgiveness that, by this time, I had run out of steam and needed cash to help fund my PhD instead.

In March 2019, I endured another painful loss – my older brother Shiran, who was forty-seven and never married, died in a freak accident in Kuala Lumpur. I caught the first flight home and barely made it in time to collect his body at the morgue and sit in the mortuary van on the way to his burial. My brother was intensely intelligent, hilarious, moody, cynical and, ever since I moved to London, developed severe depression and anxiety, which led him to estrange himself from us. He would resurface every now and then, only to retreat into his shell after getting upset by one or more of us.

I think Shiran – whom I addressed as 'Paijan', a very Penang Hokkien way of pronouncing *bhai jaan* (the respectful Urdu or Punjabi term for 'brother') – was probably slightly autistic. He hoarded cassettes of album upon album, pencilling in the dates he purchased them and arranging them in alphabetical order in his locked desk drawer. I was never allowed to touch them lest I messed up the system. But in his more generous moments, he introduced me to a treasury of musical delights, including Joni Mitchell, Carly Simon, U2, Tina Turner, Motown classics, Cyndi Lauper, Suzanne Vega and Aimee Mann. He was also a movie buff and aimed to collect the VHS tapes of all the Best Picture winners at the Oscars as well as compiling his very own book of ratings of all the films he'd ever watched. He used to get copies of chart magazines like *Smash Hits* and *Number One* for me, waiting for me to laugh at the jokes in them that he'd already read in advance. His own magazine collection was more highbrow – he got himself *Q* and *Empire,* but I could borrow them when he was done.

In a way, it's because of my brother that I started writing songs. True, my parents had sent my siblings and me for piano lessons and true, I was the only one who sincerely enjoyed them. But I wanted to do more than memorise sonatas by Beethoven and Mozart and impromptus by Schubert. Whenever I thought my tiger mother wasn't keeping tabs on my practice sessions, I would work out the chords to stuff my brother and I were listening to, even television themes – I remember plonking the *Twin Peaks* theme by Angelo Badalamenti until everyone in the house was sick of it. One thing led to another and one day, aged thirteen, a song tumbled out of me. It was in Malay and it was called 'Karim'. It was about child abuse and it was a shameless copy of Suzanne Vega's 'Luka'. Nobody's ever heard it and I've forgotten all the words but, curiously, not the music. And I've never forgotten the feeling of writing it, of creating something. I hid all my song lyrics under my mattress – they were just too raw and personal (and from a craft perspective simply too cringeworthy) to share with anyone.

I now realise that my experiences as an almost pop 'star' demonstrate one of my primary supervisor's asides during my doctorate: 'Structure tells you what you can do, culture tells you what you can't.' My English-speaking, middle-class, mixed-race upbringing in Malaysia provided the structural openings for me to acquire an abiding love of music and the means to have tried it out as a career, notwithstanding my questionable success-to-failure ratio. It simultaneously allowed me to gain access to the world of human rights advocacy in Kuala Lumpur and Petaling Jaya, which introduced a degree of complexity in my musical pathway, especially given the state of Malaysian politics back then. My background also produced complex identity baggage and personal insecurities that left me woefully ill-equipped to navigate the cultural crossfires and capitalist imperatives in the mainstream Malay music industry. All of this has taken a toll on me – I still love music and I play the piano and sing every now and then, but I haven't written any songs since moving to London.

I don't want to say never, though.

MUM AND BABU JEE

Irna Qureshi

I discovered Hindi film songs as a teenager during the early 1980s when Channel 4 began screening a Bollywood season; a film a week around 2am on a Friday or a Saturday night. The timer mode on our VCR was so fiddly that I preferred to stay up just long enough to start the recording manually, knowing that the four-hour video tape would capture the entire thing. Whilst it was an economical way of creating a personal film library, it was actually the songs I was interested in. Clutching the remote, I'd impatiently fast forward large chunks of dialogue, looking out for moments of melodrama which were bound to be punctuated with a noteworthy song. If I liked the song, I'd rewind a few scenes for the context and often find myself getting sucked into the entire film. If it was a song I loved, I'd watch it over and over again like an MTV music video.

Capturing the songs on audio cassette took a few attempts. Having queued up the song on the VCR, I'd have to remind myself to simultaneously push down the record and play buttons on the portable cassette recorder before getting the song started, all the while holding the recorder mic as close as possible to the TV speaker to get the best possible sound. No matter my efforts, the transitions were never smooth and a few words of dialogue would inevitably seep into the recordings. Nevertheless, over the next few months, I managed to compile my very first Bollywood mixtape.

Although it was the first time I hummed popular songs that weren't in English, I understood that like my mother tongue, these Hindi songs weren't to be shared beyond our four walls. Wanting desperately to blend in, I was loathe to draw any more attention to our Pakistani ways. As it was, if my classmates weren't snarling 'garlic breath' in the school canteen, then they'd be sniggering within my earshot about their favourite joke which was based on a TV ad for a popular mint with a hole in the centre:

'What's the difference between a Paki and a Polo?' my fiendish classmates would smirk. 'People like Polo!' came the punchline. It was a similar story at home. When our neighbour hurled bricks at our sitting room window one Christmas, we huddled behind the sofa trying to make sense of his drunken chant: 'Jesus Christ was born in a stable because all the Pakis have got the houses.'

'No point calling the police', Mum commiserated us in hushed tones. 'You're on the Canterbury estate love', the officer had barked last time when Mum caught someone climbing up the drainpipe in broad daylight, tempted by the open bathroom window. 'It's not Buckingham Palace, you know!'

When we'd arrived in England with nothing but our clothes bundled in a few suitcases, Christian Housing Aid sent a truckload of furniture to our council house as well as the kitchenware we needed. Armed with Vim scouring powder, Mum recited the Shahada over every pot, pan, plate and spoon, thoroughly rinsing each item three times to ritually cleanse them of any haram substance from their previous life. A machinist at Northgate Mills, Mum stitched pyjamas for Marks & Spencer. She'd also set herself a nightly piecework quota of ten doctor's operating gowns, each one earning her 50p. While the fabric dust made her eyes itch, the vibrations from the battered industrial sewing machine rattling through the floorboards lulled us to sleep every night.

Distanced from Mum's home turf, we had no sense of a family narrative. There was no history of Mum around us; no pictures or mementos of her journey into adulthood, of life before marriage, children, estrangement. Nor was there a network of uncles, aunts or grandparents within reach. But something shifted with my newfound interest in Bollywood music. Where we once sensed quiet disapproval or bewilderment directed at *Top of the Pops* from behind the sewing machine when a pop star blurred gender lines, or Legs & Co performed a racy routine in saucy swimsuits, we now noticed Mum taking her foot off the sewing machine pedal and peering indulgently at the screen over her glasses. Instead of feigning interest, she would translate if the language proved difficult, or she'd explain if we couldn't follow the plot – usually a complicated love triangle. It was a relief to have Mum's encouragement on something that wasn't cumbersome like cooking, sewing or praying. As the memories stimulated by the Indian film songs transported Mum to her formative years, I began to absorb my family history. Not only did Mum's reminiscences help me to understand my roots, I came to learn that an appreciation of Indian films and music runs deep in the family. And for my family, as perhaps for most Asian families of my generation, film and music are intrinsically linked.

Back in pre-independence Pakistan, Nana, my Mum's father, whom everyone called Babu Jee on account of his ability to read and write English, had brought home a gramophone from one of his army postings – hand cranked and featuring the famous 'His Master's Voice' logo plate on the front. Babu Jee would ceremoniously set it up on a table, laying out a cloth underneath. He had collected box upon box of Indian records, meticulously organised, many of them soundtracks of films about love and honour, duty and loyalty, justice and mercy. It was the complete audio recording of the 1939 film, *Pukar*, which Mum remembers especially. Thanks to Mum's impressionable young age, she was captivated by the nickname 'Pari Chehra' (Fairy-face) given to the leading lady, Naseem Banu, on account of her reputed beauty.

The entire family sat around on *charpois* in the yard, hands firmly under chin concentrating on the historical saga. The film told a fictitious story of Mughal Emperor Jehangir's legendary justice. The Emperor has a bell installed outside his palace which anyone with a grievance may ring to summon him. However, when his beloved wife's arrow accidentally kills an innocent washerman, the king's position is put to the test. The audio – which consisted of seven separate records housed within their own cardboard box – featured lengthy Urdu dialogues relayed in loud and dramatic style by the greatest actors of the day, and left it to the listeners to imagine the characters and draw the scenes around the music and sound effects – galloping horses, sword fighting, washer folk thumping clothes against the stones on the riverbank. Mum relished this sensory form of storytelling. She loved the sense of pomp and grandeur conjured up every time the king made an appearance, with the courtiers repeatedly announcing: *'ba adab, ba mulahiza, hoshiyar'* ('All rise. The king has arrived'). Then there was the music, especially *Zindagi ka saaz bhi kya saaz hai* ('the music of life is inexplicable') which the queen sings in captivity when she is about to be tried in the Emperor's court. Since Mum experienced the song and its singer Naseem Banu auditorily, it wasn't until decades later that she was able to put the visual component to the song.

The gathered villagers would marvel at Babu Jee's contraption, unable to comprehend where the 'baja's' voice was coming from. They referred to the flat, black, brittle disc as a 'tawa', given its likeness to the shape and colour of a chapati pan. As one part of *Pukar* ended, Babu Jee carefully removed the fibre particles worn away by the needle with his circular wooden duster, before passing the record to a member of his audience, along with a complaint that they were carelessly shoving the records in any old box meaning the multiple parts wouldn't be filed together. And before Babu Jee called out for the next part of the audio film, he'd take out one of the hundreds of tiny steel needles he kept in a special tin which everyone was under strict instructions to change after each play: 'Don't be thinking you're saving on needles', he would qualify the frivolity. 'A dull needle will damage the record and a fresh one gives a crisp sound.'

By the time Mum started college, the family had settled in Rawalpindi and Babu Jee's gramophone had been replaced with a radio. As his wife brewed his first cup of tea after *Fajar* prayers, he'd have his ear to Radio Pakistan news, switching to the BBC for verification when a headline grabbed his interest. Babu Jee would head off each morning on his bicycle along Murree Road towards Narankari Bazar, where he was a bookkeeper with one of the wholesalers close to the art deco Imperial Cinema. The empty bag he left with each morning would be brought back in the evening filled with vegetables, several newspapers as well as *Filmfare* magazine for the young girls in the household.

By the time Babu Jee returned home, the girls would be in charge of the radio. The request shows broadcast on Radio Ceylon played the best songs punctuated by the long list of names included in each listener's letter. Mum and her cousins listened regularly in the hope of hearing their song requests and dedications too, with Babu Jee imploring them to lower the volume: 'Girls! If you must have the radio on, then play it for yourselves, not for the entire neighbourhood!'

Just as my Thursday evenings in Bradford were dominated by *Top of the Pops*, during Mum's college days it was 'Binaca Geetmala' on Wednesday evenings – Radio Ceylon's weekly countdown of the most popular Indian *filmi* songs based on record sales and audience requests. As far as Mum was concerned, lyrics penned by acclaimed poets, offering different levels of meaning and written before the tune is composed were the making of a good song. Top poets had to be skilled enough to write songs for any situation and character. In recognition of the craftsmanship involved in these songs, alongside the playback singer and music director, the veteran presenter of Binaca Geetmala made it a point to announce the lyricist's name too. In turn, the success of a song determined whether or not the film was worth watching or it would at least have to intrigue the listener enough to want to understand how it had been 'picturised' in the movie.

Many of Mum's friends were forbidden from going to the cinema so they would fabricate a *Khatam-e-Quran* (Reading of the Qur'an) at a friend's house. As a keen cinemagoer himself – Babu Jee never missed any of Noor Jahan's films since she became a child star – he was happy to endorse trips to the cinema for his family members as long as prayers and studies were up to date. Going through the newspaper adverts every day, Mum knew which film was showing where. She either went with her cousins and aunts to the ladies' show, otherwise, *tasbih* (beads used in remembrance of Allah) in hand, Babu Jee would trail behind Mum and her friends along Murree Road towards their chosen cinema.

Each film they saw would have to be analysed in detail for several days – the memorable dialogue, the songs, the emotion, and most critical of all, the chemistry between the leading couple. Mum and her relatives never missed a film starring Dev Anand or Raj Kapoor, but it was really Dilip Kumar that was everyone's favourite. Because of this perhaps, Mum remembers her own mother and aunt objecting so much to his Jugnu pairing with Noor Jahan in 1947 that they continued to discuss it fifteen years later.

'She's too tall and lanky for him,' protested the aunt. 'She looks like an old woman and he's a young college lad,' my grandmother agreed, alluding to the fact that when Jugnu was filmed, Noor Jahan was already married with two young children. 'When a woman has a child, she starts to look mature,' she reasoned. 'He'd have suited a nice young girl, someone of his own height and build,' suggested the aunt. Mum eventually become a Dilip Kumar fan too, no doubt due to his charming boyish good looks and his tousled hairstyle which thousands of young men tried to copy. Mum felt that Dilip Kumar's soft spoken, understated, restrained acting style was the antithesis of stars like Sohrab Modi or Prithviraj Kapoor who were so used to projecting their dialogues with their thundering voices.

'It felt too loud, too strong, too unnatural, like they were on stage in the theatre trying to be heard on the back row,' Mum laughed. 'Anyway, no actor was better suited to a serious role than Dilip Kumar.'

Mum left Rawalpindi in 1964 to begin married life in Yorkshire. It was also the year that *Sangam* was released, with a string of memorable songs including *Har Dil Jo Pyar Karega* (Even Hearts that Fall in Love) and *Dost Dost Na Raha, Pyar Pyar no Raha* (Friend has Ceased to be Friend, Love has Ceased to be Love). The songs ensured that the film had to be seen.

Father and daughter had discussed the options: 'He's been living in England for about a decade,' he reasoned. 'He was a young lad in school the last time I saw him, so I imagine he must be well educated by now. And England's surely going to be better than marrying one of your cousins in the village'. In the days leading up to her departure, my grandmother, in the midst of her relentless chores, would repeat a sobering Punjabi saying: 'Off you go, my beloved daughter, to the other side of the River Ravi, to where no-one goes and from where no-one returns.'

The *nikkah* (marriage) ceremony took place on the phone, so it was only when Mum arrived in Keighley a few weeks later that she finally met her husband. He took her to Leeds and bought her a coat and appropriate shoes. They also visited a photo studio. The sepia toned 'wedding' picture sent to her parents features Mum looking demure in a sari gifted by an aunt, with the *pallu* (one end of the sari) draped over the wrong shoulder – it was the first time she'd worn one. Crucially, the gold bangles sitting snugly on her left wrist are clearly visible, and the strap of an oversized handbag draped over her right arm finishes the look. Her husband – tall, lean, handsome, with thick wavy hair, in a dark suit complete with a plain white pocket square tucked into the breast pocket, stands proudly just behind her right shoulder.

The following evening, he grabbed his tiffin box and disappeared down the snicket towards Yorkshire's oldest cotton mill.

'Machines don't stop,' he explained, returning the following morning. 'Only shifts change.'

'Is it easy to stay awake?' Mum wanted to understand.

'I'm on my feet all night. I have to walk around the machines, inspect the combs, make sure the cotton doesn't snap. If it breaks, I have to repair it as fast as possible. Otherwise it will ruin an entire bail of cloth and they can trace it back to the worker.' He broke off another piece of the butter-soaked paratha. 'And if that doesn't keep you awake, the noise does.'

Over the coming weeks Mum learnt that if her husband wasn't home as she was getting up, then it simply meant he was topping up his regular twelve hours with an extra half shift. 'No news is good news. That's what you should assume,' he assured her. 'If my hand gets caught in the machine, I'm sure someone will come and tell you.'

My father had bought 1 Alpha Street, Keighley, furnishing the modest terrace with several beds in the two bedrooms and two attics, as well as the lounge, and taking in fifteen lodgers. A rota system determined who slept when. If you finished work early, you waited for a housemate to get up for his shift before you could use the bed. The men were probably awake for no more than an hour or so at either end of a shift, which would have been a blessing because there wasn't much personal space to be found. The last lodger moved out the day before Mum landed at Heathrow Airport. So while her husband slept, Mum spent her days giving the house a thorough clean, climbing the stairs on tiptoe and not daring to flush the toilet.

On Sundays, her husband changed out of his grubby overalls into his English suit for a trip to the cinema. He was part of a group that had negotiated a deal for Sunday matinee screenings of Indian films at the Essoldo Cinema when it was usually closed. It was an imposing building just a couple of doors away from the famous Busby's department store on Manningham Lane in Bradford city centre. The screenings had become so popular that men came from as far afield as Newcastle and Sheffield, standing three deep on the pavement in their Sunday best waiting for the cinema doors to open. It was a chance to connect with the homeland, a cultural refuge. They offered the men a lifeline, a chance to reconnect with home. Prints of the latest films were difficult to come by so they screened whichever films they could get. Dilip Kumar was very popular and they were screening *Andaz (1949)* and *Aan (1952)* which Mum had seen a decade earlier when the films were first released. It didn't matter if they screened the same film week in week out, the men still bought the 2-shilling ticket – they were grateful to have something to do.

For many men, the Sunday matinee in Bradford was their very first movie experience. Like my dad, the majority hailed from rural areas with conservative values, meaning films were shunned or they simply didn't have access or the means to watch them. After screening *Anarkali*, the tragic story reduced one of the men to tears. He'd never seen a moving image before and didn't understand it was fiction: 'It makes you want to cry, doesn't it,' he bellowed. 'They've buried the poor woman alive!'

Mum was astonished to learn that her elderly father-in-law was a regular at the Sunday screenings too. It was the only social life he had but he was too embarrassed to admit to his daughter-in-law that he enjoyed watching romantic films.

Mum knew a trip to the Sunday matinee at the Essoldo was impossible. For Dad, the idea of going to the cinema with his wife to watch a film about a love triangle was scandalous. As it was, Dad avoided public transport when he was with her, preferring instead to take a taxi even though he insisted she wear a bhurka. It was because he didn't want to be seen with his wife that he had chosen a photographer's studio in Leeds - nobody knew him there. On a rare outing to Bradford, at great expense in a taxi, they had visited friends of his extended family who lived in a huge honey-coloured sandstone villa on Manningham Lane, with more bedrooms than Mum could even imagine. She could see that the cellar – the old servants' quarters – and enclosed back passageways were perfect for this conservative community, affording them the sort of privacy they wanted for their women. While Dad used the front entrance, he instructed Mum to head to the back, into the women's day quarters in the cellar. It was cosy, with a big log fire and settees set against each wall to maximise the seating. The women of the house set about making tea for the men upstairs. When it was ready to be sent in, one of the women tapped a broom handle on the basement ceiling which was directly beneath the lounge. This alerted the man of the house to come and relieve them of the burgeoning tray.

A few weeks later, Dad organised another Sunday outing to Bradford, paying the £2 taxi fare which was probably a few hours' wage. The taxi took them through Manningham Lane and past the Essoldo towards Legrams Lane. Dad had located a cinema in a different part of Bradford which also held Sunday screenings, but had a very different clientele. Even though she was in a bhurka and would have gone completely unrecognised,

Dad found her a seat with a group of Sikh women. And there she sat to watch *Sangam*, no doubt mesmerised by the voice of Mukesh:

Har Dil Jo Pyar Karega,
Voh Gana Gayega
Deewana Sekdon me pehchan jayega

Every Heart that Loves
Will Sing
The Demented will be Recognised
Amongst Thousands

Five minutes before the end of the film, her husband indicated that it was time for them to leave.

SUFI SOUNDS OF SENEGAL

Estrella Sendra

Senegalese scholar, writer and musician Felwine Sarr suggests that the African continent is shaped by the 'delocalisation of its presence in a perpetual future', that is, a vision of what it will be; an incomplete present. An Afrotopia possible only through a spiritual, musical revolution.

One prominent figure inspiring spiritual revolution through music in the nation is Cheikh Amadou Bamba (1850-1927), the Sufi founder of the Murid Brotherhood. The much loved Sufi leader is often referred to as 'The Servant of the Messenger', and 'Serie Touba' as he established, in 1887, the city of Touba, regarded as the Senegalese Mecca. Murid devotees gather there to pray, perform *zikr*, and take part in an annual pilgrimage and music festival, the *Grand Maggal*, which attracts millions of people from across Senegal and the diaspora. However, his influence goes beyond the *Grand Maggal*. His portrait, which is based on a single photograph discovered in 1912, can be found all over Senegal, not just on T-shirts, necklaces, postcards, posters and stationary, but in street art, carved on trees, painted on walls, and on *car rapides*, a popular mode of public transport in Dakar – the iconic image is revered and believed to offer protection. Cheikh Amadou Babou was a prolific writer who produced works on the Qur'an, rituals, meditations and an extraordinary number of poems. He led a non-violent cultural struggle against French colonial rule with emphasis on a reinterpretation of Islam based on black African cultures. He represents a past projected on the present.

A celebrated disciple of Cheikh Amadou Bamba is Cheikh Ibrahima Fall (1855-1930). His image is also to be found everywhere in Senegal; and he too has disciples, known as *Baay Fall*, or *Yaay Fall* if they are women, who express their religious and spiritual devotion through music. The devotees consider music as both a way to reach the Divine and to spread the message of Islam using sounds inspired by Arabic-Muslim and black influences and quotations from the Qur'an.

Murid festivals have played a crucial role in the popularity of devotional music, making it accessible to the wider public. One example is the *Festival des Musiques spirituelles*, founded in 2011, whose two initial gatherings, in partnership with the Town Hall of Dakar, were open to all religions as well as Sufi, sacred and spiritual music. Renowned artists such as Carlou D, Iba Gaye Massar, and Aïda Faye Bou Baay all participated. More recently, in 2015, the most famous Senegalese artist in contemporary times, Youssou N'Dour, founded *Festival Salam* in Dakar, the only music festival in Senegal taking place during the holy month of Ramadan, designed to celebrate the life and legacy of the Prophet Muhammad and Islamic tradition. It is televised on N'Dour's own television channel, *Télé Futurs Média Réligion* (tfmRéligion). An array of Senegalese artists feature, plus musicians from Turkey, Egypt, Morocco, Algeria and Tunisia, and other parts of the Muslim world.

Many musicians dedicate songs to their spiritual guides, either to Cheikh Amadou Babou or his disciple Cheikh Ibrahima Fall. They combine a mix of different styles, including jazz, blues, folk, afrobeat and salsa, with acoustic guitars and a combination of modern and traditional instruments. Papis Samba, the first scholar to ever edit a monograph entirely devoted to Senegalese music, argues this is a defining feature of musicians in Senegal, including Souleymane Faye, Viex Mac Faye, Ismaël Lô or Pape Niang defining their music as Afro or African, influenced by jazz, soul and other genres.

Such musical diversity as the embodiment of Muridism is arguably best represented by the legendary multifaceted musician Cheikh Lô. Born in Burkina Faso in 1955, he left the country to study in Senegal before returning to play drums with Volta Jazz. Travelling back and forth between Burkina Faso and Senegal, in 1989 he surprised Senegalese audiences with a spontaneous salsa performance of the song *El Guantanamo* by Barroso. That kicked off his prolific music career: he signed with the record label Jololi, and then with UK-based World Circuit. Since then he has toured internationally. His appearance at a festival programme or concert in Senegal guarantees a sold out event. His charismatic personality and strong religious beliefs contribute to his special place in the Senegalese music

Cheikh Amadou Bamba painted over a wooden panel in Ngor Island, Dakar.
Photo: Aurea Puerto

world, a loyal disciple devoted to his marabout, Mame Massamba NDiaye. He produces a hybrid sound influenced by eclectic styles, incorporating salsa, jazz, and *mbalax,* which is a fast form of drumming and dancing characteristic of Wolof celebrations, fused with an intimate and spiritual

A poster of Cheikh Ibrahima Fall, and painted of one of his disciples, Seriñe Fallou Mbacké. On the right, a typical Baay Fall outfit, made out of patchwork, in the Médina, Dakar. Photo: Áurea Puerto

sound. Cape Verdean *morna*, Spanish flamenco, and Zairean rumba, can all be detected in his album *Ne la Thiass*, first recorded and produced in 1996 in Dakar by Youssou N'Dour.

One of the major festival centres in Senegal is the city of Saint-Louis. It hosts many long running music, dance and film festivals. In 2016, the *Festival Saint-Louis Jazz*, one of the longest running music festivals in the country, faced severe challenges. A series of disasters, including the false reporting of a potential terrorist attack in Senegal, caused audiences to stay away amid fears the headline acts would cancel. However, Chiekh Lô stood firm and on the night he performed, the festival vibe could be felt all over the city of Saint-Louis, not just on the main stage, but in the streets and 'OFF' performances across different music venues. It was the talk of the town for months.

The Murid spirit infused in Cheikh Lô's performances can also be sensed in the broader Senegalese music scene, with local endorsement key for success within the industry. Throughout the year, there are continuous performances courtesy of the younger generation, such as Takeifa (a band of siblings) Marema and Maïna. Takeifa derives from the Keïta family, originally from Kaolack but established in Dakar since 2006. Marema, born in Dakar to a Mauritanian father and Senegalese mother, won the Jury Prize StarAfrica Sounds in 2014 for her first single *Femme d'affaires*. Maïna, originally from Saint-Louis, was recently awarded artistic residence in France as part of the *Visa pour la création* 2019 programme.

They have played with famous Senegalese and international musicians, such as Baaba Maal, Youssou N'Dour and Daara J Family; and both are regular performers in Dakar and Saint-Louis, where they establish close bonds with the local population and cultural scene. It is not rare to meet them hanging out at the *Institut Français* in Dakar, or in the audience at Just 4U, a legendary music venue in Dakar, listening to Cheikh Lô, or at the Bazoff Restaurant in Dakar, invited to sing along, as I once witnessed. Or drinking Ethiopian coffee or local juice at the ndar ndar music & café, lounging at the Siki Hotel, or performing at the Flamingo Restaurant, in Saint-Louis, establishing friendships, networks and authentic connections.

Cheikh Lô during the 24th Festival Saint-Louis Jazz in 2016.
Photo: Estrella Sendra

Cheikh Lô featuring in the "IN" and "OFF" programme of the
24th Festival Saint-Louis Jazz in 2016.

This is how, in the spring of 2016, I met Sahad Sarr, a musician, who
divides his time between Dakar, his birthplace, and Kamyaak.

At the time I was screening a documentary on migration which I had
co-directed with Senegalese journalist, Mariama Badji, *Témoignages… waa
suñu gaal*, in Aula Cervantes in Dakar. The documentary generated a
heated debate and Sahad had asked a question. After the event, he
introduced himself and told me about his work, not just as a musician but
as the manager of a sustainable project of spiritual training, education,
renewable energy and organic farming in Kamyaak village.

He was due to perform later that summer at Just 4U. I had friends visiting and we decided to all go. As we were arriving, we realised something was going on. Cars were being diverted, and there were few people by the door. Students were protesting at the Cheikh Anta Diop University, and because of the proximity to the music venue, there were rumours about the potential cancellation of the concert. Sahad stood outside, staying as optimistic as usual, so we chatted and waited. By midnight, things had calmed down and, as more and more people were arriving, the concert finally started – Sahad Sarr and the Nataal Patchwork performed songs from their first album, *Jiw*, recorded in 2016 and released the following year. *Jiw* is the Wolof word for seed, an apt name for the association he manages, *JiwNit*, symbolising the idea of an Afrotopia promoted by his brother, musician and novelist Felwine Sarr. His book, *Afrotopia*, won the Grand Prix of the Literary Associations (GPLA) in 2016. *Nit* means person, reflecting the project slogan of 'seeding humanity', which is exactly what happened that night at Just 4U: an embodiment of the mission through a mixture of jazz, folk, Afro highlife, and Murid inspiration.

Sahad and the Nataal Patchwork during the 7th Festival Coeur en Or.
Photo: Estrella Sendra

We have been in touch ever since; and I saw him perform again in the spring of 2019 at the *Festival Coeur en Or* in Saint-Louis. By the time I arrived at the venue, Sahad and the Nataal Patchwork were already on stage, playing the latest single, *Wall of China*, released just a few months before. What a concert! It was the headline and highlight of the festival. Sahad and his band had refined their performance, with a rich variety of registers ranging from jazz, to folk, mbalax, afrobeat, highlife, Malian blues, rock, and what Sahad Sarr himself defines as 'afro spirit'. Murid inspiration was evident throughout the performance with his generous approach of sharing and spreading his talent and views.

Sahad Sarr has already played over fifty international concerts abroad and over four hundred in Senegal, and I was keen to know how it all began. 'My relationship with music started at a very early age', he said. 'We used to play with so many musicians, just to have fun. It was when I was at university a producer was passing by, listened to us, knocked on the door and went: "wow!". He asked me if I was a musician and I said: "No, I don't do concerts." And he replied that I should, and I started to combine my studies with my musical career. That was in 2010. And we started playing many concerts and festivals in Dakar, for about two years. Before I had only played in the different festivities at school. We started little projects in Europe'.

In 2014, he applied to be considered for the *Journées Musicales de Carthage* Award, an important music award in Africa, with his first EP, *Nataal*. The band went to Tunisia to represent West Africa. They played and were awarded the first prize (*Tanit d'Or*); and their career took off. In 2016, the band was shortlisted for the finals of *Marché International de l'Edition Musical* in Paris, and won another award. Since then they have toured in Germany, Belgium, the USA and Switzerland; and signed with French record label Mektoub.

'I've been living in a Sufi world for about 16 years now, with devotion for Cheikh Amadou Bamba', says Sahad. And goes on to explain: 'Within the Baay Fall symbolism, there is music. Music is the food for the soul. Today, we have to link the temporality with the spirituality. Our soul needs happiness and love. It needs food, just like we do. Today, within the Baay Fall symbolism, music is always present. Everything we do as human beings has to do with music. If you go to the street, you will hear birds sing. Music

Sahad Sarr in front of some sand artworks in Saint-Louis island.
Photo: Estrella Sendra

is sung by the universe. What we do is to emulate what the universe does. Life is music, actually. Life is symphonic. Everyone does its own symphony. Through music we speak about what is going on around us'. African people, Sahad says, 'look up to the European model, which does not belong to us. We talk about how it is not about living in a beautiful building, but rather finding oneself, as a cultural and spiritual being. We are hybrid beings. Even if we share similarities, we have our roots somewhere. It is not that we judge Europe. Our position is, 'ok guys, you have your own way of doing things. Yet, there are other ways of doing things'. There are also other ways of being Muslim, says Sahad. Our 'spiritual leaders shared that the kind of Islam which arrived from the north was a sort of imperialism or colonialism. We are not Arabs. It is much more spiritual than anything else'.

I ask Sahad about the band's new single, 'Wall of China'. In the song, he says, 'we speak about the wall of Berlin, the wall in China and all those large walls that prevent people from moving and mixing. We speak about that fear that becomes ignorance. It is only through encountering the other that we can get to the truth, because each person has their own truth, their own seed. And in order to achieve certain knowledge, we need to open up

to others'. There is also a big wall in Morocco, called Black Mamba, says
Sahad. 'All migrants have to go through it. We are all sold an image of
Europe… The first time I went to Europe I was shocked. I found
individualist people. Where was the joy and happiness I found in Burkina
Faso, in Senegal? People were cold. This was in France. In Africa, we are
sold an image of a rich continent. Everything that makes happiness,
however, can be found in Senegal. We are very rich here, but we are not
even aware of that'. Sahad believes that 'music has a role in the
decolonisation of the mind'. This is what Senegalese music is all about. 'We
do jazz, folk, afro highlife. Yet we still remain within an afro spirit. There is
a sense of accomplishment and mindfulness in Senegal. When we play, we
try to show and share that energy. That is how I understand the afro spirit.'

LED ZEPPELIN AND ME

Hafeez Burhan Khan

What seems a lifetime ago, I was working for the Birmingham University Field Archaeology Unit. My cousin, Shaiz, came up for the weekend looking for some action. Having nothing to do on a particularly fine Saturday, I flippantly suggested that we visit Robert Plant's home. This was before online stalking was even a thing but I had in fact discovered that he lived in a village in Worcestershire while leafing through a Led Zeppelin biography in a bookstore the previous week. Surely Shaiz would say no, I thought to myself. To my surprise he was up for it.

So we took the train from Birmingham to Kidderminster, only about an hour's journey or less. Once we were out of the station, it was as though time had stopped at 1975, everything about the place screamed 1970s. From the way people dressed to the flock curtains adorning their windows. We roughly knew where Robert lived but weren't exactly sure so went straight to the library as it occurred to me that we could check the electoral records. A stroke of genius on my part as we found his address. Hearts pounding, and feeling like kids going to watch our favourite football team, we then took a bus to his village. Within fifteen minutes we were there.

Wolverly is a one street village so we started walking. I remember the road was lined with trees on either side with a backdrop of gentle rolling hills covered in green fields. It was quiet except for the sound of birds chirping. As we got nearer, I started to have doubts, this was a bit silly. I'd only mentioned it as a lark, I had no idea it was going to be this easy to find out where he lived. I just wanted a day out. After what seemed like an eternity we finally reached our destination. By now I felt a complete idiot. 'I can't do this,' I told Shaiz. But he was adamant. We had come all this way and now that we were here, we had to see Robert (so now we are on first name terms are we?). There was no turning back.

With Shaiz taking command, we walked up the path of the unassuming house. I was praying that no one would be home, I looked down and my palms were sweating. Shaiz rang the bell and we could hear the sound of a dog barking from inside. Through the glass door I saw a figure with big hair approaching.

'Oh my god', I thought, the door opened. Was this Robert in drag? No, it was his mum. 'Is Robert in?' asked Shaiz as nonchalantly as a car salesman attempting to sell you a clapped out banger. Suddenly, I was transported back to my childhood when I used to knock on my friends' doors to ask their parents if their child could come out to play. What a preposterous thing to say – 'is Robert in?' Should I have brought a football with me and some jumpers for goal posts. This was frankly getting ridiculous. I felt like a foolish child. His mum looked us over and just as nonchalantly replied: 'No he's in Ibiza, he'll be back next week.' So started a bizarre ten minute conversation. All the while, I felt dumbstruck and rather mortified, letting Shaiz do all the talking. Mother Plant must have seen plenty of our kind before as she cast a beady eye over us. For some reason she mentioned how Asians look after their parents, we nodded silently wondering what on earth she meant. I can't recall much of what was said, it was all far too surreal for me. Shaiz did most of the talking; he was as cool as a cucumber. I was so nervous I got my words mixed up. 'We've not come to meet Robert star the rock Plant, but the person.' Did I really say that? Now was a good time for the ground to open up and swallow me.

Mother Plant said we looked like good boys and suggested we come back next week to see Robert when he would be home. Er… After saying our goodbyes (she was a really pleasant lady) we scarpered, I don't know if Shaiz felt as stupid as I did but I muttered to myself there would be no repeat of this. Some years later, I spent a Friday night sitting in my car outside Jimmy Page's house in Kensington.

In the early 1980s, like many kids, I watched *Top of the Pops* every Thursday evening at 7.30pm even though there was no discernible style that captured my imagination. I didn't mind pop songs but no band really grabbed me. One day my sister gave me Queen and Black Sabbath's Greatest Hits. From the moment I began listening I was completely blown away. I realised that I loved the sound of the power chord fused with strong melody and a good vocalist. I'd just started secondary school and began developing friendships mainly through shared music interests. Records and cassettes were swapped as my musical education began, primarily in the rock genre. In those days, there was no YouTube or Spotify where an album is a click and five second download away. Albums were expensive so we would record the ones we had on cassettes and pass them around our friends, and also listen to our favourite radio shows. While many people of my generation cite John Peel as a life-changing musical influence, it was Tommy Vance's Friday Night Rock Show I would look forward to hearing. He would play new releases as well as a mixture of classics from the 1960s and 1970s.

I knew that the contemporary hits of that era were no match for the music that emerged in the 1970s. I really can't explain how exciting it was to listen to something new for the first time without any reference point or background knowledge. Looking back, it was an exhilarating period as I embarked on an aural carpet ride traversing sonic landscapes and textures. Classic, blues, folk, art, soft and punk rock to name but a few and then there was heavy metal. Diverse in style and nature, I lapped it all up. It was the music first and lyrics second that appealed to me. Sure, many bands didn't speak to me lyrically but that didn't matter. I wasn't some kid who felt suffocated in a dead end town, or wanted to make some political statement or needed to express some deep underlying insecurity. It had nothing to do with image or teenage rebellion. I had a happy childhood and was a well-adjusted kid, but was also aware of society's problems. There were no 'factors' in liking rock music. It just sounded good to my ears.

There was one band that my friends spoke about with unrivalled awe and reverence. They were the holy grail, the band all rock bands aspired to. I'd never heard or seen any Led Zeppelin apart from the *Top of the Pops* theme tune so one day I went out and bought *Led Zeppelin 2*, as friends swore blind I had to have it. If you want to get into heavy rock, then this is the heavy metal bible. The first time I heard the opening song, 'Whole Lotta Love', it exuded an energy that consumed me, a verve that was untamed, it was dangerous, even unnerving. There was something about this band that was different to every other band I had listened to; they had an otherworldly edginess. It was the vocalist. His voice electrified me. It was primordial, wild and savage. It hit me right in the gut and when he wailed, the hairs on the back of my neck stood up. I had never experienced such a physical reaction to any music before. It was visceral.

What was it about this record? *Led Zeppelin 2* contains some utterly recognisable guitar riffs. It's not all fist pumping. There's the folksy 'Ramble On', the ballad 'Thank You' but it's mainly a study in dynamics. One moment hushed and taciturn, the next second a cacophony of fire and breathlessness exploding in devastating fashion. Above all, it was the power in the sound, I don't think any band at the time produced such bombastic sounds. Over the next few years, I bought or was lent Zeppelin albums so by the time I was around seventeen, I'd heard all their studio albums. There were always a couple of songs that would take months for me to fully appreciate. The effect upon me was diffusive, there were too many textures and soundscapes to deal with, which over time would reveal even newer layers and sounds. They sounded different, the guitar tone had an eastern vibe and Plant began to adopt the vocal gymnastics of Indian and Arab singers.

What about the members of the band themselves? Jimmy Page – the wizard and visionary, the top session guitarist at that time. Listen to any pop hit from the mid 60s and the chances are that Page had played on it. The list is a who's who: Val Doonican, Shirley Bassey, Cliff Richard, Lulu, Brenda Lee, Herman's Hermits, Joe Cocker, Dusty Springfield, Rod Stewart, The Rolling Stones and Donovan to name but a few. He would later join the Yardbirds playing with Jeff Beck when Eric Clapton left. Page's versatility and experience in the studio was what gave the first Zeppelin album heft. Couple that with Robert Plant – the original rock god who was already a student of the blues, had played in several bands around the West Midlands, and was renowned for his voice, which was regarded as too visceral when he sang live. Then you have John Bonham – a good friend of Plant and sometime band member. His drumming was considered too loud on the Black Country live circuit. Along with Keith Moon of The Who, he shifted the drums to the forefront of the recording of music. Finally there was John Paul Jones – the quiet genius who, like Page, was a highly regarded session musician, a multi-instrumentalist and music arranger. He played with Page on many of the aforementioned sessions. In my opinion it was Jones who sprinkled stardust on Zeppelin as his musical versatility and compositional arrangements in the studio made Zeppelin more than a rock band. In all probability he was the most musically talented member of a group of virtuosos. Plus he was part of the greatest rhythm section in rock history. It was the combination of Jones's bass and Bonham's drums that created the heaviness and groove. It's not guitars that make a band heavy. It is how the rhythm section combines with the guitar. So many heavy rock bands do not recognise this and what is considered heavy is actually loud, distorted guitars but without the 'bottom' of the rhythm section to uphold it.

It was one day at school, I was in Sixth Form, that my friends told me Led Zeppelin would be reforming for Live Aid. To say I was jubilant is an understatement. There was very little footage of Zeppelin on television as they hardly gave TV performances or interviews. I'd seen snippets of them playing but that was all, and for a Zep starved fan, I couldn't wait. I stayed up to watch the whole event, mesmerised by Queen's jaw-dropping set. At night I watched the American segment. Phil Collins, whose increasingly annoying mug was everywhere at the time, introduced Led Zeppelin. The audience (and me at home) just went crazy. The reception was like nothing else I'd seen, ten minutes after the band left the stage, the crowd were still chanting for more. This is despite the set itself being beset by problems. Firstly, someone had forgotten to tune Page's guitar, Plant had a sore throat and there were two drummers, Tony Thompson of Chic and Phil Collins, who were drumming out of time. I recently re-watched it and the sound is terrible. It all seems a bit messy. Nonetheless, at school the next day, we all agreed they had been brilliant. For a new generation of fans like me and my friends, we loved it. For us, the mystique had finally become a reality and we wanted more.

The next best thing was to see them live as solo artists. A couple of years later, Robert Plant played at St Georges Hall in Bradford. It was the beginning of my many live experiences with the Zeppelin performers. When he played the Zeppelin numbers, the audience including myself went mad. I recall jumping so high that I almost ended up on top of the person in front of me. It was that kind of night. And it's as a live band that Zeppelin excel. Three hour sets were the norm. Most bands will play the same set every night with no deviation. Zeppelin would play instinctively and improvise the songs on stage. There was a zest to do something new and be unpredictable. No night was ever the same. Small wonder then that you can always hear Page play 'bum' notes every night due to his willingness to take chances. They never played it safe. The sound of a twenty minute drum solo may be rather indulgent but their shows were legendary for the energy, the musicianship, the improvisation and the fanaticism of the audience. By their last tour of Europe in 1980, they had stripped down the playing time to a mere two and a half hours, jettisoning the extended workouts and solos. The phrase 'tight but loose' was coined to describe Led Zeppelin performing live.

Rock purity was not the total sum of the Led Zeppelin sound. The influence of Indian and Arabic music emanates throughout their discography. Page had been fascinated by Indian classical music early on in his musical odyssey and Plant had spent his teenage years in Asian neighbourhoods in West Bromwich where he had been introduced to Indian music, plus his girlfriend and eventual wife had been Anglo-Indian. Both Plant and Page visited India several times in 1971–72 to record with the country's finest artists. The fruits of these trips can be heard on the Bombay sessions where a couple of Zep tracks are accompanied by Indian classical instruments. The results are a wonderful insight into the workings of these great musicians. Page and Plant explained what they wanted to do. The sole English-speaking person in the ensemble then explained to the others who would converse in Urdu. There seemed to be initial confusion as musicians from different musical traditions attempted something unprecedented. Eventually, it comes off and the results are remarkable. Instead of guitars, we hear the sarangi, shehnai, sitars and tabla. What appears isn't clumsy fusion but beautifully steeped in the Indian classical tradition. I remember playing it to my parents who were impressed and commented that the songs definitely had a *ghazal* like quality. Plant was deeply influenced by Umm Kulthum and declared that Abdel Halim Hafez had the best singing voice he had come across. No surprise because both Plant and Page had visited Egypt during their Zep years and Plant, who is conversant in Maghrebi Arabic and spends considerable time in Morocco, has been spotted sporting Umm Kulthum and Hafez t-shirts on many occasions. I've seen it myself.

Led Zeppelin also established a connection between the blues music of the Mississippi Delta, which had been brought over by African slaves, and the music of the Gnawa tribe who were slaves sent to Morocco from West Africa centuries ago. They believed the DNA of the blues lay with Gnawa music which encompasses themes such as healing and spirituality, themes also prevalent in Berber music, which Plant and Page both cite as influences. It figures then that Plant's solo ventures have increasingly looked towards the Sufi influenced music of North and West Africa rather than the European tradition over time. When I heard that Plant and Page were going to collaborate in 1994, I felt as if it was the second coming. The idea was to reinterpret some of their earlier folk and eastern songs in a live setting by adding classical musicians and an Egyptian orchestra. 'The Battle of Evermore' was recorded with ghazal singer Najma Akhtar, and they also recorded with local musicians in Morocco to create songs including the electric composition 'Yallah'. The video comprises a live performance in the Jemma el Fnaa in Marrakesh with Page's buzzsaw riff overridden by Plant's azan-like wailing. Overall, it gave the songs a dimension that wasn't available to them two decades previously. I saw them a few times on the No Quarter tour with a full Egyptian orchestra. Most of the set-list comprised eastern-influenced tracks such as 'Friends', 'Four Sticks', and 'In the Evening'. They sounded spectacular with an Arab lushness and vigour that enhanced the original songs. Oh, and 'Kashmir' was positively transcendental.

In a class of their own live, the band's first studio album is no less phenomenal. Regarded by many as one of the greatest debut albums of all time it was recorded in thirty-six hours of studio time. *Led Zeppelin 1* is a mixture of heavily distorted electric blues, yet was roundly panned by the critics for its lack of subtlety; I can only imagine they must have skipped 'Babe I'm Gonna Leave You'. Steeped in heavy blues, it isn't as diverse as later albums but contains the proto punk 'Communication Breakdown' and the Indian folk instrumental of 'Black Mountainside', which features a tabla. Plant's vocals are raw and demonic and the musicianship is electrifying.

Their next album knocked the Beatles off their perch. *Led Zeppelin 2*, which was panned by critics, particularly *Rolling Stone* magazine, contained riffs, which constituted some of the most famous in rock music. Like its predecessor, this is influenced by heavy blues with a touch of psychedelia. The guitar, drums and bass are tighter here, though it is a heavier sounding record. The Tolkein influenced folk-fest 'Ramble On' continues the development of the light and shade dynamics that became a staple of Zeppelin songs throughout their career, and it is this album that contains the greatest guitar riff in music history: 'Whole Lotta Love'. The next album, imaginatively titled *Led Zeppelin 3*, kicks off with the blitzkreig riff of 'Immigrant Song' which pulverises the listener into submission but veers sharply into the Indian folk of 'Friends' before segueing into the warped multi riff of 'Celebration Day', eventually flirting with the sublime blues majesty of 'Since I've been Loving You'. Side one ends with the riff rocker that is 'Out of the Tiles' but the soul of the album belongs on side two. Suddenly, everything is acoustic from the manic folk thrash of 'Gallows Pole' to the tender melancholy of 'Tangerine'. Plant really comes into his own as a vocalist and lyricist. It is on this album that he begins to sing in scales used by Indian and Arabic singers. Probably their most important album as everyone expected more of the same but Zeppelin demonstrated that they were much more than just a heavy rock band. Confounding both fans and critics, this wasn't too well received at the time but was essential for an outfit unconstrained by simple labels.

The band were so big by the time *Led Zeppelin 4* came out that they didn't even include their name on the cover. Probably their most balanced album in terms of diverse music, it was peppered with folk, rock and roll, blues, eastern and stoner rock. Each genre complemented the other as Zeppelin furthered their interest in medieval folk mysticism epitomised by the ethereal 'Battle of Evermore' where Plant duets with Sandy Denny of Fairport Convention. This is an epic album full of grandeur and drama which reaches its pinnacle in the iconic 'Stairway to Heaven' The best track on the album is 'When the Levee Breaks', with its opening apocalyptic drumbeat the most sampled in history. The seismic rhythm section underscores the hypnotic heavy blues guitar which reaches a frenzy as it accompanies Plant's banshee howling. If the term dinosaur rock is attributable to any song then it's this one because it is truly a lumbering monster. Outselling the Rolling Stones and The Who by a ratio of three to one, *Houses of the Holy* was even more eclectic and expansive. Plant had by now developed his vocal scales more in common with Arab and Indian singers while Page creates shimmering layers of texture in his playing represented by the opening track of 'The Song Remains the Same'. The highlights of the album both belong to Jones, whether it's the delicate string arrangement on the ballad 'The Rain Song' or the haunting keyboards of the gothic 'No Quarter'. Zeppelin, who by now had shed any semblance of being a heavy metal band further annoyed critics and fans alike by their tongue in cheek pastiche of funk and reggae in 'The Crunge' and 'D'Yer Mak'er'. The most compelling track is the Indian influenced 'Dancing Days' with a backward style droning riff that sounds plain odd at first but is an example of those weird Zeppelin songs that over time are revealed to be masterpieces.

The following years saw Led Zeppelin rule the world. In 1975 *Physical Grafitti* was released and this double album became their most diverse yet. The result is Stalingrad meets Laura Ashley, which reaches its pinnacle in their finest ever song 'Kashmir', written about a road trip they took in Morocco. The songs are epic in scale from the Stevie Wonder-on-steroids sound of 'Trampled Underfoot' to the eleven minute twisted blues of 'In My Time of Dying' with drumming that threatens to explode out of the speakers. However, they could be intimate on songs such as 'Ten Years Gone' and 'Down by the Seaside'. There is a real campfire spirit to the album.

Barely a year later, after a life threatening car accident had kept Plant in a wheelchair for several months, *Presence* was released. A very heavy guitar album it lacks the variety of earlier albums. The guitar-playing is performed with an urgency, which culminates in 'Achilles Last Stand' boasting a level of musicianship so astounding it seems an almost telepathic interplay between Jones and Bonham, and it is this interplay which forms the bedrock of the work. Though recorded in only eighteen days, the album deals with bleak and dour themes epitomised in 'Nobodys's Fault but Mine' and 'Tea For One'. A gloom that reflects the band's sense of malaise at that time.

Robert Plant had to be coaxed back into the group after the death of his son and what emerges, in the form of the band's final album, is a world away from the swaggering bombast of a decade before. Synthesisers are on an equal footing with guitars as Zeppelin appear to anticipate the 1980s. A diverse modern-sounding record with samba rhythms and Texan hoe-downs it jostles with blues and progressive rock. Its strength lies in its diverse musicality and experimentation due to the influence of Jones. One song that hinted at a future direction is 'Carouselambra'. A galloping guitar and synth epic that undergoes several stylistic and time changes ending with a disco fade out. Some fans thought that Zeppelin had gone soft, the music press in pure Maoist fashion called it obsolete. Today, it stands as one of the most compelling albums of that period.

December 2007. 'I don't believe it!' Shaiz is screamed in my face as Led Zeppelin kick off their show at the O2 with 'Good Times Bad Times'. Apparently twenty million people applied for tickets for this reunion show, crashing the internet when they went on sale. By luck or by an act of God, Shaiz managed to get a pair of tickets. It was a surreal experience as I watched three ageing rock stars, along with the son of John Bonham, create an unholy racket that had the building shaking at its foundations. I concentrate on each member of the band. Jason Bonham, who sounds the closest thing we will ever get to his father. Jones, a quiet intensity as he stands beside Bonham's drum set glancing at the drummer from time to time. Plant, the grizzled survivor who acts as a musical historian when he gracefully introduces each song. Though he doesn't have the range of forty years ago, he still has 'that' voice, still the greatest living frontman. And James Patrick Page, probably, the most exciting live guitarist of his generation; the guy who wrote the handbook on the guitar hero as he gurns his way through shredding solos and rambunctious riffs. Light and shade, tight but loose. When people say that Zeppelin are the greatest, I always believed it but now I have experienced it. As we walk into the cold December night I know I have witnessed something special, profound, magical. But there remains a nagging feeling, a sense of an incomplete performance. 'They didn't play an acoustic set, it was all electric,' I grumbled. There's no pleasing some people, eh?

MEENA KUMARI

Leyla Jagiella

It is perhaps not well known that Meena Kumari, the legendary Indian actress, had a remarkable voice, often commented on and frequently described as hauntingly beautiful. A voice that seemed to embody the full extent of melancholy in the universe in its cadences. We know it well through her movie dialogues, also through the interviews and poetry recitations that she recorded. Rarely do we actually hear that voice singing. Once in the song 'Aisa Hoga', a half sung and half spoken duet with Manna Dey from the movie *Pinjre Ke Panchi* (1966). Another, far more captivating example, is her recitation of a few lines of a ghazal in *Benazir* (1964). She starts to recite the poem, set to a simple melody, in the middle of a *mehfil* led by Ashok Kumar, when a dashing Shashi Kapoor enters:

Phûlâ chaman khushî ka jân-e bahâr âyâ.
Ânkhon ka nûr âyâ dil kâ qarâr âyâ.

Blossom O Garden. The spring of my happiness has arrived.
The strange light has brought peace to my heart.

In most, albeit not all of her movies, Meena Kumari performs to songs sung by Lata Mangeshkar. And it is these two women together that created a magic that has enchanted us for decades. It is, in fact, difficult to think of Meena Kumari without invoking Lata Mangeshkar too. When people talk of Meena-ji, they will inevitably conjure up an image of her performing to the songs of Lata-ji. Whether it is the songs of *Pakeezah* (1972) or from *Sahib Bibi Aur Ghulam* (1962). It is strange how in the imagination of the viewer the voice of Lata and the performance by Meena merge into an integral whole. But Meena Kumari's talent for acting certainly soared the highest when she made her body and face give shape to the melodies sung by another tongue. The playback song has been a standard of Indian cinema almost from its beginnings, of course. Viewers are very much used to this set up. But only rarely does a perfect dynamic between actor and singer make us forget entirely that we are witnessing the work of several artists here. Meena-ji and Lata-ji were able to create such a resonance. When reflecting upon this feat of beauty, I am reminded of a scene from the Bette Davis film *All About Eve* (1950): A playwright and an actress have a severe argument about who actually owns the role performed on stage. The playwright asserting that the actress is just a mere body with a voice, reciting his lines. But the actress holds that her work consists of much more. Through her performance, she rewrites the lines of the playwright, giving them fresh intent in meaning. Indeed, Meena Kumari is doing much more than just temporarily lending her body to Lata Mangeshkar. It is her performance which gives these songs the meaning that made them so popular.

It was while on the trail of Lata Mangeshkar's voice that I was first led to Meena Kumari, set on discovering the remarkable woman whose performance would forever be connected to '*Inhi Logon Ne*' ('These people') and other mesmerising songs from *Pakeezah*. I haven't stopped watching Meena Kumari's movies and listening to Lata Mangeshkar's songs ever since. In fact, even though I have probably watched *Pakeezah* more than a hundred times by now, I am by far not yet finished with discovering performances by Meena-ji that I have not seen before. I can never get tired of watching her, crying with her, finding strength with her.

It is for the songs, melodies, hypnotic singing voice and truly enchanting dancing that, for the past two decades of my life, I have watched *Pakeezah* (1972), Kamal Amrohi's masterpiece on the tragic love life of a courtesan, at least once every single year. A classic of the genre usually called the 'Muslim Social', of which the Courtesan Movie has become a very common sub-genre ever since, each scene, every song, whispers to my heart at every viewing. To this day I continue to be moved as much as I was when I watched it for the first time. In Kamal Amrohi's era, the story of the golden-hearted but socially oppressed and exploited courtesan had not yet been the cliché that it would eventually become. What Amrohi wanted to do with his movie more than anything else was first and foremost to provide witness to a world that was slowly disappearing from the face of our planet. A world of culturally refined Urdu-speaking urban upper class

Muslims of Northern India. What he also attempted to do with his movie was to give a grand stage to the woman that he loved, the actress Meena Kumari. And, indeed, it is her who is the breathing (and sighing) soul of the movie, playing the heartbroken courtesan Sahibjaan.

Much has been written already about how the movie, which from 1958 to 1972 took more than a decade to reach completion, in many ways mirrored the troubled and tragic relationship between Meena Kumari and Kamal Amrohi. Much more has been written about how the pining character of Sahibjaan seemed to embody the fulsome tragedy of Meena Kumari's own life. What is often missed in those writings is how Meena Kumari embodies much more, not so much the Sahibjaan of the movie, but even more the Sahibjaan after the final '*Khuda Hafiz*' of the screen. The courtesan she depicts suffers from the stigma of her profession and dreams of true romance and the safety of an acceptable marriage. Despite tragedy upon tragedy, her dream finally comes true. In the closing scene of *Pakeezah*, Sahibjaan is carried off from the *kotha* to the house of her husband. In real life, Meena Kumari certainly also spent a long time pining for romance and married life. The stigma that as a woman on stage she experienced at that time was not too far away from the stigma of the courtesan. In fact, many Indian actresses of her generation came from courtesan families and there is much to indicate that her own family had such connections as well.

As soon as Meena and Amrohi fell in love, she would not experience the happily ever after we wish for Sahibjaan once the closing credits had rolled. Kamal was a controlling and often abusive man who wanted her all for himself. She consented to become his second wife at some point, but their relationship remained an on-and-off affair until her death during the making of *Pakeezah*. Meena Kumari realised that marriage and love were not worth the dreams she had once cherished. She felt imprisoned in her relationship with Amrohi. Meena-ji, who was not only a gifted actress but also a poet, once wrote the bitter line:

> *Talâq to de rahê hô nazar-e qahr ke sâth,*
> *jawânî bhî merî lautâ do mahr ke sâth*
> You divorce me, with hateful eyes.
> Do not just return my dower to me, also return my youth.

In another poem she wrote:

> Pyâr ek khwâb thâ,
> *is khwâb ki ta'bîr na pûch*
> Love was a dream.
> Don't ask about that dream's interpretation/unfolding in reality.

Meena Kumari passed away shortly after Pakeezah's premiere. I am myself soon turning thirty-nine, acutely aware that my idol passed away at that age. The story goes that the troubles in her relationship with Amrohi led her to seek comfort in alcohol. Allegedly first on the advice of her doctor who told her to drink small amounts to calm her nerves. She was soon drinking more regularly and increasingly large amounts. Her physical health deteriorated rapidly until she was diagnosed with liver cirrhosis. It is said that from the day of her diagnosis she did not touch a single drop of alcohol again but it was already too late. Her liver could not be saved and, in the end, she passed away before entering her forties. Pakeezah gives witness to this slow suffering as well. The Sahibjaan of the later scenes of the movie appears genuinely broken and one easily gets the sense that this is not just an act. In the last song of the movie, '*Aaj hum apni duaon ka asar dekhenge*' ('Today I will see the results of my prayers'), Meena-ji is barely visible and the more vigorous dance moves of her character are actually played by a double.

It is no surprise that to aficionados of classical Indian cinema, Meena Kumari will always be known as 'the tragedy queen'. It is likewise no surprise that the tragedy queen has uniquely attracted the love of those who have experienced their own encounters with romance to be deeply tragic. Granted that is a common human experience for many, plus in many South Asian societies, with often unromantic arranged marriages still widespread, even more people would relate easily to such tragedy. But in particular those people who identify with Meena Kumari and her tragedies both on screen and in real life, similar to the *filmi* courtesan, empathise deeply with the longing for romance and even marriage that is frowned upon by society. In that context, my infatuation with the movie, the songs and even more so with the actress is a bit of a cliché. If you ask around amongst my generation of South Asian trans women and gay men, you will find a heightened obsession and infatuation with Meena Kumari, and if not with Meena-ji, then with the other legendary actress of classic Indian cinema Mumtaz Jehan Bagum know to the world as Madhubala. Described as 'the Venus of India cinema' and 'Beauty with Tragedy', she too was a tragic figure and involved with Kamal Amrohi. These beautiful female stars of Indian cinema's black-and-white and early colour era once used to be the heroines of many queer South Asian dreams. Their melancholy songs of longing offer comfort in broken-hearted times and strength in moments of desperation. Both in the characters that they have portrayed on screen and in their private lives they often combine moments of rebellion with submission to fate and society in a way that must feel very familiar to anyone who does feel like (at best) an exception or (at worst) an aberration in society. In that sense, my love for Meena Kumari is a cliché, despite my not being South Asian in origin.

What emanates from Meena Kumari, her voice, her words and her story is universal, attracting all those who perceive themselves as outcasts of society, not only those of South Asian origin. She embodies grace in moments of humiliation, beauty in the face of the ugliness of life, strength in moments of utter defeat. She perfectly symbolises the tragic but strong feminine woman; the ubiquitous glamorous heroine of yesteryear's cinema.

Like many queer kids of my generation I harboured an early fascination with such tragic but strong feminine women on the nostalgic silver screen. Two of the first that I loved from a young age were the Hollywood stars Bette Davis and Vivien Leigh, soon to be accompanied by graceful Egyptian dancer-actresses like Samia Gamal and Taheya Carioca, who became the stars of my primary school days. I became notorious for imitating their dances at every other school kid's birthday party. My encounter with yesteryear's Indian cinema and with Meena Kumari came later, in my teenage years in the 1990s.

I started watching Indian cinema and became enamoured by classicial Indian film songs many years before I encountered Meena-ji. The first Indian movies that I was able to see were recorded on scratchy video tapes and had a terrible Russian voice-over dub, an unpleasant type of synchronisation in which the original Hindi/Urdu audio track of the movie was not erased but merely toned down, and then the monotonous voice of a Russian narrator was added as a voice-over to offer translations of the dialogue. These kind of tapes were regularly shared in the Russian-German community of the small German town that I grew up in. At that time, in the late 1980s and early 1990s, that was the only access that I could have to Indian film songs. These Russian versions of Indian movies were a product of the Soviet era, when, on the one hand India, as a 'non-aligned state' was working with the Soviet Union on many political levels, and on the other Hollywood and other western movies were frowned upon in the Soviet Union. Indian movies became highly popular in Russia in Soviet times and were actively promoted by the state. Most of the films were either based on stories that could easily speak to and for Soviet Socialist sentiments, such as the iconic Raj Kapoor movie *Shree 420* from 1950, or were naïve and politically unproblematic romantic comedies, like the 1972 Hema Malini twin flick *Seeta aur Geeta*.

Pakeezah was not one of these movies. There is a Russian version of the film (aptly titled *Kurtizanki*, the courtesans) but I don't think it ever gained too much popularity. I also imagine that its nostalgia for a lost feudal age and its visual abundance sometimes reminiscent of the work of Sergey Paradhzanov would probably not have sat too well with Soviet censorship boards. Although there used to be a certain demand for the Muslim Social genre amongst Russian Tatars and Central Asian Muslims in particular; an Uzbek grandpa might have recognised a lot that would have once been familiar to him in a movie like *Pakeezah*.

In any case, my first encounters with Indian cinema quickly created a passion in me as I would sing the hits and learn the dance routines, it inevitably led me to look out for more. A well-travelled and, like me, slightly orientalising grand-aunt of mine had already introduced me to Classical and Filmi Indian Music. I then fell in love with that unique cinematic world which so beautifully combined engaging stories with music and dance. Further access to that genre was finally enabled via the magic of a shortwave radio that I acquired roughly around the age of twelve. With that shortwave radio I listened for many years, religiously I can say, to the 'Old is Gold' transmissions of All India Radio. And, a bit later, also to Southall's Sunrise Radio.

In *A Person of Pakistani Origins*, Ziauddin Sardar presents us with a rather unflattering critique of how Sunrise Radio brought together members of different religious and national factions of the South Asian community in Britain while at the same time maintaining and constructing borders and differences without ever connecting them in a meaningful way. For me, sitting in my German small town, the panorama of different faiths and nationalities that met there rather seemed like a much better alternative to the largely monocultural parochial world that I had to face every day. And as a Muslim I deeply appreciated the little nods to my own faith that I witnessed there, such as the *azân* being played during Ramadan. Or even the odd and displaced qawwali at *fajr* time. In Germany, we did not have any such publicly visible displays of immigrant culture or Muslim religiosity at that time at all. And through that medium I not only learned to appreciate the beauty of the voice of Lata Mangeshkar or Mohammad Rafi, but also the brilliance of Iqbal Bano, Mehdi Hassan and Farida Khanum.

This was the time when I first heard Lata Mangeshkar's *Inhi Logon Ne*, the iconic first song from *Pakeezah* that introduces Meena Kumari's character Sahibjaan to us. My knowledge of Urdu was still very rudimentary at that time, but I still roughly understood what the song was about. I think there also may have been some discussion of the movie by radio listeners calling in. Somehow, the song stuck to my heart, and the names *Pakeezah* and Meena Kumari emblazoned on it.

I gained a greater insight into the world of those names when the internet finally reached my home in the course of the 1990s. Those of my generation or older will remember that the internet was still a decrepitly slow affair in those days. Nobody would have even dreamed of uploading, downloading and watching whole movies back then. There was no 'Netflix and chill'. But short videos of song sequences from Hindi/Urdu movies were probably some of the first cinematic contributions that started to appear quickly online. I remember watching *Kuch kuch hota hai* – the song, not the movie – with the screeching sound of an internet modem in the background. And I was finally able to see what *Inhi Logon Ne* looked like in pictures and see Meena Kumari. I quickly moved on to other songs from *Pakeezah*. And just as I had been caught by the dance of Samia Gamal before, my attention was quickly absorbed by the steps, the poise, the extraordinary grace of Meena Kumari.

It was the early 2000s by the time I finally got my hands on a (probably pirated) DVD copy of *Pakeezah*, in Old Delhi, from some stall close to the Jama Masjid. I was not a teenager anymore by then. I was a young woman living in a transgender/hijra community in Delhi, and *Pakeezah* had been on my mind for a long while as a movie that I desperately wanted to see in full. I was not disappointed, and continue not to be disappointed each and every one of the many, many times I have watched it ever since. Around that time, in Delhi, I also learned that I was by far not the only trans woman who saw in Meena Kumari someone she could identify with. Almost all of my sisters in Delhi broke out in sighs when her name was mentioned. All of them knew the words of all the songs of *Pakeezah* by heart. Many of them were able to give dazzling performances to *Inhi Logon Ne*, *Thade Rahiyo* or *Chalte Chalte*. I started to realise that Meena Kumari was somewhat of a patron saint of the broken hearted. There was so much about the star, Meena Kumari, the vision, and what that vision means, that spoke to me, to us.

Behind that tragic figure was someone else too. A woman born in the year 1932 as Mahjabeen, into a humble family of Muslim performers, although with some grand connections to the Tagore family on her mother's side. Her father's name was Ali Bux (*Bakhsh*), her mother's name Iqbal Begum. She started to act professionally and contribute to the earnings of her family as a little child, appearing as *Baby Meena* in several movies based on Hindu mythology. When, much later in life, a naïve interviewer declared 'From an early age on you have chosen to be an actress...', she replied 'I have not chosen to be an actress. I'd rather have gone to school and become something else.' Throughout the late 1940s she starred as a minor actress in several movies, cast for the first time in 1946 as 'Meena Kumari'. Her big success came with *Baiju Bawra* (1952), in which she played the female lead. At that point it was probably decided that she would not become 'something else'.

Despite my longtsanding and faithful infatuation with *Pakeezah*, I cannot deny it is not Meena-ji's best work as an actress. Its value lies, however, in being a *Gesamtkunstwerk*, as we say in German, using many different art forms to produce a work of exceptional aesthetic quality: Kamal Amrohi's dream-like vision, paying witness to a disappearing world, the brilliant camera work of Josef Wirsching (German-born, like me), the dazzling colours, and the tragedy of Meena Kumari on and off stage. The pathos of a talented actress already very sick during much of the filming, evident when her dances become sedate and laboured and instead of her vigorous movements we find her reclining or lying down in several scenes. Her acting in *Pakeezah* conveys a sadness, a tragic aura that belies everything that is happening to her off-screen; she just seems to *be* Meena Kumari rather than acting. As far as acting is concerned, the strongest performance in the movie probably does not come from Meena-ji but from Veena, who plays Sahibjaan's maternal aunt Nawabjaan.

Despite her iconisation as a tragedy queen, Meena Kumari was a versatile and gifted actress. Certainly, her most iconic roles were those in which she brought all the pain of the world to the silver screen. With all her talent and strength still at her disposal, she excelled in *Sahib Bibi Aur Ghulam* (1962). Likewise remarkable in that regard are her performances in *Dil Apna Aur Preet Parayi* (1960) and *Benazir (1964)*. In movies like *Ek Hi Rasta* (1956) and *Yahudi* (1958) we see her laugh and be happy as much as cry and suffer. In *Kohinoor* (1960) she shows us an entirely jolly and comic side. The most unusual and maybe also most underrated role she ever played was probably Chavli in *Char Dil Char Rahen* (1959). Performing in a blackface that we nowadays would probably find objectionable (although the porcelain tone that she shows in other performances may also not be entirely natural) she is a widowed Hindu Dalit girl who falls in love with a man from a higher caste, played by Raj Kapoor. *Char Dil Char Rahen* is an odd film in that this work by Khwaja Ahmad Abbas is such an obvious piece of Soviet tinged Socialist propaganda. Four couples, amongst them Meena Kumari's Chavli and Raj Kapoor's Govinda, struggle to stay together even though an oppressive society does not have any space for their love. Tragedy ensues several times in this movie as well, Chavli is separated from Govinda and has to endure a number of terrible ordeals, including rape by someone who, in the context of this film, is probably best described as a 'capitalist pig'. In the end she reunites with Govinda, and also awakens to the truth of Socialism. Meena Kumari's depiction of the personal journey from a slightly naïve uneducated village girl to a young woman who discovers her own social and political agency is something to behold. Something very different from the eternally pining courtesan of *Pakeezah*.

In her dance performances, Meena-ji again shows her greatest skill not so much in *Pakeezah*, even though her graceful postures and facial expressions in many songs of the film have become iconic, but elsewhere.

Most beloved to me are her performances to *Baharon ki mehfil* in *Benazir*, and to *Chalo gori pee ke milan ko chali* in *Ek Hi Rasta*.

Meena Kumari is somewhat of a patron saint of the broken-hearted. And I do actually often invoke her, like an actual patron saint. I have done so often in my own times of heartbreak. But also in far more mundane moments. In moments when I need the strength of a woman who has never stopped giving beauty to the world even though the world broke her. A woman who continues to offer her allure to the world even beyond her death, through her heartfelt and exquisite songs that offer comfort to those of us who have ever longed for a love that society seeks to deny.

RAVING IRAN

Interview with Rim Jasmin Irscheid

Rim Jasmin Irscheid grew up in Berlin, arguably renowned as the European capital of techno. Think endless thumping beats as revellers traverse the streets of the iconic city, negotiating their way into clubs that bow to the altar of pure unadulterated decadence. Enter vast communist-era buildings and the scene that awaits is one of ecstatic bodies, wide eyed and writhing to the bfff bfff bfff sound of industrial bass.

The daughter of a Palestinian-Jordanian father, her background ignited an interest in the way in which, what is perceived as traditional music from the Arab world, is fused together with dance music culture. This was piqued while studying in Heidelberg, where she met Iranian friends who introduced her to a site of cosmopolitan youth culture that was, for those who weren't in the know, unthinkable: the Iranian rave scene.

A rich tradition of music has long existed in Iran, with Persian folk and classical genres celebrated as part of the cultural heritage of the nation. The revolution of 1979 changed this entirely, however, and music was outlawed, viewed by the authorities as a lascivious and corrupting tool that needed to be strictly regulated. All forms of music perceived to be Western in their source or influence were regarded as antithetical to the religious identity the theocracy sought to promote. This stance softened by the turn of the century but was revived once again, when in 2005 Iranian president Mahmoud Ahmadinejad banned all Western music from state media outlets.

Despite the crackdown, the music scene in Iran managed to survive by evading the attention of the authorities. Much has been written about the thriving rock scene and the emergence of Iranian hip hop in recent decades, but less well-known due to its covert nature, is the rave scene. Irscheid became interested in the uniquely social aspect of raves in Iran, and the intensity of shared experience felt by those drawn to the reverberating sound of electronic dance music. The intimacy inspired by dancing to techno and the sense of unity that is a component of collective motion opened up questions surrounding the rave scene's role in political resistance. Keen to understand more, she looked at 1990s rave culture and theories of escape and youth resistance 'to demonstrate how rave-goers in Iran belong to a shared music community sustained by invisible activities that give rise to particular forms of cosmopolitan culture'. It became apparent to her that, 'the unlawful Iranian rave can be understood as a "counter-site" of youth resistance'.

Irscheid found she wasn't the only one intrigued by an illicit music community in one of the more austere theocracies of the world. Underground raves in Iran, which are illegal under Iranian law, have been lauded by international music journalists and academic researchers as sites of urban youth's resistance to the regime. The stakes are high, she explains, anyone taking part in these events faces the prospect of prosecution for 'transgressions' that are defined as the inciting of the inappropriate movement of a person's body and inducing a state of rapture or even just the appearance of joyous delirium in a person.

As well as extensive fieldwork cataloguing the experiences of her Iranian friends who frequent the country's rave scene, Irscheid's research was informed by the 2016 documentary *Raving Iran*, produced by German filmmaker Susanne Regina Meures. Praised by critics and audiences for its 'courageous' and 'brave' portrayal of two Iranian techno DJs, known as Blade&Beard, as they seek to bring the defiant tones of techno to the youth of the Islamic Republic of Iran. The film offered Irscheid a window into the way in which young Iranians are navigating their circumstances in order to have a good time, just as any young person around the world might seek to do. Combined with her own experience of Arab and Muslim culture Irscheid expanded on this raw material to provide an insight into the rave scene in Iran that steps back from presenting a purely Western gaze and uncritical platitude of 'dance music as resistance', which was a criticism of Meures' film. She does this by exploring the subject as part of her research interest in electronic dance music (EDM) as a social form of music consumption and performance.

How accurate can it really be to describe the rave culture in Iran as politicised? The rave scene in London is one that exists in unofficial spaces on the margins of urbanity, buildings in transition such as derelict structures reminiscent of a once-proud and thriving industry that has been rendered redundant. Casualties of neo-liberal government policies and symbolic of the gentrification of once-affordable areas that are now being cleansed of all traces of the past as, once planning permission has been granted, luxury flats sprout out of every latent crevice. No doubt there are many ravers who are oblivious to any added dimension to their party, but for many it feels like a political statement to enter these spaces and appropriate them for a use that is in such defiance of the one that is intended. For Irscheid, any comparison with European rave culture cannot be a neat one. 'It's different because in Europe you can make use of abandoned spaces but in Iran it's trickier because you can't really go somewhere like an actual house where people would know what's happening because there is a fear that you could always get caught, because it is far more criminalised. This is why I use literature on 1990s rave culture and the gay scene in New York and Detroit for example because it was interesting to see how these minority groups were able to find places where they could be social and intimate at a time when it was not socially acceptable to be themselves'.

Young people in Iran set about organising raves in much the same way as techno enthusiasts elsewhere, just under the cloak and dagger of darkness and subterfuge. 'The people in Iran I talked to drive out to deserts, they hire coaches and sound equipment under the pretence of some other event, not a techno rave. Everything is done in secret, and then they drive out to the desert just outside of Tehran. The spaces they go to are places where you know nobody will come and nothing can happen to you. Some of the spaces are completely unlikely, like greenhouses, any place you would least expect a rave to happen. It's very different to European raves where you would not be surprised to find a rave underneath bridges or in disused warehouses. In Iran the fear of getting caught is so strong that they seek out the most improbable venues.'

The location of raves in Iran may be contrasting, but the feeling of subverting authority and indulging in symbolic acts of civil disobedience is universal, that feeling of "we are in it together" connects everyone at the rave and establishes a common purpose, like a counter culture for behaviour and social attitudes that is at odds with what is happening outside. Everything, from the way you dress, is completely different and an act of defiance because, of course, in Iran women have to wear a veil. In the documentary Meures describes how women arrive at the raves in a headscarf wearing no make-up and then they get changed, take off their veil, put on their make-up and their hot pants and transform into the opposite of what is acceptable to the religious police. We all know that the West has an endless fascination with Muslim women's bodies and how they do or don't conform to the tropes of Muslim attire. Irscheid is aware of the ease with which anyone researching a topic as explosive as the Iranian rave scene, can be drawn into orientalist clichés of victim narrative and emancipation through the rejection of Iranian or Islamic identity. 'The danger exists of Western researchers exoticising what is happening in places like Iran. Many of my friends from Tehran told me they don't want to be recognised for just going to these crazy raves and the DJs would rather be recognised for the quality of the music they produce. It may come as a surprise to learn that for many of them it is actually apolitical, they are just youngsters having fun. They want to enjoy what we all enjoy so it is more of a thing of people coming together and the only intention is escapism'.

An analysis of rave culture in Iran leads Irscheid to Foucault's notion of heterotopias and is further informed by Brian Wilson's ethnographic research on techno raves in Canada, in which he writes about escape through pleasure. In his study, Wilson takes a closer look at studies on youth culture focusing on pleasure-seeking as subcultural resistance, as seen in earlier writings of Angela McRobbie and Steve Redhead. 'Raves do frequently get busted and people get lashes and are put in jail because techno and electronic music is accused of fostering a demeanour which isn't natural, and encouraging immoral behaviour'. The notion of heterotopia casts the rave space as entirely opposite to the usual social surroundings and mental states. Rave culture is characterised by the hypnotic beats of repetitive trance music and sounds of techno music that diffuse into your body and move it in a particular way. Combine this with possible drug-taking and the heightened state of intimacy that invites disorientation, social bonding and the feeling of acceptance, and you are somewhere other than the norm.

A taste of uncomplicated freedom is the sensation that drives the atmosphere at Iranian raves, not dissimilar to the global rave scene but with an added gravity, as Irscheid explains. 'In Iran, you do have music concerts but they are tightly regulated. Security will be watching over the audience, scanning the area to look out for people moving inappropriately to the music. Even the act of standing up from your seat will cause someone to come over and tell you to sit back down. You literally have to sit there and you can't do anything with your hands. The emphasis is on always being in control of your emotions and feelings and behaviour. A techno rave is all about losing yourself to the music and not caring how you look or how you are dancing, you just move to the beats without any constraint.'

There is, of course, the added dimension of free mixing between the sexes and the sexually expressive vibe of techno raves. It is interesting to note the distinction between the drunken atmosphere of mainstream nightclubs around the world where the music is secondary, and what takes place is more predatory and aggressive sexual behaviour with rather more misogynistic overtones. Sexual expression within the techno scene has traditionally been in a space of equality, a safe space largely devoid of aggression or violence, where the quality of the music and losing yourself to a higher state of consciousness is a primary goal.

While the rave scene in Iran imbues this message of equality, it is undeniable that privilege is a factor in participation, although it would be unfair to then dismiss the scene as the playground of the elite. If anything, for Irscheid, it is unsurprising that the young people coming along to the raves are largely liberal, secular and middle class. 'Raves attract people with access to the internet who can circumvent restrictions on the internet through proxies and by changing VPN. YouTube is banned. Spotify is banned. Soundcloud was even banned for a while. So it is the middle classes with their access to technology and education in operating sound equipment, and also the means to bribe themselves out of jail, should they find themselves arrested, who are willing to undertake the risks. People who fear punishment because they don't have the money or the connections to get themselves out of jail can't afford these risks.' This is in some contrast to the birth of the rave scene in Europe and the US, which emerged out of working class urban environments and street culture.

How does a rave scene come about in Iran? Due to the highly risky nature of organising such events, it is trusted friends with a shared passion for EDM who co-ordinate together, with each person implicitly aware of the utmost importance of discretion. These networks are driven by enthusiasm and a sense of purpose, with everyone involved incentivised to work for the successful completion of the project without falling foul of the authorities. The co-ordination of groups with different skills and responsibilities to put on the rave is particularly compelling for Irscheid: 'I'm always interested in how people from different backgrounds come together and socialise. It's a circle of friends thing with people finding out about raves through word of mouth, text messages and sometimes Instagram. As far as I am aware you have to know someone involved, usually the DJ or the person producing the music so it is their friends who will come along to the rave.' The raves are not on the scale of a clubbing experience in London or Berlin. Sometimes there will be just thirty people involved, which heightens the intimacy of the setting as it is a close-knit community of people taking part, who have proven that they can trust one another. It may seem somewhat exclusive to restrict information about an upcoming rave to just a handful of known friends and acquaintances, but this is purely to ensure their activities remain undetected. 'You have to be very careful, which is why it is not promoted in the same way as a rave in London or Berlin. In Iran you have to be part of that circle of friends to even know a rave is going to take place.'

The popularity of raves in Iran is increasing, but is still worlds away from the mass marketing of raves advertised among the global music scene, with adverts on billboards, in the music press and on social media. 'It's a particular interest but is growing as people are working out how to circumvent internet restrictions and are becoming aware of what's out there and what works and what doesn't work in order to pull off a rave without incident.' Iran is becoming more globalised in cyber space, while it remains static in the public space. This is why digitisation is key to the rave scene and is fuelling many underground movements and subcultures. 'Everything is DIY in the Iranian rave scene. You can't sign up for classes in music production so instead you look online and teach yourself. There are so many internet tutorials so if you want to learn how to produce music you can watch an online video. There's a lot of literature out there on how Iranians have skilfully utilised online resources such as YouTube tutorials because it is so difficult to access training in real life and so we have a generation that is relatively 'self-taught' because physical borders are sealed, whereas borders in cyberspace are more easy to breach. A couple of decades ago there was a thriving black market for cassette tapes, which kept the music scene alive, but now online music is widening access.'

People go to raves and there is little information about the event other than their experience. There are no photos on social media or write up on Resident Advisor. The secrecy heightens the mystery, and reduces the risk of getting caught. 'It's not like you pay an entrance fee and enter a rave because it's just there and you want to go. It's more about becoming a part of a community and working for a cause that you believe in – which in this case is a love of electronic dance music. This is what distinguishes the Iranian rave scene from the European one. In Iran there is a feeling you're all part of this one community and this collective risk taking is a unifying factor, which really sets the tone of the atmosphere. The bonding with people you may not have known before is amplified because there is so much at stake. The fact that these young people are having these exceptional experiences that remove them so far from their everyday mainstream lives and create a space which is just in the moment, and only those that have had that same shared experience can relate to it.'

The irony is that it is the attempt to demonise electronic dance music, casting it as a moral crime, the listening choice of the unbeliever, which increases solidarity among techno devotees and galvanises their determination to outwit the Iranian police. Irscheid's view of the rave scene in Iran has been impacted by this background of labelling, and she expands on it by drawing on the work of subcultural theorist Howard Becker who talks about the criminalising of youth and how deviant practices, once they are labelled thus, form subcultures in response to the description imposed on them. So when the Iranian Ministry of Culture and Islamic Guidance and local media labels these young people as illegal and casts them as 'kuffar', it gives meaning and therefore enables their existence through criminalising them. That labelling ties the rave into a 'heterotopian space', a realised form of a utopia. It is a real place in real space and time but is not part of the current present. Instead it finds itself a little bit apart and separate because it has been stigmatised by the state and the media. This only empowers artists who wear these labels as a badge of honour and reclaim their status as underground actors by declaring that it is in fact their wish to remain underground and not be co-opted into the mainstream.

What's more, according to Irscheid, those who are part of the EDM rave scene illustrate that it is possible to carve out an alternative social order from within, undetectable and alive. This sanctuary is cultivated by the producers of music and the rave organisers as well as those who merely show up to dance. Techno music enthusiasts mark out a space of resistance purely through the fact that the act they are indulging in is criminalised. Young people in Iran taking part in a global cultural phenomenon that is locally invisible, arranged via social media and streaming platforms, occupy fissures brought together in spaces of commonality, which are physically, socially, and culturally distinct from the everyday existence of the majority, but also distinct from the visible life they convey to those authorities that scrutinise their personal lives. They offer an alternative to acceptable social spaces that operate within the margins, such as those spaces that play legal forms of pop music, but hover out of sight, whether that be far from the authorities in the desert or in digital cyberspaces. Politicised or not, these are young people determined to enjoy their lives according to the dictates of so-called western culture, navigating the social and religious conventions that provide them with the boundaries they choose to transgress. This, surely, is the epitome of resistance and escape through pleasure, and what could possibly be a better 'high'?

YESTERDAY

Zia Chaudhry

'A world without the Beatles is a world that's infinitely worse.' One of the more memorable lines from 2019 feel-good movie *Yesterday*. The story revolves around Jack Malik who awakens from an accident to a world in which nobody has heard of the Beatles nor of any of their songs. So when Jack starts singing them, they regard him as a musical genius – a persona he reluctantly runs with for the time being. The film, and especially that line, made me think of the impact music has had on me and in general, and of that band in particular.

My family moved to Liverpool when I was seven years old and although the Beatles had long since disbanded, it was evident just how much they still meant to the city. To this day I remember school trips when the lads would all be singing Beatles songs in the coach en route. At that time, in the early '80s, the music of the 1960s seemed a long time ago, but I have to remind myself that it was no more historic then, than me now listening to tunes from 2004 – just the other day for my middle-aged sensibilities. I also recall how around that time one of the boys from my school ended up singing 'Yesterday' on the kids' TV quiz show *Blockbusters*, and how much I admired his courage, and the fact that he kept winning (Can I have a 'p' please Bob?).

Thinking of the Beatles also reminds me of my (albeit somewhat imagined) recollection of my parents' arrival in the UK in the 1960s. Certain parts of that recollection are unequivocally based on facts: it was true that they came from a tiny, forgettable village in the north-east of Pakistan, situated in a district from which my father was the only person to have escaped with an education. It was also true that they encountered opportunities in the UK which were simply unavailable to them 'back home'. The fact remained, however, that I hadn't discussed with them all the details of those initial years, so it remains questionable just how much of my picture of their early life here in the 1960s was accurate.

I imagined a bleak, smog-ridden Northern town where locals wandered around in flat caps sipping pints, whilst the Pakistani immigrants looked on, shivering, in bewilderment. I recalled that those terraced streets of two-up, two-downs were certainly not furnished with the mod-cons we have since become so accustomed to. I was also painfully aware of the blunt racism that those early immigrants had to endure as the shouts of 'Paki' were very much part of the memories of my own early years. And I also have a semblance of my growing understanding of the priorities for all immigrant families, or so I assumed. Those priorities revolved around gaining an education and bettering yourself, priorities which in turn afforded little time or space for luxurious pastimes such as music.

Not surprisingly, that recollection of a monochrome era devoid of joy does not convey the real picture. As ever, often the details are provided by the things left unsaid. Conversations involving me may well have been about working hard and gaining an education, but they were held against a background of photographs of smiling Pakistani men (and they were always men back in those days) posing by the flower beds of local parks. These photographs painted a picture of life outside of the factories. Life at the weekends, during brief snatches of leisure time, where hard-working immigrants caught up with their pals and were able to relax and find moments to enjoy in a land very different to the one in which they had grown up. And boy did those guys look smart! Sharp suits and dark sunglasses were definitely picked up from the Beatles and suggested that these men were taking on more of the cultural life of their new home than perhaps they were being credited for. Occasionally I'd pick up a disparaging hushed reference to someone outside our circle of family friends, who was rumoured to be frequenting pubs and clubs. Looking back on it now it seems obvious that such visits would have exposed these more-adventurous immigrants to the music that their white workmates were listening to.

Those park poses in the photographs adorning the Punjabi mantelpieces of the 1960s and 1970s were undoubtedly derived from the movies of the day, and implied an accompanying soundtrack, perhaps not in the language that everybody else was twisting to, but a soundtrack nevertheless. And perhaps that is what music does best, namely, provide the soundtrack that not only accompanies and punctuates our life with a chronology of reference points, but also instils it with meaning. How many films of the lives of Pakistani immigrants in the 1960s ought to have opening credits accompanied by the cultural reference points of a Beatles or Elvis medley, before settling into the dulcet tones of the legendary Bollywood play-back singer, Mohammed Rafi. This would capture the new world they were encountering.

The human memory is a fascinating and complex phenomenon, subject to a plethora of triggers and prone to awakening by a multitude of stimuli appealing to different senses. Although many of our memories are provoked by visual imagery, it is often the most delicate and subtle influences which add to the richness of the human experience. What may be a barely perceptible scent to one person, may evoke a particular place or person to another, bringing into the foreground either a particularly painful or joyful episode, or simply marking out a point in time. For me for example, Old Spice aftershave will forever be associated with memories of visits to my uncle's house in the late 1970s, whilst the far cooler Kouros defined my 'trying-a-bit-too-hard' adolescence and rather nervous entry into adulthood in the '80s. Music, however, by its very audible nature, provides a far clearer commentary on life. While certain songs can speak to our innermost thoughts, others simply serve to remind us of past events from our lives. And they can also provide an introduction into somebody else's life, a window into the soul of another individual or a gateway to a different culture. How many of us are transported back to holidays abroad as a result of a chance encounter with a particular song, with that three minute interruption in our existence able to bring back the sights and smells, as well as the sounds, of distant lands.

As I am forced, reluctantly but inevitably, to accept the fact that I am just another balding middle-aged man, I obviously indulge in middle-aged pastimes such as reminiscing about my youth, particularly about how I could do x, y and z so easily before but now x, y and z are becoming increasingly difficult, not to mention beset by side-effects and consequences. And such reminiscing is often accompanied by a musical commentary. There are the obvious and memorable musical demarcations of decades, but also the more subtle musical signposts which have all served to influence my life in a myriad of ways.

I have no musical training whatsoever as, much to my shame, music was the one lesson I stubbornly refused to attach any importance to at school. I was utterly blind to its benefits and concluded that my mental energies were better expended elsewhere. In my childhood and youth, therefore, this meant that music was something I consumed passively rather than actively. It was there. Some tunes may have been more pleasing to my ears than others but they did nothing more than form the background rather than foreground of my life. And a large part of that background was provided by one Mohammed Rafi.

As a young child of Pakistani immigrants growing up in the 1970s, I rarely encountered British or American music. Our family just did not listen to it. Our friends did not listen to it. And so we children had no exposure to it. The music which we did encounter was from the Indian subcontinent. This was a time before the boom of Bollywood videos in the 1980s so there were no films which could be viewed at home. There were the odd forays by the adults to see Indian films at the cinema and they reminisced about films they had seen 'back home' and listened to old *filmi* songs, which meant nothing to us kids but seemed to really animate the adults, and none more so than songs by Rafi. If I had a pound for every time I heard an adult say 'What a voice' when describing Rafi I could probably have dispensed with a career at the Bar.

Although my family was not in the habit of playing music at home, I was exposed to it at the houses of friends and, more likely, when in a car driven by my uncle. When I listen to Rafi today, I can still feel the heat of the plastic seats in summer and the slight whiff of petrol emanating from my uncle's Ford Cortina. Rafi provided the soundtrack for many, probably most, Pakistani families in the England of the 1970s. The sheer effort of trying to establish new lives in a foreign land which required hard work on the one hand and a wariness of National Front abuse on the other, set against the general greyness of the decade, was all forgotten when Rafi was singing. So many Pakistani men spent their nights working shifts in local factories, doing as much overtime as was available so that they could provide for families here and in Pakistan. Their down-time, such as it was, simply consisted of catching up with their friends. Television had nothing to offer them in those days so all they had was the music of Rafi. There existed an obsession with him, which for a long time I simply put down to his being called Mohammed rather than Mukesh and it was only many years later that as an adult I was able to confirm for myself, 'What a voice'.

The 1980s saw me enter high school and although music as a subject did not interest me, I was now more aware of the sounds around me. Well before the days of downloaded music and even before the advent of CDs, music was purchased in the form of records and cassette tapes, and high school was where tastes were formed and such purchases discussed. My school was within walking distance of WH Smith, Woolworths and Penny Lane Records, all of which helped fill many a lunch hour for teenagers who were after the latest tunes. And unlike today it was much more of a communal experience. There wasn't the excessive individualism of the twenty-first century encouraged by an on-demand culture which allows you to walk around with your entire personalised collection of music tucked away in your pocket. Not only was this physically impossible back then, but it was also incompatible with an era of a few television channels and, therefore, much more culture consumed collectively rather than individually.

Perhaps we all think this of our teenage years but to me the 1980s was a particularly rich period for popular music. From the New Romantics like Spandau Ballet and Duran Duran to rock bands like U2 and Simple Minds, the excess of the 1980s was epitomised by stadium-filling big bands. This was also the decade that saw me go to my first concert, along with over 125,000 others who gathered at Aintree racecourse in 1988 to see Michael Jackson. This was music as a big spectacle extravaganza which you would remember for the rest of your life.

Surprisingly, one of the bands that I recall most fondly is The Eurythmics. The combination of the musical talent of Dave Stewart, combined with the vocal skills of Annie Lennox helped the band produce a string of pop chartbusters, but their impact was far outweighed for me by one of their live performances. The live concert video that was produced of the Australian leg of their Revenge tour in 1987 was shown on TV that Christmas and, as was common practice back then, I set the video to record it. I don't particularly recall why because I was hardly their biggest fan, but I do remember watching the performance and being amazed by one member of the band in particular. Jimmy Zavala not only had an exotic name but also possessed the cool, yet exotic looks I wished I had back then (and hair that I would kill for). More notably, however, he played harmonica on 'There Must Be an Angel', and saxophone on 'When Tomorrow Comes' – both of which were mesmerising performances for me and, for the first time, began to stir in me an appreciation of the musical talent on display, without necessarily having any understanding of the music itself.

Although the key to the band's success lay largely with the amazing voice of Annie Lennox, particularly on the hauntingly beautiful 'Miracle of Love', in those days it was upbeat music that I was more interested in. Teenage years are the period where you can be both bursting with joy and a sense of fun and simultaneously saddled with the weight of the world. A sense of optimism about the future is tempered by the realisation that it still seems a long way off and in the meantime nobody seems to understand you. I suppose a lot depends on your personal outlook on life and, being the glass-half-full kind of guy I am, my memories of the 1980s are rose-tinted and conveniently overlook the painful self-consciousness which sometimes affected every step I took. So the parts of that decade which I recall most clearly are the joyful moments, and, therefore, the uplifting tunes.

For me, many of those joyful moments were supplied by one Eddie Murphy – but thankfully, not the uplifting tunes, because although his character's performance of 'The Greatest Love of All' in the 1988 film *Coming to America* was a work of comic genius, his actual musical career was defined by the more forgettable *Party All The Time*. What he did do, however, was burst onto the comedy scene with a stand up show called *Delirious* which provided the perfect antidote to studying for exams for us impressionable teenagers. His profanity laden sketches were repeated ad nauseam by me and my friends, albeit well out of earshot of our parents, and he quickly became one of our heroes.

For many Asian Muslim youngsters growing up in the Britain of the '70s and '80s there were few, if any, heroes and role models from a similar background. This void was often filled, therefore, by Black Americans. I remember being given the Autobiography of Malcolm X by my father, and although I was totally impressed by the integrity and eloquence of his struggle for his fellow African Americans, not to mention his cool back-story, he was of course long since gone. Muhammad Ali was another hero co-opted by Asian Muslims - for several years as a small child I assumed he was a Pakistani bloke like my dad's friends – and although he remained so until his death in 2016, in the '80s he was a once-great boxer in decline whose greatest achievements remained before my time. Other sports stars such as Magic Johnson and Kareem Abdul-Jabbar had a more limited following among my peers so it wasn't until Eddie Murphy that we found our own contemporary young black star to follow.

His early films were amongst his best work, combining the effortless natural comedy of his stand-up routines with the sort of violent action which was the staple for teenage boys back then. And for me, the Eddie Murphy film which had the greatest impact was *Beverly Hills Cop* (1984). As is so often the case, when I occasionally revisit this film now I am somewhat nonplussed by its ability to stir much of a laugh in me, perhaps inevitable after the umpteenth time of hearing the same joke, but what I remember vividly is the effect it had on me back in 1984. Slap bang in the middle of my teenage years it provided me with everything I wanted my life to possess. Humour, action, and entertainment set against a glamorous Californian backdrop was pretty much the stuff of my teenage dreams and the scene when Axel Foley, Murphy's character, arrives on Rodeo Drive to the accompaniment of Patti Labelle's deliriously upbeat 'Stir It Up' remains one of the most inspirational episodes of my youth, convincing me that my future lay in Beverly Hills. Even today, although my middle-aged self may be somewhat more aware of the darker side of the American dream, that particular song never fails to make me feel good about life.

And American culture was certainly able to make you feel good. Ignorance was definitely bliss if you were able to put to one side many of the actions of that country, and judge it by its entertainment industries alone. Just as the world was being wowed by a gyrating Elvis at the same time as the Vietnam war, in the same way all the ensuing American crimes and misdemeanours highlighted even more the need to have our minds distracted by talented and beautiful people representing the optimism of youth rather than the corporate greed that was behind the world's conflicts. And I must confess that I was completely taken in by it all, packaged, as it was, perfectly for the young people of that decade who were just embarking on their own journey of consumption. It was easy to convince myself then that just as inequality was inevitable when some people were prepared to work harder than others, similarly we could not expect all of the world's nations to behave in the same way. Some had surely earned their right to wage war, dominate and pollute. The decade of winners and losers closed out with me being utterly convinced that the soundtrack to the future sounded (and looked) better when it was played by Bon Jovi rather than Status Quo.

At the start of the 1990s I began my career at the Bar. Just as the '80s were my years of education, my working life commenced neatly at the beginning of the next decade. Disposable income coupled with no serious responsibilities meant that finally I could see the rewards which my parents said would be waiting for me if I got a good education. And for me that just meant one thing. I have always been fascinated by cars and now I was able to afford one that suited a young barrister. A silver BMW 325i sport was cool enough anyway, but when it had £1500 worth of Alpine sound system added, it became a very desirable object indeed and now just needed the right kind of music playing in it. The look was completed with the RnB tunes of the 1990s which were the choice of the discerning young man about town back then. Ok, perhaps that should read discerning young Asian man about town because it certainly seemed to be the default music for that particular demographic. The choice of music was one of several similarities between those young Asian men and their Afro-Caribbean counterparts. What was the point of doing a demanding job if you weren't able to enjoy the trappings of that success, and what was the point of enjoying the trappings if you did not show that to the rest of the world? The demands of the new job were now at least partially offset by my, admittedly superficial, enjoyment of life as depicted in some of the music videos accompanying my chosen RnB tracks.

Happily we don't have to remain superficial forever. Although I hope I can be forgiven for being a bit shallow in my interests when I was in my twenties, I would expect less sympathy if those interests were to define the remainder of my life. I can now appreciate that one of the keys to a fulfilling life is probably ensuring that it is occupied by as many diverse experiences as possible. Even so, I have to admit that it was with a sense of trepidation that I accepted a colleague's invitation to join a group of them to go and see a performance of *Les Miserables* in Manchester in the early 1990s. I figured this was the kind of thing that barristers did and I should make the effort to join in, for the sake of my career if nothing else, although I'd be listening to my R&B all the way there and back.

Well, what an unforgettable experience that was. I was simply blown away by the songs and the sheer emotional intensity of the performances. This was the kind of music that previously I would not have dreamt of listening to yet here I was thinking it was the best thing I'd ever witnessed – so much so that I went to see the show again a few years later when it came to Liverpool and now, some twenty years later I'm planning on taking my children to see it when it revisits our city this year. This was music as storytelling, soul stirring and inspiring and I could not believe there might be people out there who would object to it. The fact remained, however, that in those days I was still somewhat inclined to the view that religion was a straightforward affair involving obeying the rules and although I did not hesitate to ignore any such 'rules' about music, in the back of my mind I was aware that for many Muslims it was a thing to tolerate rather than celebrate.

I think it was perhaps after witnessing this performance that I began to regard music as something to be celebrated, and celebrated because of my faith rather than despite it. The performance had certainly felt like some kind of spiritual experience for me and served to make me realise that you really did not have to look very far to find God, often to be found in the unlikeliest of places. He had, in fact, provided us with so many sign posts pointing to him – or at least pointing to an opportunity to contemplate Him. Throughout the ages art had been used to express the Divine and although I had not really appreciated why, now I was beginning to understand that there are certain things for which words are simply insufficient. A direct appeal to the heart had to be made and that, perhaps, is more readily done through an artistic medium. Don't get me wrong, I'm not suggesting that I went straight from watching *Les Mis* to opening the doors of Sufism, but for the first time I began to directly connect music with an appreciation of the Divine, and to consider my faith as more than the sum of my observance of the rules.

I also began to develop a more eclectic taste in music. I'd always had an ear for pop music but it was the contemporary stuff that appealed. Yet now I was revisiting the 1960s. And I was completely fascinated by the simplicity of many of the songs from that era and how despite this, or maybe because of it, they seemed timeless in their nature. I rediscovered Motown which provided songs I could listen to forever - to this day The Elgins' Heaven Must Have Sent You remains my favourite song. I was living on my own and had the time to listen to music, but also I could actually afford it now. Over the decade I amassed a large collection of CDs which included everything from Frank Sinatra to NWA via Nusrat Fateh Ali Khan. And although I was still more attracted to the slickness of RnB, my superficiality in that regard was tempered by my appetite for some of the more forthright Hip Hop that also came from the States. Bands like Public Enemy with their clarion call to 'Fight the Power' were particularly attractive to a young man making his way in a career in the legal system. Being confident, fearless and willing to confront the injustices of the world are probably appealing to young people and some of this music was really spurring me on to stick it to the man.

The man survives, however, and we grow older. Of course one of the advantages of doing so is that you learn that there is often more than just one way to achieve an objective. Many people, for example, do not realise that the music and Sufi poetry of qawwalis played a significant role in spreading Islam in the Indian sub-continent. I had had to endure many hours of listening to them on the seemingly interminable car journeys we undertook when I was a child, wondering why my dad was so enthralled by a song which often felt like it hadn't ended even by the time we'd reached our destination. Years later I was able to appreciate this music, and although my understanding of the lyrics was partial, I was intrigued by the fact that the music was often composed in a way that facilitated inducing a trance-like state, thereby representing the union with the Divine which many mystics were seeking. It was this music that led to me becoming more interested in reading about Sufism and its attempts to focus on the underlying reality rather than the apparent form and opened up for me a whole new way of thinking about Islam.

And these Qawwalis also reminded me that it was not just the pop music of the 1980s that I found inspirational. Although the hymns I had to sit through at school seemed to be a tedious start to the day, I have since discovered that they somehow carved out a little niche in my soul, from which they have continued to uplift and inspire. If it wasn't the music it was the stirring lyrics that surely served their purpose in reminding us of the Divine, albeit through a Christian medium. And to be perfectly honest, what is life about if not remembering our Lord? Yet now that I have young children in school myself, I can't help but think that the more user-friendly songs that they have in their school assemblies will never influence them the way 'Jerusalem', 'Praise to the Lord the Almighty' and 'Amazing Grace' did me. But then I guess my children will be moved and influenced by their own musical tastes – even if, somewhat bizarrely, my younger son has an uncanny appreciation of songs that I enjoyed as a child, varying from Mohammed Rafi's '*Kya Hua Tera Vada*' to Joan Armatrading's 'Drop the Pilot'. Strange though this is, it is a complete joy to watch and hear him sing along to anything pleasing to his ear regardless of it being in a foreign language.

And that perhaps is the key to music – the ability to stir the emotions and make us feel. What exactly it makes us feel is no doubt down to the individual's mood and the nature of the music but it certainly awakens emotions which are often lying dormant. 'God is beautiful, and loves beauty' is a well-known tradition of the Prophet but it is perhaps one that we too readily ignore. Life is indeed beautiful but easy to miss when you're doing the school run. Easy to miss when you have work deadlines to meet. Easy to miss when you're busy making plans. So it is sometimes the musical interlude which makes us pause, perhaps reluctantly and against our impulse to motor along, and reflect for a moment - about our lives, our loves, and our blessings. Ultimately music is any sound which is pleasing to the ear. The giggle of our toddlers is rightly regarded as a blessing from our creator, as is the voice of our beloved, sounds which we never tire of hearing. But introduce some musical instruments into the equation and suddenly we encounter a plethora of rules about exactly what is permissible and what remains forbidden. And through all the enervating halal/haram debates the beauty of life ebbs away.

Now, having finally reconciled myself to the fact that the baldness, declining speed and diminishing dexterity are here to stay, and that it's not just my heroes of the 1980s who have aged, I have developed a greater appreciation of the beauty of life and its presence in everything around me. My allegiance to Kisstory may not have totally yielded to Classic FM just yet, but when it does I'd like to think that it will be a seamless transition and another chapter in my evolving appreciation of beauty. It is human nature perhaps to dwell on the few negatives in our lives, and forget the multitude of positives, but music helps to focus on the latter in the way we are meant to. Even sad songs are beautiful in their own way. I may struggle to hold back the tears whenever I hear Dance With My Father, or Father and Son, but that is only because they remind me of my late father – and those are always beautiful thoughts.

We may smugly celebrate not having to worry about the playlist for our funerals (thank God, for now), but if the efforts the young generation of Muslims put on their wedding soundtracks these days is anything to go by, then even that day may not be far off. For the time being though, let us just rejoice in the beautiful sounds available to our ears, and recognise that truly 'a world without the Beatles, is a world that's infinitely worse'.

ARTS AND LETTERS

POETRY AND MUSIC

Paul Abdul Wadud Sutherland

I use 'music' as a metaphor with a similar weight to the use of architectural forms or elements of nature to communicate more than the selected words permit. Musical inferences have a slightly more reflective connection than most metaphors or tropes because the words of poetry anticipate musicality as a further method to convey the poetic subject. T.S. Eliot went so far as to claim that 'musicality' infused its own intelligence into a poem and that a composition's rhythmic pattern of word-sounds suggested for the alert reader/listener an understanding that surpassed intellectual analysing of the piece.

In music there is an implied invisibility. The visible figures of language on the page or spoken need a harmonious power that is unseen to ensure the poem's completeness and elegance; words cannot achieve this excellence. John Keats, a century before Eliot, wrote 'Heard melodies are sweet, but those unheard/ Are sweeter; therefore, ye soft pipes, play on; /Not to the sensual ear, but, more endear'd,/ Pipe to the spirit ditties of no tone'. Keats is not only employing music as a metaphor to describe the Grecian Urn, he's signifying to the reader that we can best value the words when we listen to the less overt semantics of the poem's musicality. If we cannot understand the meaning of the words we can intuit their inner notes. I hope in my lyrical writings that the reader will leap beyond intellectual comprehension to find something akin to the Sufi masters' practice of listening to the speaking melodic heart.

Keats knew that what he was inspired to communicate couldn't be realised through an order of words, a more elusive sounding, a mode of 'music of spheres', was necessary to serve his readers. The master teacher, Maulana Jalaludin Rumi, six centuries before Keats, took music as a metaphor to a higher vision when perceiving in the song of a reed flute, the ney, a sign of our separation from the Creator. He heard our grief at this estrangement in the reed flute's cadences that both veil and reveal. My writing too fulfils its profound realisation when the written language of words somehow gives way in a reader's mind to a more refined and whole message. These pieces of poetic discourse also are veils that hide and express our separation from the love of the One. Love, of course, is the ultimate signature tune in beautiful poetry.

Burda and Nasheen From A Rooftop

A hot Kerala sun in twilight haze, a semi-circle of da'wah students sing with no pages to refer to; one pads and taps a tambourine-like drum. Arabic phrases disperse beyond the unfinished building. I fear I can't sit unsupported on the prayer fabric. The youth's music and sincerity braces. A scholar and imam with me feel the merging of respect and wonder. We're settled on the top of a half built structure, a breeze weaves over the flat roof to accompany their soprano voices. We listen. They perform. They stretch this ghost edifice toward future realities. Crude essentials of concrete and steel grow supple as the Burda chanters reveal: a song in praise of Muhammad (saws). The un-whole building absorbs every movement written by a wounded poet, unable to walk, whose prayers were granted centuries ago. If you heal me, he bargained with the spirit of Muhammad, I will compose a great eulogy in your honour, an ever-lasting song-poem. Now we listen to those forgiving and warning words.

It's All Jazz

Along village roads a family ensemble might patter out at night without fear of being run down. They know their swinging steps are protected and more precious than a four-wheeler or two or three. Out of the busy twin lanes again men and women walk and do not flinch within inches of crescendo-zooming motorbikes and rifts of honking cars. The deep shaded enclaves that you don't know exist until you're inside one, are ideal for the three-wheel half-car-size auto-rickshaws. Their rattling putt-putt is a frequent jam-session among bird trilling and muttering residents. Each dweller will have their way to reach out into that new nation, breeding a new nationalism, zinging along another national highway, more kilometres of paved roads criss-cross India than any other country except the United States. 1.3 million kilometres in Kerala. A colossal repair job follows each monsoon's tabla-pounding but new by-passes and six lane highways are perennially under construction, further fly-overs designed with more workers' drilling. The region's developing nature is visible in the unexpected leap from apparent recklessness and disorder that must orchestrate each initiative until its sudden pristine completion, and yet with some residual builders' mess, heaps of unused sand, broken bamboo scaffolding poles, discarded laterite blocks – maybe someone will create a pool or a rocky terrace in which lightning-streaked kingfishers might make their homes. That launch from frenzied first movement to a polished coda is the transformation that travellers observe everywhere. The buildings will be erected to shimmer in a tropical sun and its inhabitants will stay cool with state of the art humming fans and air conditioners endearingly nicknamed AC.

A Nocturne for my Man

I ache to share his slow steps – a dance before nightfall in a large dim-lit white room.

Who's intruding? Wishing to take my love's hand? Then calm greyness again we waltz inside, outside, under the moon.

A she moon invades – snatches him up – the greater dancer; flings and ravishes him over the sky. I'm alone. The chandelier flickers.

The first intruder joins we sit with up-turned brows puzzling at his nocturne's frolicking – escape and fate.

A flute sounds – a shadow of love's costume his blue dancing suit.

An Interlude

The shiny plywood chairs were a bit loud with nothing but a rubber thimble to cushion their legs' contact with the hard floor, but the annoyance was soon eclipsed by the collective music of many dialogues proceeding at the same time towards very different destinations. The fugitive listened, it was his gift to listen, until used cups and saucers, half-empty glass sugar bowls and the side cake plates had voices which might be decoded if one could listen forever.

Fantasy on The Rite of Spring

Emerging from the infinite
sounds of a solo bassoon
unnerve silence of remote
valley; a child-sage stares
far ahead deep into the past.
From unspeaking beginnings
light surges; fragments wing
towards home before landing
reversal back to conception
intrusion of strings – chaos
behind order, force behind
calm, death in back of light.
Return to mystic observer
for short soothing – before
fury consumes earthlings
rapid insistence on change
violent rioting notes descend
ascend – crash, crash toward
the barrage of cannon tubas
gun-flash, battery of trumpets
and rata-tat-rat of percussion.

Marchers thrust on and on
until conflict's made sacred

before next transformation.
And everything must alter
no resistance tolerated and
landscapes crumble under
rhapsody of swirling missiles
the treeline is made treeless
undulating field's grouched
pastures turn into morass.
Shrill strings re-introduce
the arrival of innocence
war ends, peace prevails
the seer weeps the dream
of origins in sub-heaven
then human hands cover
the sky in his blasted eyes.

Revolt of passion, water's
turbulence, air's collision,
earth's ache 'consumed
by fire or by fire', patterns

smoulder. Bell echoes warn;
high timbre can't hold clefts
lets flee to further preferred
violas, woodwinds or horns.
The watcher cannot slumber
who knows what must invade.

No theme survives before
flying hands pluck at cords
soar to cliffs of cellos and bases
too soon another starting
demands sacrifice with fresh
episodes of curses and praises
then so lowly muttered as if
the cosmos had never awoken

into being. But that vacuum
anticipates fierce alarms of
hatred, first moving un-heard
below surface of remembrance
sand folds in water like scores
then fear and flight from new
terrors. The mystic shutters
to carry the turmoil – boom
of trombones, cymbals clash
that plummet to a raging trance.
And before – one more perhaps
last speechless transfiguration –
straining pipes of Pan, flutes
and oboes proclaim a monster
clawing out of its clayey abyss.

But it cannot conquer for long.
From so many spring offences
peace re-breathes only in pain.

To our too slow returning to life
the now old sage lifts a reed to lips
and blows into the human heart
that the source of love is humility
that 'the meek shall inherit the earth'.

A Final Evening in Kerala

The dinner is over. The cuisine was moreish and stylish. My host is pleased
his home has been cluttered with visitors to serve a looking forward with
hope to futures the students seek and the photographer, the best around,
has been invited to give a fleeting image of the marvel of transfigurations
taking place. It's a long journey to the departing airport. Three years' time
it might take half as long. The table still carries more than hints of beautiful
tangy food sunk in heirloom bowls, in covered plates and on loaded
spoons. All sitters at the table except me employed their right hands in

dainty manoeuvres of shepherding morsels, dry and wet, into loosely formed balls before lifting them into their mouths. Hand-users ate more quietly than me handling my steel fork and knife. The sweet earthy aromas linger among remnants of the photographic session. Let the food, companionship and of course the music of love play on.

THE PRODIGY

Nadira Babayev

Baron Arild Rosenkrantz was likely to have been immersed in the philosophical meanderings of anthroposophy while commissioned to create the stained glass windows adorning what is now Cadogan Hall. A 'spiritual seeker', he was prominent within the Rudolf Steiner branch of philosophy. The movement assumes the existence of a spiritual world, which may be intellectually experienced through a process of heightened imagination and thinking rather than sensory experience. Previously a member of the Theosophical Society, Steiner had become frustrated by the Eastern, specifically Indian, influence upon the Society's teachings. In an attempt to counterbalance the diminishing influence of Western thought, he founded Anthroposophy, which was instead based on Christianity and the natural sciences. The theosophists, however, persevered with their post-west pursuit of esoteric philosophy and became influential in the Indian Independence movement as well as Buddhist modernism and Hindu reform. In a subtle nod to theosophy, the architect of Cadogan Hall, Robert Fellowes Chisholm, was also deeply influenced by Eastern philosophical and artistic traditions, defining the skyline of Chennai in India with what became known as Indo-Saracenic or Muslim-style architecture. In a departure from the Greek-inspired architecture of colonial times, he utilised local aesthetic trends and materials traditional to buildings across the city, transforming the city's urban design.

Gazing at the gallery of the former New Christian Science Church that Baron Rosenkrantz and Chisholm helped to design and create, I am struck by their diverging approaches to East and West. Could their paths have crossed sufficiently for a philosophical deliberation to have occurred?

These and other musings preoccupy me on a sweltering June evening, the stuff of Indian summers, as I wait backstage in Cadogan Hall, the setting for a performance I have waited and worked years for. To calm my nerves I visualise myself, a tall, thin, intense young man with a concentrated gaze striding onto the stage oozing an air of reassured confidence. How different I must seem from the casual youngster who had everyone doubled up with laughter at a dinner party in East London just a few days ago. That evening I was on form, entertaining everyone with raucous stories of generational spats from my homeland, and dangerously extravagant acts of chivalry in the sun-soaked nightclubs of Ibiza, hoping to impress. With a flourish I would acknowledge the applause and position my instrument. A hush would descend in the auditorium. My subtle nuance of touch majestically captivating the audience with such miracle of verve that they would be in rapture.

A few months later I am sat in an organic, vegan cafe in South East London that serves the best fairtrade coffee in town. Shabby chic decor and sprawling sofas on which we lounge construct an ambient vibe that wouldn't be out of place in a backpacker hostel in Pushkar: a sprinkling of Western fusion in the East. But here we are, in reverse, as eclectic sounds from Transglobal Underground to Alt-J drift into the aural space around us. Conversation intersperses with questioning, to which I submit with the grace of a man well-used to navigating the politics of performativity.

Up until the age of six I was a carefree child who would play out in the streets of the capital of the Soviet Republic in which I was born, day and night. That year saw my father abandon the family and the death of both my grandparents. My mother's response to tragedy was to become one of the few per cent of women in our country to wear the hijab. People would tell her not to wear it or they would recommend that she wear it in a different style but the more they said these things the more she would rebel and defy them. By the time I was seven, I recall my mother explaining that, while struggling with multitude layers of grief and loss, financial hardship and constant objections to her choices, she had completely neglected to enrol me into school. An unruly child and not well-behaved, she struggled to get me into good schools without success, and she didn't have the money to bribe anyone so her only option was to persuade her former specialist music school to take me. An improbable prodigy, I was unable to read, write or count, never mind read music, and had not once even held a violin. My mother was undeterred. She bought a violin and all of a sudden I was expected to practise for hours and hours endlessly. Determined that I gain entry into the class of *the* internationally-renowned violin teacher in our country, barely literate and a novice, I was driven to compete with students who had been practising since the age of three years old. My mother enlisted the help of a friend who taught me to play and, against all the odds, I was admitted, one of just a handful of students, at the relatively mature age of nine years old.

I could never attribute this achievement to talent. Instead I credit my success to intense training from a young age and a mother who reinforced the discipline of practise as instilled by the teacher. My theory conjures up images of the hot-housing of young maestros by communist countries battling Western cultural imperialism. I would practise incessantly and could never convince my mother to be less strict about my hours or economical with the truth when asked to report the details of my practise sessions to my teacher, who would easily be able to tell anyway because there are certain exercises that we would have to do in a particular sequence and we had to do all of it without missing any part out because otherwise a certain twist of the neck or something that we hadn't worked out would come up and she would just know that we had practised much less or without concentration. She would be very cross and constantly threaten to kick us out of her class, and she did actually kick people out of her class who were not getting A+. A or A- just wasn't good enough. We had to get A+.

While she poured her energy into the music studies of her young son, supervising my practice and accompanying me on international music competitions, my mother found herself simultaneously grappling with theological misgivings. People were constantly telling us that music is *haram* and my mum was forever trying to figure this out. Someone would send her some *ayats* (verses from the Qur'an) claiming to prove music is *haram* and my mum would be so anguished, but then someone else would send something else that proves music is not *haram*, to her relief. She would also be constantly consulting Imams and one told her that music was fine as long as you don't profit from it. She was always grappling with this issue and trying to ascertain a semblance of absolute truth. I still continue to receive text messages of religious guidance from relatives. They send them sincerely because they genuinely worry for my soul, but I tell them ok I am just going to play music a little while longer don't worry I won't do it forever, and that soothes their concern.

The government of the former communist republic I am from, enthusiastically supported my precocious talent, providing funding for me to travel to music competitions abroad. However, with no other source of income, these lauded trips overseas were actually an illusory lifestyle that navigated a path of penniless fame. Instead of staying at five star hotels with other entrants, my family and I would head somewhere cheaper and opt not to have breakfast included, buying food at the supermarket instead. We were immersed in this bourgeois existence, where it was perceived that luxury was free to us. I was as little as twelve and people would greet me with great formality and respect. They would always make sure they never said anything wrong in front of me. Everyone was formal and deferential because I was a student of the most famed violin teacher of my region and because I had travelled abroad. It was assumed that we dined in fancy international restaurants and visited expensive bars when in reality we would eat packed lunches in the park and stay in budget hotels.

The price of accomplishment was a childhood dominated by immense pressure. I was no longer allowed to play out because I was required to practise incessantly and when I wasn't practising I was expected to read a book on Jascha Heifetz or study classical music. I had no access to television or the internet and would relish the occasional times I could venture out of my house on the premise of going to buy bread or to put the rubbish out. My mother had good reason to restrict my movements. Men in my neighbourhood like to brawl, so if a man passes you on the street and somehow feels slighted by the way you looked at him, he immediately wants to fight. I was a very bad fighter but if someone wanted to exchange blows I would never refuse and would always end up with black eyes and considerably worse off than the other guy. As my teenage years approached, men would fight me more aggressively. If they knew I was a violinist they would demand respect for no reason, and obviously I would not give it, so they would try to break a finger.

Only one opportunity existed to escape the endless hours of practising – prayer. I would do the longest prayers just to have a break from the violin and from music. It was really enjoyable. It was more of a meditation and escape from the monotony and pressure of constantly practising. On a Friday I would make sure that I went to the mosque and sit there for hours, elated by an intention to practise only for two hours instead of four that day. When I would get home my mum would be frantic and ask where I had been and when I told her I had been at the mosque she couldn't say anything. It was not long before even this loophole was closed when crackdowns on alleged Islamist terrorists caused my mother to worry that I would get picked up by the security forces or be mistaken for an extremist, so she put a halt to my mosque visits. My mother's ambition for her son drew unkind whispers alleging exploitation but I swear this wasn't the case. It was she who sacrificed so much, putting my music study above everything.

The spiritual serenity and peace that I had experienced in mosques in my home country, was something I was keen to emulate upon my arrival in London, with less happy results. On visits to the UK capital I had been to Regents' Park Mosque but soon after my arrival as a student I decided, with a friend who was interested in Islam, to visit another, more local mosque that I had admired for its distinctive dome. Me and my companion were met at the entrance by men wearing green turbans. They saw that we were new and young. I was only sixteen, and they pressured me to stay after the prayers, which we reluctantly agreed to do. Suddenly we found ourselves in a gathering with a small group of Salafis who were expressing very anti-Western sentiment and ultra-conservative opinions. The experience shocked and frightened me, particularly as the men insisted on driving me and my friends back to school. I was terrified they would come back and ask me to attend another meeting or that the embassy would discover I had been to this meeting or my teachers would find out or even Islamophobes in my profession who would seize on this. It was a few years before I went to a mosque again.

From the moment I got into my violin teacher's class, and as long as I managed to remain in her class, I understood that my destiny would lead me to travel outside my country. She had been teaching students for 50 years and many of them had attained great heights. For a long time I dreamed of a future studying in France. People used to say you go to Paris and you walk into a cafe and you have all of my country's elite sitting in there. However, I ended up winning a place at a prestigious music school in London. I didn't like it, it was gloomy, everything was on the right-hand side, the taps were tiny and either very cold or scalding hot. People were in the street smiling even though the weather was so bad and I couldn't understand how they could possibly be cheerful. My school was one of the most prestigious music institutions in the world, yet all I could imagine was that I must have not done well in my auditions at various schools to have ended up there. Everything was alien. In the morning assembly the headmaster would read from the Bible and the choir would sing. Adapting was very difficult. I was used to being treated in a deferential manner, which is why it was such a culture shock when I came to study in England. I had been a highly respected figure but as soon as I arrived in the UK, all that was gone.

A Muslim teenager from a former communist republic, I found this acclimatisation acutely fraught. The cultural chasm between myself and my schoolmates seemed achingly vast. English people like to make jokes about anything and they get over those jokes almost instantly but the way that I was brought up there are just some things you do not joke about. When I first arrived I couldn't take a lot of jokes and I had never been exposed to people who would say something just to get a reaction out of you, just for a laugh whether they meant what they said or not. I just didn't get it at all. Culturally it was completely alien to me and as a consequence I came across as humourless and reactionary. I studied with many talented musicians but was scandalised to see the majority hardly practised, often distracted by the illicit pleasures of teenage partying. Aesthetics training, discipline and professionalism had been drilled into me from a young age but when I arrived in London that all faded away. Yet, confusingly, despite the relaxed attitude of my fellow students, there existed a fiercely competitive environment, like a constant psychological warfare. It was never encouraged to be a team player. I didn't know English very well and I didn't get the social references of my peers. Being a violinist, I just obsessed over the few opportunities I would get to achieve validation and the respect that I craved. I didn't want anyone to hear me practise or to know that I practised often, so I would try to get a key to another building and practise from 4–7am in secret. Before long, I came to realise that there were times when I did not need to play perfectly and instead could compensate by being more social in interactions with other people. Completely locking myself away in a room and practising, which was what I did, meant that I earned a reputation of being a robot, a machine. A post-communist cliché.

This shedding of my former self became apparent to me during a recent trip back home, my first visit in ten years. I was asked a question in a typically allegorical way. An acquaintance whispered: 'In the UK do you have too many blue skies?' In Russian slang 'blue' means 'gay' so it was their way of asking whether there are many gay people in the UK, except they didn't want to actually use the word gay! I realised that this etiquette and formality that informs what you can or cannot say depending on the status of the person you are talking to or the respect you afford those who are within earshot, was now alien to me too. I remember thinking, oh my God I once communicated in this manner, and I thought why can't you just say the word 'gay' so I started saying that the skies are very grey and cloudy so he hesitantly clarified: 'No, you know: man-and-man' and I said 'Oh you mean gay?' and the guy nearly fell off his chair and said 'don't say that word, your mother is just sitting over there'. Words are more than just a medium for description in the society of my birth. They are perceived to have such essence that if you utter a word you fear, it is almost as bad as if that word was happening to you. In comparison, the manner of communication that confronted me upon arriving in the UK, was so much more direct. Of course, the English say what they don't mean and don't mean what they say but in my country I was taught to avoid saying anything that might be remotely taboo. When I came to the UK to study, of course I met gay people and I simply did not know how to behave because I had been so conditioned to fear homosexuality. Some students I boarded with knew exactly what was going through my head and they would do things like walk into my room completely naked while I was praying. To them it would just be a joke, or a prank to wind me up but I just couldn't handle this type of so-called humour and I would lose control, which of course they knew I would, but I couldn't help but react. Sometimes it would get physical so I was lucky not to get expelled in my first week! Eventually, I realised that if I did not rise to the bait, I would no longer be harangued.

At home I was treated as if I was a great prodigy but looking back, I realise I was nothing more than lucky. I was fortunate to get into such a prestigious teacher's class. I was lucky to get into a London music school without knowing any English and I was lucky to pass my bachelor's degree because I struggled with the academic side and all I wanted to do was perform at concerts and practice. My critical inner voice sees only an abundance of compromises, which should have curtailed my success, but somehow didn't. Perhaps it was talent that kept me afloat after all. Financial hardship is not new to anyone attempting to forge a career in the arts. Combine this with the struggle to adapt to unfamiliar social conventions and the potential for a combustible situation can easily arise. I found myself constantly getting into trouble and being disciplined for my 'attitude'.

After completing my secondary school education at the private boarding music school, I auditioned for and was accepted by many other higher education institutions but was unable to accept due to lack of a scholarship. My only option was a school in Canada but two weeks before I was due to leave, I was invited alongside one of my teachers to a concert. At the reception afterwards I was introduced to a man who asked why I was going to study in Canada, to which I explained that it was only because I had failed to get a scholarship that would enable me to live in the UK. The next day a renowned higher education institution called me to offer a full scholarship, explaining that the man I had been introduced to at the concert would be covering my living expenses. They asked me to immediately send them the documentation they needed to sort out my visa, as well as my bank details so they could transfer the money into my account that moment. To be suddenly financially secure was a bewildering experience for my teenage self. Although I had been granted a full scholarship to attend the music boarding school, it did not cover the school holidays and I was unable to afford to travel back to my country. Term times were like a holiday because I had meals and a bed but half terms and end of terms were difficult. I had been looked after by a host family that my mother had paid, having found funding from somewhere. When the money for that ran out I stayed somewhere else. It was in a basement and there were five or six other students in one room and it was awful. We were only occasionally given something to eat. Our hosts felt that it was enough that they were putting a roof over our heads. As I was under 18 my visa did not allow me to work so I got a paper round in the mornings earning £30 a week so I could buy food. It was a gruelling experience. The bag in which I carried newspapers was so heavy and I had to cycle up a huge hill weighed down on one side. The lady I worked for wanted me to arrive at 4am and I would finish my round about 7.30am. Every morning I struggled up the hill on my bike but Saturday and Sunday were the worst because at weekends newspapers have lots of supplements and my bag was so much heavier. I hated it. This unwelcome insight into the exploitation that occurs in the black market only added to my steely ambition to succeed. I did the paper round for several half-terms and summer holidays but eventually I couldn't handle it any more. From then on, I learned to get by on my wits.

Studying at university marked a new phase in my life. Fellow students came from ordinary state schools and would be hugely impressed upon learning which music school I had attended. But to me it was just a place I had become 'Londonised'. The first few months at that school had been very painful. It was probably hard for everyone but I took it extremely personally because a lot of the banter and jokes were about me being a Muslim. I didn't want to go through the same thing at university and also it took a little while to establish myself and start playing at concerts so I really got into conspiracy theories and politics to feel a part of something. I would hang around Speaker's Corner and romanced an evangelical Christian girl: Our relationship consisted of her sending me links about Muslims committing atrocities somewhere in the world and me sending her links about Christians doing something similarly cruel. My politicisation evolved into something far healthier as I gradually lost touch with my school friends and found myself hanging around with politically active and socially conscious fellow students. Suddenly I found friends with whom I could debate issues intellectually and have grown-up conversations and I finally felt at home with this worldly and internationalist atmosphere.

Political maturation was not necessarily matched by a mature approach in other areas of my life. My sponsorship did not continue after my first year at university, because I had no idea that my sponsor had certain expectations. It was entirely my fault. I was young and I didn't realise that it was the custom to call my sponsor every week. He never said it but now I realise. He had hoped I would visit him regularly and play for him but it just didn't occur to me, and no one told me that I had to nurture any kind of relationship with my sponsor. Even worse, I suddenly found my bank account was flushed with money. Instead of spending wisely and frugally, I called up my mother and told her to come to London, telling her I could take care of her. I then rented a two-bedroom flat with the funds that my sponsor had intended I should use for my music. He was very disappointed and at the time I didn't get it at all but now I feel sure he felt that I had frittered away his money. I wouldn't blame him at all for feeling that way.

Negotiating informal and formal emotional relationships is the height of intricacy. Yet British law is impossible. My visa prevented me from earning money so I could not be paid for performances. In the eight years I have been in the UK, corresponding with Britain's heightened obsession with immigration against a backdrop of Brexit, I have been astonished at how recalcitrant conditions have become for international students. Those with any plans to stay on after their studies are expected to earn unrealistic salaries and the rules are continuously tightened. When my British visa expires then I cannot fly because I have to apply for a new visa and I have to wait a couple of months and then I have to apply for a European visa, and wait another month or two. So I am missing out on so many concerts and competitions just because I have to re-apply for my visas. The bureaucracy is very communist. The authorities now check whether students are indeed studying. After each lesson, teachers are compelled to sign forms to confirm the student is fulfilling the terms of their visa and attending the lesson. It is all very big brother and communist.

The generosity of benefactors, because there is no other way to obtain a visa or to survive, is invaluable. I am from the East, and my ability to remain in the West is so awkwardly dependant on the goodwill of others in addition to the whim of government. But as far as I am concerned that tension is tolerable, because in order to realise my ambitions as a violinist, I need to be here. Maybe I have convinced myself that the culture of classical music here is not part of our culture back home. It is 'other'. I am everyone's dream migrant, the good immigrant, yet the relationship between myself and my benefactors has the potential to veer into the symbiotic. Good intentions can become oppressive or enabling as the power balance is mired in expectation. I have had little choice other than to be at the mercy of the kindness of others. My teacher of the past six years has looked after me like a mother, being ever patient during the many times I lacked maturity and didn't respond to her emails. She was the one who persuaded him to delete my facebook and Instagram and step away from Twitter as she worried my politicised posts could damage my reputation, particularly when I was going through my conspiracy theory phase. This music prodigy from the East has been wholly subsumed by the West. For now, I feel sure there is no other way to survive.

TRAGIC TIMING

Ari Haque

It started with the woman who ended detention of undocumented migrants.

'She was a second generation migrant herself, 37, and had lived in Croydon, England, her whole life, which had made commuting to Yarl's Wood in her early days as a grassroots activist easier', read *The Financial Times*, in her obituary.

'It was a tragic and unusual accident, where the car appeared to have been set alight intentionally. But the coroners concluded that it was not a suicide, for which her elderly mother was grateful, as a verdict of suicide would have nullified the life insurance policy, which had been purchased precisely a year before.'

The outpouring of grief in the days that followed from the commentariat referred, constantly, to the tragedy of the timing. Having finally closed the doors on the last remaining centre (closing ceremonies had proved a challenge to organise, for a number of reasons, as the events coordinator had learnt) only four days earlier, she had expired.

The funds, raised on a Kickstarter page (championed by the people that had been freed, plus their families and friends who awaited them just outside, tearfully awaiting the all but abandoned but much hoped for reunion), went into paying the architects, and interior decorators, to turn the detention centre into a women's refuge.

But then went the woman (42, had initially been assigned male at birth) who had finally had equal rights for transgender and non-binary people enshrined into law and implemented, successfully, across all organisations, buildings, spaces and employers. A plaque was dedicated to her at the last remaining employer to prove themselves 'friendly to all folk, whatever their presentation, or identity in both policy and practice' – she had opened it (this one was easier for the events coordinator) just three days before her death, a boating trip gone wrong, that had ended in her drowning.

And then went the survivor of sexual assault (67, retired just outside of Ebbing, Missouri) who had finally come to the end of a court case against her rapist. The perpetrator had been convicted and sent to a secure re-education facility, something like what they called 'prisons' a few years back. It was the first successful conviction of a legal client of a legal sex worker, finally proving that the idea that 'consent is not a contract' had taken hold. There were few details about her death, just some vague and lurid speculations about how the case had added stress to her pre-existing mental health conditions. The less tasteful radio hosts made blunt remarks about how 'in a way, it was almost lucky, as she'd spent her life savings paying for the lawyers, and in the meantime didn't feel safe enough return to work, having been scarred by the experience'.

It barely made the news when the Bangladeshi climate change activists had passed. They were known best for the introduction of a worldwide tax on airlines, meat producers and fast fashion manufacturers paid straight to communities most at risk of the consequences of the rising sea level. Their water-logged bodies had been drowned for days before they were found.

Then, only a few weeks later, on the day of the inauguration of the first woman-identified, queer, black president of the United States of America, who had campaigned tirelessly and met with every person in every state, in person, without eating or sleeping, literally, dropped dead just before delivering her speech, live on air. As aides, and journalists, swarmed around the almost-president to check if she was breathing, if there was hope yet, a man, who had stepped back as there was already a flurry of activity going on, spotted the president-to-be's speech.

It read, simply: 'We are exhausted.'

Such tragic timing.

TWO POEMS

Latifa Nur

The birthing of sound

My companion, cut from the reed
Carved by a master, as Fetiyhe's orange blossoms
Foretold the sweet notes of a new season
Of Love discovered
I blow into you, and you entwine with my soul
A sound is birthed, our energies mingle
You heal my separation as I heal yours
We learn to merge in each other's breath
Uniting in Takbir
There is no reality, but Yours
Recalling Yunus' Love with every puff
Into the belly
You calm my aching heart

Blowing music

From the depths
of hollowness.
Vacant of all but the
only breath.
Emptied of all but
nothingness.
Freed of life and
its pretence.
From that void

within the reed.
Music pours forth
with such force
there isn't a soul
that's not trembling.
Not a single atom
escapes the vibration.
Every *taksim*
a revelation.
Direct from the
Divine station.
Coursing through that
hollow core.
Surging into the air
I breathe it in
I can feel it working
emptying
the contents in my chest.
The script slowly
stripped away
with each note
birthed in the
same moment
it dies.
A veil pulled away
from these eyes.
In the pain:
one subtle demise
after another,
creating a blank place.
Reflecting the Face
of the eternal friend.
She takes a pen
and starts scribbling.
The secrets contained
within the abyss

that's opening
from the centre of
this broken heart.
To the surface
streams of ink
fill empty spaces.
Like breath gliding
through the holes of the reed.
Spilling tunes in the air.
She's blowing music
right there
in my breast.

POETIC PILGRIMAGE

Wasi Daniju & Azeezat Johnson

Hip hop is an art form rooted in resistance. It was created and remixed by young Black Americans who sought to take up space within the brutally anti-Black inner cities of Chicago. From the aerosol spray cans used for graffiti; the mouth manipulations necessary for beatboxing; and the 'scratching' and remixing of a family member's record collection, hip hop was undeniably founded as a critical expression of inner-city Black experiences. Young people used whatever resources they could find to create their very own Black sound and culture.

Even as corporations try to commercialise the hip hop 'sound', the culture is grounded in this history of claiming space (in spite of violent systemic inequalities). It continues to evolve alongside other forms of artistic expression in countries like Nigeria, Brazil, France and the UK. It has inspired a generation of Muslim artists and performers who use spoken word to challenge Islamophobia and social injustice (both within and outside of the Muslim community).

The Black Muslim hip hop duo Poetic Pilgrimage – comprising Muneera Rashida and Sukina Abdul Noor – have been trailblazers in the UK scene. Established in 2002, Poetic Pilgrimage demand to be heard on their own terms, and no one else's. They featured in an Al Jazeera documentary directed by Mette Reitzel in 2015, and continue to inspire young spoken word artists, rappers and hip hop enthusiasts to this day.

The duo as depicted by their friend: therapist and photographer Wasi Daniju.

REVIEWS

HARMONY IN SARAWAK

Elma Berisha

'Are you in your right mind?' reacted Hanna, my typical festival-goer best friend, in response to my invitation to join us for the Rainforest World Music Festival 2018. 'That is not an event for kids, there's hippies, and narcotics, and…it's not safe'.

'Rubbish!', responded my new friend Diana, with some annoyance. She had already convinced me to come along, particularly as her husband would be team-bound, officially covering the festival for the travel magazine he worked for. 'Tim was there last year and it is a perfectly family-friendly event', Diana said. I glanced at the official festival site once again, and was thrilled by what I saw, including many event programmes designed for children. Nevertheless, I decided to leave the kids behind. We spent the second day of the typically three-day event there, as I had to rush back to Kuala Lumpur for urgent appointments the following day. The experience was exhilarating and we both vowed to return in 2019, to attend the full programme. Come 2019, Diana and I went again, just the two of us – she didn't even bring her aforementioned husband, who had no official duty assigned that year, nor did I bring my kids, nor did we invite anyone else. Excitedly,we flew into the Borneo jungles for RWMF 2019, held from 12–14 July.

The Rainforest World Music Festival (RMWF) is an annual three-day festival held in Kuching, Sarawak, the eastern wing of Malaysia. Organised by Sarawak Tourism Board, it is supported by Malaysia's government and Tourism Malaysia; the festival has been acclaimed as one of the twenty-five best world music festivals by *Songlines* for the last six years. It is staged in the Sarawak Cultural Village in Damai Beach, located between the South China Sea and the Olympus-like Mount Santubong. Beach, rainforests and mountains form the backdrop all in one sweet spot, only about half an hour drive from Kuching city centre and the festival site offers breathtaking natural scenery of unparalleled, but conveniently accessible serenity. Celebrating diversity and authenticity in both nature and culture, the festival has won acclaim for its signature message in free-spirited celebration of human 'togetherness'. Twenty-two years ago it was a cosy gathering of a few hundred people, whereas the 2019 festival attracted more than 23,000 international and local guests. The festival featured over 200 renowned performers from thirty countries, and a wide range of hybrid performances from traditional and indigenous music, to world fusion and contemporary sounds. My particular focus was on the festival's independent music, the result of a do-it-yourself approach to recording and publishing, as well as celebrating almost extinct, rarely heard-of, indigenous musical instruments.

Sape is the iconic musical instrument of the Rainforest World Music Festival: a traditional wooden lute of the Borneo upriver tribes. Sape creates a mysteriously therapeutic and extraordinarily soft sound. Soothing sape vibes permeated our entire Sarawak Cultural Village wanderings, particularly during the daytime and late afternoon, prior to the evening main stage events. In 2018, there was a non-stop performance of sape at the very entrance of the village welcoming newcomers, and at the opening ceremony the sape was cordially presented. In 2019, additional sape performances were there to be experienced, and I took full advantage, predominantly attending indigenous recitals. I spotted an outstandingly talented and beautiful young sape dancer, who turned out to be the 2018 Miss World Malaysia, Larissa Ping, a member of the sape Warisan Telang Usan band, and who belongs to the Kenyah indigenous community. She was dancing to her tribal origin sape tune, alongside her mother and sister, and many of the other sape musicians and dancers of the band were members of her 'family'. 'We hope we have inspired you to be active in preserving your own culture', she told crowds of international audiences. We were told that just a few decades ago, sape, this captivating instrument with three to six strings was almost cast to oblivion, but thanks to the RWMF it has again become popular. Sape lessons were held at the Rainforest Music House daily, offering festival attendees the opportunity to learn the basics of playing the instrument. We also heard that, historically, women had been forbidden from playing sape. Yet with its resurgent popularity, sape-holding indigenous musicians, young and old, women and men, were seen at every corner of the village site in vibrantly coloured, predominantly yellow, embroidered outfits.

The Sarawak Cultural Village, a 17-acre site, is just the right size; not so big that it can't be fully explored, but not so small as to feel overcrowded. A pleasantly walkable area, just when you feel that you might be done with exploring you realise you have found your way back to the starting point, closing a full circle around the lake. Yet, every time you think you've seen and experienced it all, something new would appear before you, ready for exploration. Overall, the set-up offers a snapshot of Sarawakian cultural heritage, a peek at the tribal lifestyle, history, arts and crafts, music, traditional costumes, cuisine and architecture. Nine replica lodges represent every major ethnic group in Sarawak; Bidayuh, Iban and Orang Ulu longhouses, a Penan jungle settlement, a Melanau tall-house, a Malay town house, a Chinese farmhouse and pagoda. All the buildings are located around the lake, with official representatives on hand to showcase some of their cultural peculiarities. It is an exquisite living museum. Here there is no such thing as 'Do Not Touch', everyone is invited to participate and engage with all that's going on, from food tasting and batik painting, musical instrument playing and traditional games, to pipe blowing and bamboo dancing. Learning and participatory mini-workshops on various arts and crafts, musical instruments and dances, punctuate the entire village. It is anything but kitschy and dull. Everyone is catered for, whether you want to challenge a tribal leader or taste the delight of black pepper hard candy. All in all, the place is not a theme park of artifice. Many of the performers continue to live an indigenous lifestyle, scattered about in the rich Sarawakian landscape.

Furthermore, the theme of 'togetherness' is applied in full scale, with lines blurred between spectators and performers. Artists are not segregated from the audiences and can be seen walking through the site for the duration, allowing the awed spectators to approach them at any time. In one instance, I found myself mesmerised by one of the Kulintangan performances. These are ancient, indigenous instrumental forms of music composed on a row of small, horizontally laid gongs that function melodically, accompanied by larger, suspended gongs and drums. Entranced by the gong's chimes, suddenly the dance of Sangtam Nagas, a Himalayan tribe, launched right behind me, incorporating everyone present in their midst. The pan-Asian fusion enlivened me and the crowd, an empty wheelchair abandoned to my left was surrounded by their dancing and they happily made twists and turns with it, giving the feeling that there are no obstacles in the universe, especially when it comes to the fine-tuning of dance steps.

The RMWF theme of 'togetherness' came apart when it was close to prayer time. The prayer room or _surau_, as it is known, was located in the same place as last year, and was as decrepit and ramshackle as before, with no renovation even attempted. One either had to walk through the men's entrance, a more decent option, or literally trudge under the longhouse wooden staircase and into its backyard, skipping over a muddy ravine, where, if lucky, one might find an almost hidden women's entrance. *Sigh*, a typical women and mosque kind of relationship, almost anywhere outside Malaysia, but almost never in Malaysia. Malaysian mosques are very women-friendly, with almost all entrances, pathways and praying halls being shared by all worshippers, without blinders or view-blocking partitions, without shabby back doors for women. 'I'd have expected some changes this year', I told one of the indigenous RMWF guiding officers, standing in front of the souvenir shop, while trying hard not to use the men's way in to the _surau_. He gave a response, but I could not hear him clearly, his words disappearing among the predominant sape sounds echoing from all sides. Luckily the women's backdoor entrance was a few metres from the workshop stage, so, following prayer, the women could be serenaded by the ethereal song of the sape. On that same stage the legendary sape player Mathew Ngau Jau started performing with his Orang Ulu musical ensemble that very afternoon.

In the evening the two main stages, located a few metres apart for the speedy swapping of the limelight, featured at length some of the key performing artists of the event. Earlier that day, I caught a glimpse of Darmas, a Malaysian band, comprising six young musicians who got the crowd dancing to the fascinating rhythms of traditional Malay classics. While I was glued to the indigenous stage, Diana moved on to the theatre stage where she attended the spectacular fusion of a Persian and Mongolian performance. She couldn't stop talking about it. Their music sprang from natural sounds of traditional instruments and age-old vocal techniques of nomadic ancestors, where one person can produce several tones at the same time. I could only vaguely fathom what she was trying so vividly to describe in the next performance by Duplessy & The Violins Of The World of 'Crazy Horse' and 'Road to East'. The motley band featured four soloists (Mathias Duplessy, Guo Gan, Naraa Puredorj and Aliocha Regnard) from four different cultures (French, Chinese, Mongolian, Swedish), playing four different instruments, and donning idiosyncratic outfits. In another equally stunning performance that evening, Oki Kano, an Ainu Japanese folk musician, joined KILA, the Irish folk rock band, in a collaborative gig of some hyper-fusion proportions: the fusions of KILA, traditional Irish music with world and folk rock, and Oki's fusing of reggae, African and electronic with Ainu folk melodies.

One of the last to take the stage was Mehdi Nassouli's band of four acrobatic dancers and musicians on the *karkabas* (metal castanets). They were introduced as some kind of 'voodoo performance', that was Gnawa musical culture, a spiritual music of ancient and rich African heritage. This Moroccan folkish genre uses unique metallic castanets, the three-stringed bass lute known as *guembri*, as well as the mosaic gowns and caps worn by musicians mostly decorated with cowry shells. Drums are used as the main background and refrain chanting is relied upon to take one into a swirling movement, the *gnawa* trance. The regular loud rhythm of drums give a hypnotic effect. It is a combination of poetry, music and dancing. We heard how Mehdi has since fused his traditional North African style with jazz and hip hop in his own band and had collaborated with luminaries including Fatoumata Diawara and Justin Adams. Under those psychedelic beats, the saying 'one hears what one wants to hear and disregards the rest' has never been truer. I could hear him lending his voice in Arabic, quite unintelligible, but I vaguely discerned the mantra 'Allah Allah Ya Bariyah. Oh, God is pure'. It instantly reminded me of last year's GayaGayo *nasheed*-like performance by a band from Sumatra. They briefly featured a Saman dance, part of the cultural heritage of the Gayo people of Aceh province in Sumatra. Saman dancers clap their hands, slap their chests, thighs and the ground, click their fingers, and sway and twist their bodies and heads in time with the shifting rhythm – in unison or alternating with the moves of opposing dancers. Not too far-fetched from the swirling dervish dance, but this one was delivered by a fully-coordinated group of entirely seated dancers. Just as with many other indigenous performances, the underlying concept reflects a complete harmony with natural movements, whereas in Sufi-influenced mystical music traditions, 'the human body is the perfect instrument'. A concept best illustrated by a Turkish poet, inspired by Rumi's verse: 'The trees, donning their dancing gowns, supplicate in love':

> The image in me
> is a different image
> how many stars fall
> into my interior dance!
> I whirl and I whirl
> the skies whirl as well
> roses blossom out of my face
> The trees in the garden, in sunshine
> "He created Heaven and earth"
> the serpents listen to the song of the reed
> in the trees donning their dancing gowns
> The meadow's children intoxicated
> Heart
> they call you
> I look smiling, at suns
> which have lost their way…
> I fly, I fly
> the skies fly. . . .

The lasting impact of the overarching theme of RWMF 2018, 'The Awakening of the Rainforest', was visibly reflected in an environmentally conscious RWMF 2019. We were extremely impressed by impeccable cleanliness and orderliness. The Sarawak Tourism Board visibly intensified their green initiatives this year. One of the most impactful policies was the discouraging of the use of plastic water bottles. Water dispensers were provided for free flow of water throughout the village. Specially designed, eye-catching recycling bins were monumentally placed right at the centre of the main stage entrance to encourage the proper disposal of litter. At the entrance, before accessing their day passes, visitors would be thoroughly checked with metal detectors. Hanna's remarks about a potentially disorderly festival were outdated, but we understood them to be a throwback from embryonic stages of RWMF. It was clearly now a 'regulated' and extremely well-thought out, well-organised festival.

There is an irony here. Good music is often the antithesis of the highly regulated, and it springs out of a rebellious impulse against the abuse of imposed 'cultural' conventions. On the contrary, catchy musical rhymes may emanate out of submission to natural patterns. I think authentic music is in a dialogical relationship with its surroundings, be it a rainforest or a desert, it creates a sustainable musical culture that stands the test of time and geography. Just as light waves bend but never break, authentic sound waves of soul-lifting music penetrate human hearts but never hurt. Good music oscillates between submitting to nature and rebelling against the cultural straitjackets of conventional appropriateness, between proudly enjoying one's cultural identity and transcending it, and flirting with stereotypes and at the same time shattering them. Sometimes, good music can achieve what politicised modus vivendi cannot.

GOD CONSCIOUSNESS

Mohammad Shahid Alam

God in the Qur'an is the final volume in a series of three books by Jack Miles about God in the three major Semitic religions – Judaism, Christianity and Islam – commonly described as monotheist, whose followers make up more than half the world's population. The first book in this series, *God: A Biography* (1996), was widely acclaimed, and won the author a Pulitzer. It is about the development of God's character in the successive books of the Tanakh, the canonical collection of the Jewish scriptures. The second book, *Christ: A Crisis in the Life of God*, published six years later, is a continuation of Miles' seminal work and seeks to explain the dramatic transformation in God's personality between the Tanakh and the New Testament. Appearing with a lag of some sixteen years in 2018, *God in the Qur'an*, completes the trilogy.

Although these books concern themselves with God, Miles does not engage with God as a believer, theologian or literary historian. Instead, he approaches the scriptures as a literary critic approaches works of literature, but with a specific focus. His focus is on God, the chief protagonist of each of these 'literary works' –Yahweh, Christ and Allah – and what they reveal about His personality, the developments or shifts in His personality, and comparisons across the three scriptures. In *God in the Qur'an*, he undertakes a series of comparative exercises: how does Allah differ from Yahweh and God, both Father and Son?

Jack Miles, *God in the Qur'an*, Alfred A. Knopf, New York, 2018

Miles explains that he approaches the scriptures 'not through belief but through a suspension of disbelief', a concept first proposed by Samuel Taylor Coleridge in the nineteenth century. This is a bit confusing. In order to appreciate a novel, one must enter into the world of the novel as if this world, with its settings and characters, are real, that is, by accepting it on its own terms, temporarily suspending our disbelief that they are no more than fictional characters. 'You can play along in the same way', writes Jack Miles, 'even when a literary character is divine'. Not quite: for in the scriptures, God is not a literary fiction but the Creator of the heavens and earth. A literary approach to the scriptures, therefore, requires a temporary suspension of belief in God as the creator of the heavens and earth, that is, if one is – like Miles himself – a believer. And this is what he says, a bit later: 'As a Christian, by a kind of reversal, I can temporarily suspend my belief that the God of the Bible is indeed much more than a literary character.'

However, there is a difference between Coleridge's temporary suspension of disbelief and Miles' temporary suspension of belief. When reading a novel or watching a film, the suspension of disbelief occurs naturally, produced by the combined forces of the story, plot and narrative. Unless the scripture contains these elements of a fictional work, it may be difficult for a believer to suspend belief in God qua God and start looking upon Him only as a fictional character. This may be difficult even if the scripture or parts of it possess in a strong degree the elements of story, plot and character. In other words, it may be difficult to insulate such literary exercises from one's beliefs regarding God or the other characters in the scriptures. If our exercises reveal a God in the Tanakh who is inconsistent or – as Richard Dawkins sees it – 'arguably the most unpleasant character in all fiction', this may greatly disturb a believing reader whose image of a loving God may have been derived from selective exposure to the Tanakh.

This begs the question how does our author pursue his literary analysis of God? He selects passages from the Jewish and Christian scriptures and pairs them with passages from the Qur'an that deal with the same key events and/or personalities. Next, he compares these paired passages to examine how the Qur'an expands upon or corrects the Biblical accounts of the same events or personalities. Unlike previous paired comparisons, he focuses 'at every point on what Allah reveals directly or indirectly about Himself through the Qur'an's various allusions, expansions, revisions, and so forth'. It is from the modifications that the Qur'an makes to the Biblical accounts that the author infers how Allah differs from Yahweh and God, the Father and the Son. Although *God in the Qur'an* makes eight sets of comparisons – 1. Adam and his wife, 2. Adam's son and his brother, 3. Noah, 4. Abraham and his father, 5. Abraham and his sons, 6. Joseph, 7. Moses, and 8. Jesus and his mother – we will concentrate on what we regard as three pivotal sets of paired comparisons: Adam and his wife, Abraham and his father, and Jesus and his mother.

In the paired comparisons of Adam and Eve, Allah differentiates Himself from Yahweh through 'a set of selective corrections and expansions'. Allah is the omnipresent narrator of the Qur'an, speaking to Prophet Muhammad and, through him, to humanity, while the narrator in Genesis remains anonymous. In the Qur'an, the narrative of Adam and Eve unfolds in a Garden in Heaven, while the Garden is an earthly place in Genesis. The angels and jinn too are present at the creation of Qur'anic Adam, but are missing from the account of Adam's creation in Genesis. After He creates Adam, Allah commands the angels to bow to him; the angels do so but only after they protest that Adam's progeny will cause bloodshed. On the other hand, Iblis (Satan), from among the jinns, refuses to bow to Adam and he is banished from the sight of Allah. This episode honouring Adam is missing from Genesis. In both accounts of creation, Allah and Yahweh forbid Adam and Eve from eating from a particular tree in the Garden, but only Allah warns them of the wiles Satan will employ to make them disobey His command. Allah warns that disobedience will make them sinners, whereas Yahweh warns them that this will cause them to die. The Qur'anic Adam and Eve are contrite and receive forgiveness, but nevertheless Allah banishes them to a temporary sojourn on earth. Although their earthly sojourn will end in death, Allah promises to bring them back to life on the Last Day with the prospect of returning to Heaven. On the other hand, Adam and Eve, in Genesis, refuse to take responsibility for their disobedience, much less ask for forgiveness. Yahweh curses and banishes them from the Garden; and in this exile, after a life of toil and suffering, they will meet oblivion in death. Genesis as well as nearly all the other books of the Tanakh contain few explicit references to afterlife.

Allah lays out His plan for humanity in a few brief Qur'anic passages about the creation of Adam and Eve. Although their first home was in Heaven, their bodies were shaped from clay; at the same time, Allah breathes something of His spirit into their earthly bodies. While the exile of Adam and Eve is prefigured in their binary nature, it is not a fall from grace but an occasion for starting them on their earthly career, which is a time of tests involving a contest between the soul that draws them towards Allah and their earthly substance that pulls them away from Allah. In this time of testing, Allah supports humans with knowledge and guidance that He sends through His prophets. While human lives are finite and short, life on earth does not end in the oblivion of death, but, following an interregnum, there is resurrection of the dead and a Day of Judgment, leading to Heaven or Hell, depending on the balance of good and bad deeds. On the other hand, Yahweh curses Adam and Eve after their expulsion from the Garden: Adam must toil to eke a living from the land, and Eve must endure the terrible pain of childbirth. Moreover, their earthly life ends in the oblivion of death; there are no promises of resurrection, no afterlife, no chance of a return to the Creator. Yahweh does bless Adam and Eve in the first of the two accounts of creation in Genesis – 'Be fertile and increase, fill the earth and master it…' – but this blessing too is earth-rooted. It carries no promise of transcending their earthly existence, no reintegration into eternity.

We turn next to the paired comparisons of Abraham, who 'is uniquely important as a vehicle for Allah's indirect self-characterization in the Qur'an'. Yahweh is 'less absolute and overwhelming than is Allah in the Qur'an'. In support, Miles writes that Allah never speaks directly to Abraham, while Genesis often quotes Yahweh speaking directly to Abraham. In fact, Allah does speak directly to Abraham, Moses and Noah in the Qur'an (2: 260, 27: 9-12, 11: 45-48). It is true, however, that Abraham is on more familiar terms with Yahweh than he is with Allah. In trying to talk Yahweh out of destroying Sodom, Abraham, even while acknowledging his own insignificance, accosts Yahweh: 'Is the judge of the whole world not to act justly.' Coming from a prophet, this line of questioning would be crossing the line for Allah.

Other contrasts between Yahweh and Allah are clearer. Yahweh promises Abraham miraculous fertility, the gift of lands stretching from the Nile to the Euphrates, and dominion over the peoples inhabiting these lands; this is the covenant, the special relationship between Yahweh and Abraham's line, that lies at the heart of Judaism. Given his emphasis on fertility in

Abraham's line and elsewhere in the Tanakh, Miles concludes that Yahweh is a god of fertility, while Allah is a 'theolatry god,' where theolatry means god-worship. The rewards for Abraham's devotion to Allah are 'the land We blessed for all mankind' and prophecy in his line. However, Allah did not make prophesy exclusive to Abraham's progeny; he sent prophets to all peoples. At the same time, He makes no promise of fertility or dominion.

Miles' emphasis on Yahweh as a fertility god is a bit exaggerated. 'Yahweh', he writes, 'never demands worship from Abraham or expresses any indignation that another being might be receiving worship due to Him'. He quotes Yahweh speaking thus to Himself: 'I have singled him [Abraham] out...to command his sons and his family after him to keep the way of Yahweh by doing what is right and just, so that Yahweh can carry out for Abraham what He has promised him.' It is true, nevertheless, that while Yahweh demands worship, he shows little concern for humanity outside of Abraham's line.

There are other contrasts between Yahweh and Allah that are not examined. One concerns arguments to bring disbelievers to belief in a single God and afterlife. When Yahweh begins his relationship with Abraham in Genesis 12, it appears that they already knew each other, so that He can start talking to Abraham directly: 'Go forth from your native land.' Although Abraham was born among idol-worshippers, Genesis says nothing about Abraham's conversion to faith in a single God. On the other hand, the Qur'an explains how Abraham proceeds through several rejections of false gods – the stars, moon and sun – to the pure worship of Allah, the Creator of the heavens and earth. This contrast persists through all the other books of the Tanakh and the Qur'an. When the prophets in the Qur'an confront disbelievers – and this happens often – they seek to bring them to faith in God and afterlife, nearly always employing reasoning and rhetoric to draw them to the worship of God, the Creator of heavens and earth. One example of this is Moses' encounter with Pharaoh in the Tanakh and the Qur'an. 'To put the difference as briefly as possible... Yahweh Elohim wants to defeat Pharaoh, while Allah wants to convert him.' In the contest between Moses and Pharaoh's magicians, mentioned in the Exodus and the Qur'an, Pharaoh's magicians lose. In the Qur'an, after they were overwhelmed by the superior magic of Moses, Pharaoh's magicians convert to faith in the true God: this conversion episode is missing in Exodus. In the Qur'an (10: 90,

92) alone, we learn that Pharaoh undergoes conversion before he drowns; he dies a Muslim and Allah saves his body as a sign for posterity.

Then there is Yahweh's singular obsession with His people, the children of Abraham and Isaac. On the contrary, Allah's gifts to Abraham are not exclusive to his line, nor is it unconditional. Allah sends His guidance to all peoples, and he does so repeatedly. Missing from all the comparisons is Allah's stinging rebuke to Abraham when he, following his appointment as 'a leader of men', asks Allah if the gift of leadership will continue in his line. Allah answers, 'My pledge does not hold for those who do evil' as stated in 2: 124. Allah's blessings are universal, not exclusive to one people. We now turn to Miles' paired comparisons of Jesus and Mary in the New Testament and the Qur'an. These comparisons mostly focus on the 'corrections' that Allah makes to the New Testament accounts of Mary and Jesus. Although the virgin birth of Jesus is one of the cornerstones of Christology, this is mentioned in only two of the twenty-seven books comprising the New Testament – Matthew, 1: 18 and Luke, 1:34 – and in these books too Jesus' miraculous birth is mentioned only once. At the same time, however, both Matthew and Luke provide a lineage for Jesus that passes backward through Joseph, not Mary. Allah gives far greater prominence to Mary. Not only is she the only woman that the Qur'an mentions by name, but she is referred to some seventy times. She is held in particularly high esteem; in 3: 42 the angels tell her, 'O Mary, God has chosen you, made you pure and chosen you above all the women of the world'.

Allah repeatedly asserts that His essential message, sent through his prophets at different times and places, has always been the same. However, the peoples who received His message in the past – that is, before Muhammad – failed to maintain its integrity. In particular, the existing Gospels contain several serious departures from Allah's core message; for instance, in ascribing a son to God, they commit the sin of shirk – worship of anyone other than God – the only sin Allah does not forgive if a man or woman dies in shirk. According to Miles, the Qur'an underscores the altered state of the existing Gospels by 'the implicit assertion that Allah entrusted the Gospel to Jesus as He entrusts the Qur'an to Muhammad. 'He [Allah] brought me the Book,' the baby Jesus says, 'and made me a prophet, and made me blessed wherever I may be'. The Book given to Jesus could not be the 'Gospels that Christians honour as scripture, so

Allah delivers, in effect, a major challenge to the trustworthiness of the Gospels as Christians know them'.

The Qur'an repudiates more directly Christian claims of the divinity of Jesus, even though of the four Gospels only John refers explicitly to Jesus as God. Miles explains that references to Jesus as 'Son of God' do not necessarily imply divinity; for instance, Luke also refers to Adam as 'son of God.' It would, therefore, appear that the Qur'an is opposing later Christian constructions of Jesus as a divine co-equal partner with God. The contention, however, is that Allah's repeated designation of Jesus as 'son of Mary' is intended to correct the Gospels. The Qur'an also corrects the Christian belief in the divinity of Jesus more directly. This may be seen in two of the citations from the Qur'an that are referred to. When Mary, who was betrothed but not married to Joseph, brings baby Jesus to her family, the newborn allays their concerns with a demonstration of his miraculous powers of speech. He says, 'I am the servant of God. He brought me the Book and made me a prophet, and made me blessed wherever I may be (Qur'an, 19:30). Later, the Qur'an (5:116) shows Allah directly asking Jesus, 'Did you really say to people: "Take me and my mother as two gods, instead of God?"' Jesus answers, 'What right have I to assert what does not in truth belong to me?'

Miles has made forensic use of the method of paired comparisons for arriving at insights about God in the Qur'an. But this method is not without its drawbacks; it prevents the inclusion of Muhammad in his paired comparisons. It is an odd absence for a book on God in the Qur'an, whose angel transmits the Book to Muhammad, large parts of which are addressed directly to him. Miles could have overcome this deficiency if, in a final chapter, he had ventured to compare the relations between Yahweh and the three central figures in the Bible – Abraham, Moses and Jesus – with the relations between Allah and Muhammad in the Qur'an. Among other things, these comparisons would have led him to recognise that miracles, at least visible miracles, as a tool of persuasion were not available to Muhammad, whereas it would be nearly impossible to conceive of the three Biblical figures without miracles. He might also have noticed that Allah – via Muhammad – repeatedly engages pagans and the disbelieving peoples of the Book in Makkah and Medina, allowing them to criticise Muhammad and voice their objections to his message, persisting in trying to convince them of the righteousness of the message He delivers through Muhammad. It is possible that these verbal exercises in persuasion might have led Miles to conclude that Muhammad was engaging in reasoned discourse because he did not have the use of miracles, or because Allah would not destroy those who rail against him with diseases, floods, storms, lightning, and earthquakes. He would also find that the Qur'an opposes the Christian doctrines of original sin and vicarious suffering. Allah forgives Adam and Eve before banishing them. As a result, all men and women enter their earthly life with an innate capacity to acknowledge the Truth that is brought to them by the prophets. Repeatedly, the Qur'an also upholds the principle of individual responsibility, which negates the vicarious suffering of Jesus in the Gospels.

God in the Qur'an illustrates how Islam differs from Judaism and Christianity. It is a fascinating and revealing book – but perhaps not illuminating enough.

BEYOND THE BURQA

Katharina Schmoll

'Well, what you actually want to know', he replied partly amused, partly offended, 'is whether my sisters are oppressed'. It was 2011, and I was twenty-two when I dropped THE question. I asked my good friend, a Muslim Moroccan man I had got to know, whether his sisters wore hijab – or more precisely, a veil, *ein Kopftuch*. I did not even know the word hijab back then.

I grew up in rural Germany, and had been fascinated by Islam and Muslim cultures ever since a trip to Egypt with my family when I was sixteen. I had immediately fallen in love with the mystical soft-voiced calls to prayer, and secretly noted in my travel diary my plan to move to Egypt when I finished school in a couple of years. But in 2011, when I was finally ready to embark on my long-awaited journey to Cairo and Alexandria, internships arranged, the Arab Spring was in full bloom, and so I unhappily decided to do an internship in Berlin. And there we met. My first Muslim friend. By then, my longings had made space for a somewhat troubled young woman who did not know any longer what to make of Islam.

After returning from my first trip to Egypt, I was hungry for knowledge about Islam. Intriguingly, the first books I picked up were by the controversial ex-Muslim Ayaan Hirsi Ali. All I can say is really: Thank you, dear bookstores, for this exquisite selection on Islam. And thank you for planting a narrative in my head that made me blush several years later in front of my Muslim friend.

Mariam Khan, editor, *It's Not About The Burqa*, Picador, London, 2019.

I don't blame the bookstores, however. Perhaps I picked up these and similar books myself among other more balanced ones. Perhaps these books were prominently laid out because they would sell as they neatly fit into the mainstream discourse of Muslims and Islam as dangerous and backwards. But it is also true that back then, in Germany as well as in the UK, there simply were not many books written by ordinary Muslims for a non-scholarly audience that would have given me a glimpse of the lifestyles and beliefs of everyday Muslims, particularly Muslim women. This was before social media and modest fashion became big, and before mainstream media allowed a platform for Muslim voices other than that of ex-Muslims or critics of the faith. It also preceded a time when young rural Germans like myself could easily learn about Islam and Muslims through personal encounters.

Perhaps the conversation with my Moroccan friend would have been less awkward if back then I had been able to pick up books like *It's Not About the Burqa*, which illustrate Muslim women's agency and provide insights into the diversity of Muslim women's thoughts, ideas and lifestyles. Perhaps I would not have dropped THE question in front of my friend. With more books like these, perhaps THE question would not even exist any longer. The question why some Muslim women wear hijab, and whether Muslim women are oppressed.

It's Not About the Burqa is a collection of seventeen essays written by, mostly British, Muslim women and edited by the writer and activist Mariam Khan. Khan compiled this collection of essays as she was tired of Muslim women being spoken for and about in the British media, and tired of the public obsession with veiling and the burqa. She wanted to make Muslim women's own narratives and stories visible, without a filter and on their own terms. For if 'Muslim women are to progress in society, if Muslim women are be treated with respect, then it's so important that we challenge the narrative around us'. And indeed, this book beautifully shares with the reader nuanced insights into the visions, beliefs, hopes and struggles of seventeen individual, mostly young Muslim women. There are stories about faith and role models; love, family, single parenting, marriage and divorce; sex and sexuality; Islamophobia; patriarchy in the Muslim community and wider society; the representation of Muslim women in media; race and racism; veiling; the stigma and taboo surrounding mental health in the Muslim community; honour and shame; Islam and feminism. When I read the essay by Scottish writer and comedian Amna Saleem, who uses humour to tackle Muslim chauvinism, I laughed heartily. It deeply moved me when I read about the journalist Saima Mir's struggle for self-worth and living a fulfilling life on her own terms after two divorces at a young age. I was inspired to rethink my ideas about the goals of female Muslim representation when I read the essay by the entrepreneur and co-founder of the digital Muslim women's magazine *Amaliah,* Nafisa Bakkar, who questions whether the increased visibility of Muslim women in media and advertising has really afforded them a voice and a place at the table or, whether it has rather turned Islam into a brand. And I was heartened to read the essay by the writer Salma El-Wardany who, sharing the intimate story of how she lost her virginity to a non-Muslim man out of wedlock yet in the context of love, encourages her fellow Muslims to be more open-minded towards the reality of many Muslims negotiating intimacy, love and sex. For fire and brimstone theology 'serves only to oppress, alienate and traumatise, all things that will eventually be the map people use to leave Islam rather than to accept its beauty into their lives in ways that fit'.

What makes *It's Not About the Burqa* so powerful is that it does not shy away from addressing the challenges that the Muslim community faces today. Having the courage to critique one's own community when it already has its back to the wall deserves praise. While the authors' criticisms are nothing new, it distinguishes itself from the manifold public accusations in its intention. They manage to criticise without distancing themselves from Islam and the Muslim community. And they criticise because they know that Muslims, and that includes Muslim men, can do better. They criticise because they know Muslims can and will flourish if they confront and own their own issues. Surely, it is this type of loving criticism that will stipulate change rather than populist and inflammatory accusations.

Like many Muslims in the Western world, I long for meaningful and fruitful discussions about Islam that tackle far more critical issues than veiling. As such, it is admirable that this book aims to carve out a space for Muslim women to have a conversation on Islam and Muslims on their own terms. *It's Not About the Burqa* has the potential to empower Muslim women – it is really about time more narratives that are 'out there' and that they can relate to, are showcased. And I also hope Muslim men will listen. But above all, I hope this book will be picked up by non-Muslims who, like my younger self, otherwise have little access to diverse Muslim women's life stories and beliefs.

The question of audiences is critical indeed. Which audience does this book hope to attract, and for what purpose? Who benefits? The introduction clearly states that it is now society's turn to listen, meaning the book does seek to reach an audience that extends beyond the Muslim community. I would be curious to know whether the book has managed to do this, and if so, the array of reactions the essays have provoked. Since what we really need at this point in time, and this I am sure of, is an honest conversation. Not *about* Muslims. Not *between* Muslims. But *with* Muslims. In fact, with all of society. Muslims and non-Muslims, newcomers and those with long historical roots in British society, Brexiteers and Remainers, 'somewheres' and 'anywheres', progressives and conservatives. It is no secret any longer that there is a growing rift in Western societies fuelled by populism, that must be tackled. The earlier, the better. But unfortunately, I do not think *It's Not About the Burqa* goes far enough to successfully contribute to narrowing this divide. This is sadly a missed opportunity.

While the essays in this book aim to provide alternative narratives and fresh perspectives by Muslim women on their own terms, they too often remain trapped in a discourse that they essentially seek to overcome: a discourse of victimisation and 'us' vs 'them'. The authors of the essays are mostly young Muslim women who inscribe to the liberal-progressive imperative that hopes to overcome misogyny, racism and Islamophobia by strengthening group identities of the marginalised and singling out 'white men' and 'white feminism', rather than building bridges. Many essays work off the topic of societal marginalisation and discrimination in the, at times useful, but often also limiting, categories of race, gender and faith like a mantra. There is unfortunately no doubt that Islamophobes and racists exist in British and other Western societies. But there are also those who would like to listen to what Muslims have to say but may feel estranged by the accusations they often find themselves confronted with. Despite my eventual awareness of the crassness of my comment, I can certainly tell you that, at the time, I would not have found it constructive to listen to a lecture about racism and Islamophobia by my Moroccan Muslim friend when I asked him whether his sisters wear hijab. On the contrary, I would have felt pushed into a corner I did not recognise I deserved.

The book is best where it limits the importance given to categories and simply gives space for individual stories by young women who try to find out who they are and what they aspire to, much like any other young British citizen, Muslim or not. But too often, the women do not seem quite ready to leave behind the narrow categorisations they have been forced into. And maybe, we are simply not ready as society, as a whole. This is a shame.

Lately, with the rise of far-right movements and Muslim fundamentalism, I have increasingly found myself thinking about how we could foster social cohesion and tolerance in Western societies that seem to have rediscovered a fondness for binary group identities rather than cherishing individual freedoms and responsibility we once considered to be among the greatest achievements of Western civilisation. I do reflect on this issue as someone who has personally felt the societal divide within herself for too long now.

I grew up in rural Germany where my family has historic roots, but I have long lived in London and feel comfortable in many countries across the globe. I was born into a Christian family, but I feel close to Islam. I don't consider myself a feminist, but I agree that analysing discrimination through an intersectional feminist lens can be useful. I am utmost critical of Muslim fundamentalism and extreme conservatism that blames the West for everything that goes wrong in the world, but for my PhD – for which I was awarded a scholarship from the centre-conservative Adenauer Foundation – I wrote a rather empathetic ethnography on moderate Islamist female politicians in Morocco. I enjoy reading *Amaliah*, watching videos by the German Muslim satire group *Datteltäter* and British period drama. I love London, the British countryside and Islamic architecture; German cheesecake, curries and tajines; mini dresses, jellabas and hijab tutorials.

As someone who inhabits so many characteristics and views that seem to divide us, I dearly hope that we will grant more space to discover, live and share our complex identities. *It's Not About the Burqa* has been fantastic for young female progressive Muslims to voice their opinions and hopes, to give insights into their lifeworlds on their own terms, and to empower like-minded Muslim women. As Khan explains, 'this book is a start, a movement'. I hope it will encourage people like my younger self not to repeatedly engage in awfully stereotypical debates with their Muslim friends, colleagues or neighbours simply because they don't know better.

To take this 'movement' further, what I would love to read next is an essay collection by the same writers in conversation with Muslim men, women and men of all faiths and none, people of all colours, rural working-class people, white feminists, conservatives and yes, even Brexiteers to discuss a vision for our society in which all of us will have some space to breathe and flourish. A book in which we truly listen to each other in good faith. We need to. Because we happen to live in the same country. A country that many of us, Muslim or not, call home.

THE BOSS

Shaizir Aly

I remember walking into Our Price Records in Chatham Town Centre, in late 1987, and excitedly purchasing the vinyl copy of Bruce Springsteen's newly released album *Tunnel of Love*. The sheer joy I felt buying the record was in sharp contrast to the distinctly underwhelmed air of just about everyone else in the store. I was reminded of that exact moment while watching *Blinded by The Light*, based on Sarfraz Manzoor's autobiography *Greetings from Bury Park* (Bloomsbury, London, 2008). Javed, our geeky main protagonist, slips away from his sister's wedding to buy just-released Springsteen concert tickets from the local record shop in Luton, terrified they may have already sold out. Kids, this was before the days of spending hours clicking 'refresh' to purchase tickets online. We had to queue at record outlets or the box office or spend ages phoning a constantly engaged number to get the chance to see our favourite performer. I could almost feel the panic and relief as Javed's sense of urgency turns out to be in vain, as, when he arrives, he is told to calm down by his best friend's girlfriend behind the counter, who informs him that not only was there no rush on the tickets, in fact no one had bought a single one. He had ditched his sister's wedding for no reason, and not without consequences.

Watching the film I felt wave after wave of nostalgia. Or, more accurately, guilty pleasure; or horror, as the Pet Shop Boys 'It's a Sin' sung out during the opening credits. The film is set in 1987 and although the main character, played by Viveik Kalra, is a few years older than me, we both shared a love of Bruce Springsteen and experienced an awakening from the banal synth music that was in vogue at the time. The Boss was no longer cool, it was all about electric keyboard sounds as illustrated by the reaction of Javed's best friend Matt, who declared that only his parents' generation listened to the likes of Springsteen. After all, synth was 'the future'. How we rock purists turned our noses up at those artificial sounds. Little did we know that 'the future' would turn out to be all about auto-tune and button pressing.

My first memory of listening to Springsteen's songs was during the *Born in the USA* era, which in the mid 1980s was a huge record and played repeatedly on *Top of the Pops* and on the radio. I was a teenager, the summers were long and warm and his songs proved a perfect soundtrack to our lives. The music of Bruce Springsteen spoke to me, just as it did to Javed, from those days onwards, and even though the angst of his earlier albums was something I discovered later, the rawness of the storytelling in his 1987 album makes it my all-time favourite; and it continues to have a profound impact upon me. It was fortuitous that I had become a Springsteen fan, because my fate could have been quite different, considering my first ever album purchase was (ahem) *Running in the Family* by Level 42, which is mentioned in the film when 'Lessons in Love' is played on Javed's college radio. Listening to these songs was a great nostalgia fest for late 1980s kids like me but nothing more, because once I had discovered Springsteen, I had no time for the bland pop music churned out by the mainstream. Springsteen was on a whole different level. So much so that the lyrics of Bruce Springsteen moved me a few years later to write an essay for my GCSE English class about my love of the Boss, which unfortunately was marked very poorly (unfairly in my opinion) by my English teacher who decided to make an example of me to the class by reading out an extract of my essay which described Springsteen's music as 'classic'. A Springsteen eulogy-fest not unlike Javed's submission to his college newspaper, although he perhaps used rather more evocative adjectives. But both Javed and I realised that Springsteen's music had a wonderful ability to make you feel that he was speaking to you and you only, and that feeling of being an outsider connected to my experience of being part of one of just two Asian families growing up in my village, with mine being the only Muslim family as part of that subset. You experienced an empowering feeling as you put the stylus on the red CBS-labelled record and started listening to his words as you were transported to another world across the Atlantic.

Blinded By the Light is set in Luton against the backdrop of industrial decline, the National Front and the themes of racist rhetoric that Asians in Britain were all too familiar with by that time. Javed is a British Pakistani

teenager who is strait-jacketed by his restrictive father, played by the
inimitable Kulvinder Ghir, and the expectations placed upon him by his
family and the community at large. You could be mistaken for thinking that
the film is a feelgood family saga, with its fair share of cheesy moments,
but it is also hugely political with a touch of Ken Loach in its subtle
commentary on social issues that dominated the news then, and can relate
to the Brexit and Trump-ravaged times we currently live in. In an interview
with Mark Kermode, Manzoor explains that the plot is a fictionalised
version of his life rather like Bruce Springsteen describes his songs as
'emotional autobioographies'. In the same interview Gurinder Chadha
also describes how, as she had known Manzoor for a long time prior to the
inception of this movie, they wrote about the experience of feeling they
were the 'only two British Asians into Bruce Springsteen', although I
would argue I know a handful of others.

Blinded By the Light, directed by Gurinder Chadha, produced by Paul
Mayeda Berges, Gurinder Chadha and Jamal Daniel, New Line
Cinema, 2019

The film does play to typical British Asian and Muslim stereotypes at
times and undoubtedly exhibits certain *Bend it Like Beckham*-isms that gave
Chadha worldwide success in the first place. But this offering does not
attempt to emulate the formula as the influence of Springsteen looms large
in many scenes from the moment Javed is first introduced to his music by
his new college friend Roops. The first Bruce song plays against the
backdrop of the famous storm of 1987, and although it did jar a bit here
and there, it was ecstasy capturing the magic of the lyrics, banged home
even further by the appearance of perfectly poignant lyrics in the
background as Javed stumbles though the storm rather like an 1980s'
music video. For Springsteen fans, particularly those of the generation that
grew up with his music, this was a great way of bringing him alive, almost
as a co-star. I that suspect those not into Springsteen will see this as a fans'
cringefest but it is carried off with enough drama to stave off the worst
aspects of the average rock musical.

There are some, dare I say drawing on my GCSE English glory, 'classic'
Chadha-inspired sequences that transport you back, particularly to the

wedding in *Bend it Like Beckham* but with a Springsteen twist. Javed accompanies his sister Shazia to an 'all dayer' – a Bhangra club that takes place on a weekday morning so that Asian youngsters can navigate the curfew restrictions imposed by their parents and party like it's 11.55. PM. Instead of listening to the club music, he puts on his Walkman and we are all treated to the sight of Bhangra dancing to the music of 'Because the Night' from the *Darkness on the Edge of Town* album. I never thought you could ever combine that visual to one of Springsteen's most famous songs but it actually worked. There were many other moments that Chadha pulled off, where others may have not done so well, and the cameo of Manzoor in particular is a nice touch.

Springsteen is a master of painting a picture through his lyrics, which seems to be what this film seeks to achieve. Chadha did not intend to make a musical jukebox of Springsteen songs and so the storyline moves forward via the songs at certain points and for the most part this is carried off well but occasionally it does not really make sense. When, for example, Javed and Roops confront a gang of National Front racists by singing the words to 'Badlands' and they get all confused and don't know what to do. In reality, Javed and Roops would have got a good kicking but the spirit of Springsteen seemingly carried them though. The love interest in the form of Eliza is predictably serenaded with a Bruce musical interlude and disappointingly the obvious issues confounding both their backgrounds are not explored to the full. The extreme awkwardness of Javed being invited to dinner and refusing alcohol will chime with many Muslim viewers, as the oh-so familiar disbelief of Eliza's father, who still pours him a bit of alcohol, is thoroughly entertaining in its predictability.

What is outstanding about the film's portrayal of weighty topics including race, religion, class and social justice, is the consciousness of the complexity of these issues throughout. No character in the film is uncomplicated and although some of the themes may appear clichéd, the awareness of this is redeeming. Javed's father is portrayed with empathy and humanised, Javed himself is forced to confront his own contradictions and sense of victimhood, while Eliza is asked by Javed whether she is with him only because she wishes to provoke her parents, to which he adds the amusing caveat that it would be perfectly fine with him if she was. This nod to intersectionality and resistance to lazy stereotypes is a credit to the writer and director.

The supporting cast is mostly excellent. Javed's best friend Matt, Dean Charles Chapman of *Game of Thrones* fame, gives a solid performance and Meera Ganatra as Javed's overworked but ultimately empowered mother, is a much understated role. The actor that really transcends everything that he has done before is Kulvinder Ghir as Javed's father – but can we forget him as Chunky Lafunga from *Goodness Gracious Me?* The heart of the film is the relationship between Ghir's character and his son Javed. The final address from father to son is a powerful statement of the issues surrounding growing up as a second-generation Pakistani and it is carried off with an earnestness. There is great warmth and nuance in the film that makes the few gaping holes in the plot and the tilt towards the saccharine easier to stomach.

Blinded By the Light may not have made up its mind whether it is a musical or a comedy with a Springsteen soundtrack, but ultimately it has great fantasy elements borrowed both from Bollywood and rock musicals. The end result is a triumph that should reach out not only to Springsteen fans but all those who can identify with the outsider who strives for something more. I had hoped that at least one track from *Tunnel of Love* would actually end up on in the film, but alas it didn't. Still, it will be my personal soundtrack to 1987 even if it isn't Javed's.

ET CETERA

ON RECYCLED MUSIC

C Scott Jordan

It's happening again, isn't it?

You have that one song stuck in your head. You know, either a treasured classic or that *one* song that the radio and/or general cacophony of everyday life sees fit to play ad infinitum. I apologise dear reader as I've played a dastardly psychological trick on you and ask that you forgive my exercising of that bit of the brain that is not so easily quieted. But let me tell you that the average human being spends forty percent of his or her days falling into constant, spontaneous cognitions. As many of you are undoubtedly attesting by the clear sign of how you are tapping your foot along to that one song – at this very moment. The phenomenon is commonly called an 'ear worm', yet goes by the technical name of involuntary musical imagery (INMI). Other little tricks have been optimised to really take advantage of the ear worm phenomenon. Various studies in neuroscience have noted the impact of repetition on memory and recall; music definitely benefits from such a nature. Because of this, that one song can become very powerful deep down on the neurological level.

Repetition in music has been criticised time and again dating back to the late nineteenth century. In 1882, Ferdinand Praeger published a paper 'On the Fallacy of the Repetition of Parts in the Classical Form', where he stated that other artists, such as authors, poets, and painters do not repeat in their work out of fear of being labelled the ultimate insult – 'uncreative'. Yet, music has a nature of repetition. Diana Deutsch advanced this notion through coining the 'Speech to Song Illusion' in 1995. While working on mixing her own album she found that through the repetition of words in simple spoken speech, the listener naturally perceived something as more musical. In fact, repetition grooves with our brain's stimulation patterns. As a song repeats a beat or line of lyrics, the brain lights up in sync with the music's frequency. Even more interesting is that multiple brains listening to the same song also manage to fire in synchronised rhythms. This explains why different people tend to gain similar feels from a given song over vast differences. So that one song has not only a tremendous power over the individual's brain, but the masses' as well. As you head towards your nearest music-making device, you might be tempted to ask, are you pressing play or is the music itself in control of the 'play' button.

As music, particularly of the more popular nature, has evolved, it has developed several techniques that can foster the greater effect of repetition to make that one song a true sensation and even come to define a genre or era. In fact, since the 1950s, at a rate of every ten years, small pits and techniques would be capped by the increase of repetition within songs towards the end of the decade until it becomes monotonous and demands the next decade's artist to step in and try to make something new. Yet, a repetitious nature must be maintained. Also, thanks to those ear worms, old eras tend to be resurrected in the new. This has happened right now as we speak in Western popular music. As you listen to music today you may even think it sounds oddly familiar. This can sometimes be seen when direct beats and lyrics are taken from one song and inserted into a more contemporary context. Sometimes it isn't simply familiarity, it might actually be a direct cover of an old song. Right now, the 1980s is the vogue. Why? Well nostalgia is a phenomenon that will require several dust-til-dawn conversations for me to illicit. But in brief, Netflix's *Stranger Things* and a generation of Steven Spielberg fanboys are beginning to create their love letters to the living legend (for instance, the filmography of JJ Abrams). Likewise, governments tend to be more imposing and right-winged than they have been since the good ole days of Reagan and Thatcher. Social unrest is hot again from racial tensions to religious turmoil and the LGBT+ community is equal parts under fire and at its heaviest level of militarisation. Not to mention tight clothing, cleavage, and wild hair is back in style as well. Plus, everyone just seems to be really afraid again and no doubt for good reason. But of what? Well, I also think nostalgia works because we tend to take memory as known and the more we obsess, the more 'sure' we are of it and with unknowns and ignorance cast aside (whether truly or illusory), one can focus on the bliss and romanticise the good bits. That one song couldn't ask for a greater deal.

One of the greatest techniques that allow that one song to hang out in your ear is the fade out. When done right, a fade out makes a song live forever. The first fade out was used in 1918 by Gustav Holst in his piece 'The Planets' where he used the technique to characterise the great distance between planets in outer space. To do this he had his choir set up in a separate room and had an assistant slowly close the door to the room that held the microphone. A clever move no doubt, but something that didn't come into play for popular music until the 1950s and 1960s when radio required songs to be three minutes or less, so the fade out allowed for a 'radio edit' of a given song to be made. Otherwise, it could also be used as a postproduction editing technique such as in The Beatles' 'Strawberry Fields' where a producer who wasn't a fan of the percussion at the end of the song faded that out, only to also create a fade in as the rest of the band has a lovely instrumental at the tail end of the song that he couldn't omit. In fact, the Beatles so loved the fade out that it made their timeless classic 'Hey Jude' that one song for many of us, even today. The fade out, lasting longer than the rest of the song before it (over four minutes!), was so effective an ending that when they wanted to do a television presentation of the song it required copious editing and the show actually had to use a fade to black, lest the song be compromised by a clunking ending. The 1980s loved fade outs and by 1985, every billboard hit had one. Yet a rumour started that fade outs were uncreative or lazy, so the 1990s moved radically towards hard endings or the use of a closing instrumental sound to add closure. When audiences tap their foot to a song with a cold ending, they actually tend to stop before the song has concluded, yet with a fade out, one's foot keeps tapping for several seconds after the ear perceives the last note. Anyone listening closely today may have noticed a resurgence of the fade out that works with repetition to make a song live beyond the actual playing. Rihanna and Drake's 'Work' not only relates to the daily grind of the Protestant Work Ethic, it combines repetition and the fade out to make one of those songs that, again, sorry, you may now be tapping your foot to.

Fade out is combined with the repetitious nature of music to recreate the feel of the 1980s along with a few other techniques, such as the use of synth and reverb. Reverb was invented by accident in 1979 by Peter Gabriel and his band, Genesis, while working in their state-of-the-art recording studio. The new studio had a special microphone that allowed the booth to communicate directly with the band. During play back, Peter Gabriel fell in love with the way in which this little microphone captured the drum. Prior to this discovery, drums had always come off as rather stale in recordings, but now the reverberations of the drum could be captured. Peter Gabriel used this happy mistake as the basis for their next album and one of the most famous drumbeats in the world, the thumping of 'In the Air Tonight'. This drum reverb, known as gated reverb, was capable of taking sound waves and giving them the impression of hitting a brick wall. It was a sound that could not be naturally produced, only through technology and the 1980s played it to death from Prince to Duran Duran and John Cougar Mellencamp, making for a 1990s filled with more stale, yet familiar, drumbeats. Listening to Carly Rae Jepsen, Lorde, or Haim today, it can be safely said, that this little invention is coming back in a big bad way. Now that music technology can be found in apps only a download away, the full sound of the 1980s can accompany the rest of the world's attempts to prove the point, that as the more things change, the more they really just stay the same.

Well, are you still tapping your foot to that one song?

In that case, let's talk about K-Pop. Korean Pop designed for feet tapping. What ought to send a shiver of dread down your spine from the beginning is the fact that to define K-Pop is quite a chore. It is not simply popular music from South Korea. No, K-Pop is a phenomenon, a movement, a style, a genre, a feeling, a life style. From the hair, to the coloured contact lenses, the intersexual faces, the fantastical costumes, the complex choreography, and hyperbolic lighting, K-Pop is a strange beast indeed. And like the Tao, any attempts at trying to define it as such results in a failure of imagination in comprehending its nigh omniscience (and heaven forbid potential for immutability). Long story short, K-Pop is yet another of the long list of American inspirations that have made the world anything but a better place. After fighting for independence from the ruthless dictatorship of Japan, and then breaking from the dictatorship of communism in the north, the Republic of Korea was left in ruin and would fall into a dictatorship of its own. What did I say about things changing and repetition again? In the ruins of South Korea, American GIs started blaring popular music from the US all throughout the country. The first popular Korean music took the popular stylings of 1950s America and sang old folk songs to the beats. Much of this music was, as you'd expect, abhorred by parents and the government alike. Dictator Park Chung Hee banned most K-Pop songs and was even known for dispatching police with rulers to ensure lady's skirts and men's hair were of modest length. Following Park's assassination in 1979, his replacement Chun Doo-Hwan only allowed two television channels, both set to 24/7 state propaganda, and in keeping with the dictatorial precedent of his forebearer, public modesty was enforced. The tapping of teenage feet to K-Pop songs was the hymn of rebellion and democracy. The oh so lovely 1980s saw the birth of democracy in the Republic of Korea in 1987, yet popular culture continued to be highly monitored by the government. Those one songs pertaining to love and relationships were held to a level of prudence that would even have Victorian England screaming 'lighten up, man'.

The frozen-in-time feel of Korea with 1950s beats and longing looks being the closest thing to dating in the cultural consciousness melted by 1992. K-Pop as we know it today began with Seo-Taiji and the Boys. In Korea at the time, the way everyone was exposed to music was through the television, thus, it was not just about the sound, but the look and the presentation. Looking like Korean preteens going as the Beastie Boys for Halloween, Seo-Taiji and the Boys donned baggy clothes and sideways hats, taking to the stage with a mix of breakdancing and other intense choreography. They fused Korean-language lyrics with western concepts of rock, rap, and techno. Their lyrics spoke to the youth, criticising the government, parents, and schools. And the teens loved it. They could not get enough and the older generations saw this as the end of times. Only moral decay could result from this! The arrival of Seo-Taiji and the Boys not only broke the trajectory of Korean popular music, but it disrupted the tight hold that governments and music producers had on the cultural production within South Korea. A studio system that would put any of Hollywood's worst ages to shame was defeated overnight with Seo-Taiji and the Boys rising via independent means. Men with money watched as the grandfather of K-Pop tore down the old world, leaving them a new one to capitalise.

One such producer, Lee Soo-Man put his money into his own Frankensteinian project. All he needed was an attractive young person, good production value, and some meaningless, yet catchy tunes for the pretty face to sing. His first K-Pop star Hyun Jin-Young was an overnight sensation. Older generations cried out in condemnation as teens poured money into his albums. Yet the older generation underestimated the power of institutional prudence over the prior three decades of their country's history. When Hyun Jin-Young was caught in possession of marijuana not only was his career abruptly ended, but the youth who once adored him, roundly hated him and publicly shamed him for living such a heinous and immoral life! And just like that, K-Pop nearly died on launch.

But Lee Soo-Man was determined to make his investment back. He needed to take the Frankenstein-in-the-garage model and turn it into a factory, not only for attractive and talented musicians but ones moulded in his preferred image. He created the first of what would become specialised schools where kids would go to become K-Pop stars, which came to be known as Idols. Academies began springing up to teach children everything they would need to become the next K-Pop Idol, the latest number one desired career of Korean youth. The militaristic schools involved a rigorous curriculum of singing, writing, producing, instrumentalisation, and intensive dancing and choreography and all of this was mixed with the essential standard core classes required of a Korean education. The idea was for these academies to not only produce pretty talents, but upstanding, model citizens. Manners and the approved and trending 'poses' were amongst their lessons. They are also given intensive language courses in English, Chinese, and Japanese. Naturally, their diets were also highly restricted. Beauty isn't easy as the old mantra goes. Plastic surgery would be recommended and paid for without much of a thought, just another piece of the training. The student must be willing to do anything to be the next Blackpink or H.O.T. Known as the 'Big Three', JYP, SM, and YG have allowed these schools to be the assembly line factories for their next clients. The more things change, the more they really just stay the same. Korean children can even begin pursuing their dream of becoming the next K-Pop Idol at the ripe age of ten.

All this is given a big boost by the Korean government which has a very large and very powerful Ministry of Culture with a $500 million a year budget at their disposal. Their goal is to produce annual cultural exports of $10 billion. Anything and everything can be monetised. By the new millennium, the second generation of K-Pop Idols set their eyes abroad, first taking Japan by storm and then on to the rest of East and South East Asia. Breaking land in America and the UK, their eyes are well set on Western domination and teens of the world are eating it up. Psy's 'Gangnam Style' planted the South Korean flag in America, but in becoming one of the most highly viewed YouTube videos of all time, he only began what looks to be a long lasting musical trend. Now the pilgrimage to Korea is becoming a rising trend that the Ministry hopes to take full advantage of. One in thirteen tourists to South Korea state it is for BTS, the latest K-Pop Idol sensation that took K-Pop to the global stage with their sweeping wins at the 2019 Billboard Music Awards. While physical album sales around the world have been on a direct route to the planet's core, in Japan and Korea they are not. In fact, thanks to including posters and personalised messages from the bands, buying the CD is still a deep and intimate ritualistic part of being a fan, downloading is too impersonal. Oh and have you noticed how records are making a comeback?

Now, you maybe thinking that I have become an old curmudgeon who yells at kids to stay off his grass. That I have embraced my inner Nancy Reagan and joined the rest of my 'old folks' in denouncing K-Pop for the corruption of the youth. Yes, this may be true, and even as a millennial, I am too old for this distinctly Gen. Z problem, but I might make one more point. I believe corruption is as much akin to the nature of youth as repetition is to that of music. And there is a distinct difference between Elvis Presley shaking his posterior and recycling the music of marginalised black musicians in the hopes of creating something that might tear it all down in order to make something better and soulless corporate executives abusing Korean children on their path towards becoming K-Pop Idols. The producers of K-Pop closely monitor youth trends and with a well-oiled machine producing their minions, are allowed to flex power of the popular, over the messages we hear and the standards of beauty we are expected to uphold. They welcome repetition and the power it invokes within the mind. That is a corruption I disagree with. This manufactured standard, defined by bleached white skin, platinum coloured hair, thin and ripped body shapes and plastic moulded beauty and androgyny is tantamount to child abuse. And covering it up as 'cultural preservation' with cute indeterminate cartoon characters, Bubble Tea and other diabetes inducing boutique delicacies puts these executives-cum-gods in the same respects I put murderous dictators and prize-winning Eugenicists.

But do not forget that music is powerful. All it takes is one song to consume almost half our day. All it takes is another Seo-Taiji to tear it all down. In their 2007 hit 'Videotape', Radiohead used the technique of syncope to create a song with really solemn lyrics into something upbeat for dancing. Syncope is created by setting the rhythm off by a beat. Radiohead not only set their song off the typical stressed and unstressed pattern of contemporary music, but they also speed the pace up. This causes the untrained ear to clap to the wrong beat, which causes a rhythmic confusion that the listener may not notice, but their brain does and let me tell you it creates a really cool sound that stays with you. Creative disruption, even within the repetitious nature of music. A simple move, yet a revolutionary result. This will be the challenge of us all in the ever-changing world, both musician and music listener alike. There is still power in our choices (for the time being). The choices we make will set the stage for a much more defined and controlled world by powers even more shadowy and indistinguishable than music executives. As the Radiohead song asks, 'when I'm at the pearly gates, this will be on my videotape.' As we tap our feet along, will we play that next song, or will that one song play us for the fools we chose to be?

TEN NON-WESTERN
ONE HIT WONDERS

One-hit wonders are disappointing occurrences. A new artist breaks onto the scene with a fresh and innovative sound. Much excitement abounds as they capture the zeitgeist for all of five seconds, only to flounder at any attempt to replicate success. It's doubly deflating when the artist descends from a music tradition that isn't confined to Europe or the US, only to fizzle away as vanilla tastes continue to dominate. Often, an artist regarded as a one-hit wonder may well be a superstar in the country of his or her birth, which makes it rather galling to then be dismissed as a flash in the pan. One is reminded of the Trinidadian reggae artist Queen Omega who teamed up with Manudigital in 2017 to record the instructive *Don't Call Me Local*, in which she laments being sidelined as a 'local' artist when performing at music festivals around the world. As she sings it: 'Don't call me local. I'm internationally blessed wid my vocal. Don't call me no local artist.' Queen Omega will no doubt resonate with our list of musical artists, in no particular order, who created temporary waves in the West. Some of them even managed to create hefty musical legacies in their own countries.

1. 'Jai Ho' by A R Rahman

What happens when a legendary Bollywood composer and acclaimed British film director come together to create an international film sensation? The result is a catchy feelgood song that has people shuffling their bodies and miming lyrics all the way from Mumbai to Barcelona. 'Jai Ho', which roughly translates as 'let the victory prevail', is the perfectly poppy theme tune to Danny Boyle's 1998 sensation *Slumdog Millionaire*, and was written and composed by AR Rahman, the genius behind a plethora of unforgettable *filmi* songs including 'Chaiyya Chaiyya' and a mesmerising collaboration with Talvin Singh titled 'Mumbai Theme Tune'. Such was the mass appeal of 'Jai Ho', the song was picked up by The Pussycat Dolls, who recorded their own version that achieved chart success around the world. Keen to pay homage to the song's origins in the film, The Pussycat Dolls recreated the final scene of Slumdog in the accompanying video of their version 'Jai Ho (You're My Destiny)'.

2. 'Ye Ke Ye Ke' by Mory Kante

Mory Kante stormed to the top of global pop charts in 1987 with his rousing score 'Ye Ke Ye Ke'. Of Malian and Guinean heritage, he belongs to a family of griots, a long line of musicians skilled in the playing of intricate traditional instruments. He is a kora harp oficianado, having mastered vocal ranges characteristic of the performance of griots, and receiving formal griot training in Mali from the age of seven. 'Ye Ke Ye Ke' was taken from his album *Akwaba Beach*, which also featured the devotional song 'Inch Allah', and another track, 'Tama', which formed the basis for the Bollywood film *Thanedaar*'s anthem 'Tamma Tamma', and 'Jumma Chumma', which featured in *Hum*.

3. 'Im Nin'alu' by Ofra Haza

1987 was obviously a year for a taste of the exotic. But pop music fans in the West were not so discerning that they could differentiate between Arab, Hebrew or Indian songs. So it was that when Ofra Haza's dulcet tones wafted across radio airwaves, it was assumed that the 'ethnic' lyrics she sang were attributable to the language of the homogenous and mystical East. All brown persons were expected to understand and therefore translate the song for their eagerly expectant counterparts. In fact, Ofra was a Yemeni-Israeli artist who was huge in her home country and widely referred to as the Israeli Madonna. The song itself is a seventeenth-century Hebrew poem by Rabbi Shalom Shabazi, which opens with the words: 'Even if the gates of the rich are closed, the gates of heaven will never be closed'. Ofra's hypnotic voice was sampled widely by Eric B and Rakim, Public Enemy, Coldcut, Snoop Dogg and Panjabi MC.

4. 'Mundian To Bach Ke' by Panjabi MC (Knight Rider Theme Tune)

Talking of Panjabi MC, his pumped up offering 'Mundian To Bach Ke', featuring the Knight Rider theme tune, has been lifting floors in clubs around the world for the past couple of decades. One of the best selling singles of all time, it was first released in 1997 by the bhangra DJ from Birmingham. Various remixes later, including a sprinkling of star dust courtesy of Jay-Z, and this track is so recognisable that if you ever catch someone asking you the name of 'that totally cool Indian song that's played in all the discos', you instantly know which song they mean. The title roughly translates to mean 'Beware of the Boys' and if you've been fortunate enough to witness David Hasselhoff (of *Knight Rider* fame of course) in his *Baywatch* days, you'll know what we mean.

5. '7 Seconds' by Youssou N'Dour and Neneh Cherry

Senegalese artist Youssou N'Dour was described in 2004 by *Rolling Stone* magazine as 'perhaps the most famous singer alive' in Africa. His fame had by then already crossed continents due to his duet with Neneh Cherry, to which listeners swooned in 1994. '7 Seconds' exudes a sultry and brooding sound complete with delectable lyrics celebrating the initial tender moments in a newborn baby's life: innocent and unaware of the tribulations they are set to face in the world. It reached the top of the charts across Europe and stayed at number one in France for a whopping sixteen weeks. N'Dour is not just a singer/songwriter. Born into a Muslim family of the Wolof tribe, he entered politics in his native Senegal, unsuccessfully running for president, before being appointed Minster of Tourism in 2013.

6. 'Awaara Hoon' by Mukesh

Who would have thought that the Soviet Union would have such an enduring affection for one of Bollywood's giants, the inimitable Raj Kapoor. In 1960s Russia, he was indeed, bigger than the Beatles and decades later is idolised by young and old alike who will on request reel off all his greatest hits. Recently, the president of former Soviet Union republic, Uzbekistan, gladdened the hearts of devotees of retro Indian cinema by apparently regaling an audience at a cultural event with the classic Kapoor anthem *'Awaara Hoon'* ('I am a vagabond') in a YouTube video that went viral. It is the title track of the 1951 film, directed by and starring Raj Kapoor. The song is actually sung by the legendry Bollywood playback singer, Mukesh; and written by the noted Bahari Dalit lyricist and long-standing collaborator of Kapoor, Shailendra. But it has become associated with the persona of Raj Kapoor. One story now mythologised in the Kapoor-Russian love affair occurred during one of Kapoor's many visits to Moscow. He was getting into a taxi outside the airport and was soon quickly recognised by star-struck fans. Before he knew it a crowd had gathered and lifted his taxi off the ground, carrying him off to beat the traffic!

7. *'Woh Humsafar Tha' by Qurat-ul-Ain Balouch*

Qurat-ul-Ain Balouch, also known as QB, rose not just to national acclaim, but even became a familiar voice to the ears of the world over, with the theme song to the highly acclaimed 2011 Pakistani television series, *Hamsafar* (Fellow Traveller). The drama revolves around a battered wife, abused by the mother-in-law and neglected and mistrusted by the husband. The song is in fact a *ghazal*, written in 1971 by Naseer Turabi, and first performed by the legendry Abida Parveen. It is a lament about the succession of East Pakistan (now Bangladesh) from Pakistan. In the Hum TV drama, the song portrays the parting of ways between husband and wife: *Woh Humsafar Tha*, He Was My Fellow Traveller. QB's version became a global hit and made her an international star. Without any formal education, QB developed her voice listening to Sufi and Sindhi Pakistani vocalists. In fact, doing covers was how she began her singing career and was eventually signed to Coke Studio Pakistan. QB most recently took to the world stage being featured in Jason Derulo's 2018 FIFA World Cup theme song 'Colors'.

8. *'Gangnam Style' by Psy*

Emulated in prisons, in hospitals, in schools, in supermarkets and even government chambers, this insanely catchy pop smash dominated the music scene of 2012. What's more it left everyone seemingly possessed with the need to flail their arms around and dance like a waddling duck – we all know the moves even if we can't quite manage them. 'Gangnam Style' was the genius K-pop offering from diminutive South Korean rapper and music producer Psy. The song topped the charts in over thirty countries around the world and was the first YouTube video ever to ratchet up one billion views. A commentary on the Gangnam District of Seoul, the song parodies the rich, self-consciously cool and hyper hip inhabitants of the neighbourhood. Psy's attempt to subvert the concept of Gangnam 'class' left him rich enough to snap a penthouse in that exclusive area of Seoul and thus become a living parody of himself.

9. 'Mustt Mustt' by Nusrat Fateh Ali Khan

Nusrat Fateh Ali Khan, the renowned Pakistani vocalist and musician, has rightly been described as the greatest voice ever recorded. He was an exponent of Qawwali, the Sufi devotional music performed at shrines throughout South Asia. Nusrat brought Qawwali, essentially classical mystical poetry sung in the love and longing for the Divine, to the West. Before he became an international star, Nusrat sung 'Mustt Mustt' without musical accompaniment at various shrines and festivals. In 1990, he collaborated with producer Michael Brook and rock musician Peter Gabriel to produce a fusion version and 'Mustt Mustt' became a sensation during the 1990s, voted the Top 100 albums of the decade. Numerous versions of 'Mustt Mustt' followed, each draining the Qawwali of its spiritual content: a decent enough remix by the British band Massive Attack, a string of Pakistani pop variations, a number of Bollywood versions, and the final insult – a version for a Coca-Cola advertisement. The sublime was eventually reduced to the ridiculous.

10. 'Now We Are Free' by Lisa Gerrard

Now wait a minute, you might be thinking, yes Lisa Gerrard is an Australian which, while geographically is about as far from West as it gets, cultural-politically it is the most Western nation in the world, perhaps the galaxy. But hear us out! The child of Irish immigrants living just outside

Melbourne, Gerrard grew up listening to traditional Mediterranean music and gained her footing in the post-punk Melbourne experimental music scene. She is also a specialist in the Chinese instrument the *yangqin*. She broke onto the world stage when she collaborated with famed composer Hans Zimmer to produce the score for the 2000 film, *Gladiator*. From this film came the song 'Now We Are Free' that not only gained global appeal and popularity, but was commonly mistaken for having lyrics from what popular opinion figured was some non-Western language. In fact, the lyrics were written in an idioglossia. An idioglossia is an invented language used by one or a few people. Idioglossias are common amongst young children, evidenced frequently with identical twins, who make up languages amongst themselves to communicate with a bit more privacy. Children exposed to multiple languages at a young age are more likely to create idioglossias. Lisa Gerrard calls her idioglossia the 'language of the heart'. Perhaps her claims are not so hyperbolic as music itself is a language more common amongst humans and fit for such creations. No doubt, the bravado and timbre of Gerrard's music in *Gladiator* won her awards and the acclaim of audiences in both the East and the West, despite no one having a clue what she was singing about.

CITATIONS

Introduction by Samia Rahman

Josh Wink's 'Higher State of Consciousness' was released in 1995 and came to my attention that same year when I sneaked into my first ever dance festival, the UK Tribal Gathering at Otmoor Park in Oxfordshire, by hiding under a blanket in the back seat of a car. Headline acts included The Prodigy, Orbital and Moby. For further reading on the effect of music on the brain's regulation of dopamine visit PNAS research papers at https://www.pnas.org/content/116/9/3793 and https://www.pnas.org/content/116/9/3364. Muslim lifestyle magazine, *emel*, ran from 2003 until 2013. The 1984 mockumentary *This is Spinal Tap* was directed and co-written by Rob Reiner and features a fictional British heavy metal band on tour in the US. Jim Marcovitch (9/3/74–17/10/08) co-founded klezmer band She'koyokh in 2001. Thank you Jim for all the memories from Kathmandu to New Cross.

Hidden Windows by Jeremy Henzell-Thomas

I have referred to the following in my essay. All websites referred to were accessed during May 2019.

Jeremy Henzell-Thomas, 'Reaching for the Sublime: The Power of Music to Open the Heart', *emel* magazine, June 2007; 'Memories of Sarajevo: The Healing Power of Art and Music', *Emel Magazine*, April 2012; Roger Cohen, 'Music Helps Sarajevo Stay Sane During the War', *The New York Times*, 23/10/1994, https://www.nytimes.com/1994/10/23/world/music-helps-sarajevo-stay-sane-during-war.html; Bonnie C. Wade, 'An ethnomusicological study of music, art and culture in Mughal India' (University of Chicago Press, 1998); Martin Lings, *A Return to the Spirit* (Fons Vitae, Louisville, 2005), 48. Sharon Bryant, 'How Children Benefit from Music Education in Schools', 9/6/2014, https://www.

nammfoundation.org/articles/2014-06-09/how-children-benefit-music-education-schools; Laura Lewis Brown, 'The Benefits of Music Education', https://www.folsomlakesymphony.com/music-education-benefits; Ketki Karanam, 'Music, The Universal Language of Mankind', 16/11/2015, http://syncproject.co/blog/2015/11/9/music-the-universal-language-of-mankind; Oliver Sacks, *Musicophilia: Tales of Music and the Brain* (Knopf, 2007); Interview with Oliver Sacks by Andrea Seabrook, 21/10/2007, https://www.npr.org/templates/transcript/transcript.php?storyId=154 72815&t=1556435530870&t=1557327113175; 'Prof. Oliver Sacks Discusses Healing Power of Music', *Columbia News,* 10/6/2012, at https://news.columbia.edu/news/prof-oliver-sacks-discusses-healing-power-music; Vincent Dowd, 'Afghanistan's first all-female orchestra Zohra visits the UK', *BBC News*, 15/3/2019, https://www.bbc.co.uk/news/entertainment-arts-47571463?SThisFB&fbcliVincetnd=IwAR0Uh SaeF6V3dbUg8R9JOJIznvn0XBNjiAxQOfFtjHWKwopNEIK94HBJRVM; West-Eastern Divan Orchestra at https://www.west-eastern-divan.org; Omar Kasrawi, 'Study: Memories of Music Cannot be Lost to Alzheimer's and Dementia', *Big Think,* 29/4/2018, https://bigthink.com/news/ever-get-the-tingles-from-listening-to-good-music-that-part-of-your-brain-will-never-get-lost-to-alzheimers?fbclid=IwAR2YKp3WAPsuhmzvuIo6Y R7jcNgrbizC7lLvDikcU75CoGKmu6q_WMpv4Dc; '5 Reasons Why Music Boosts Brain Activity', 21/7/2014, https://www.alzheimers.net/why-music-boosts-brain-activity-in-dementia-patients/; John Rampton, 'The Benefits of Playing Music Help Your Brain More Than Any Other Activity', 21/8/2017, https://www.inc.com/john-rampton/the-benefits-of-playing-music-help-your-brain-more.html?fbclid=IwAR2DL; Howard Gardner, *Frames of Mind: The Theory of Multiple Intelligences* (Basic Books, New York, 1983); Shaykh Saleem Bhimji, 'The Status of Music in Islam', https://www.al-islam.org/articles/status-music-islam-shaykh-saleem-bhimji; 'Is Music Haram in Islam?', 11/12/2017, https://hadithoftheday.com/is-music-haram-in-islam/; Abdal Hakim Murad, 'Music in the Islamic Tradition', talk given in April 2017 at the Cambridge Muslim College Retreat, https://www.youtube.com/watch?v=5qJdhhOCv04; John Taylor Gatto, *Dumbing Us Down: The Hidden Curriculum of Compulsory Schooling,* (New Society Publishers, 1992); *The Essential Rumi*, translations by Coleman Barks with John Moyne

(HarperCollins, 1995); Oludamini Ogunnaike, 'The Silent Theology of Islamic Art', *Renovatio*, The Journal of Zaytuna College, 5/12/2017, https://renovatio.zaytuna.edu/article/the-silent-theology-of-islamic-art ?fbclid=IwAR18fuuDEmE51HAquSei5de gKn_qE2DuZMkT9bdVgB_oSExODeGMuXu5EEI.

Qawwali by Ziauddin Sardar

Nusrat Ali Khan's qawwalis are widely available not least on YouTube. On Qawwali see, Regula B Qureshi, Sufi Music and India and Pakistan: Sound and Meaning in Qawwali (University of Chicago Pres, 1995). See also: Inayat Kham The Mysticism of Sound and Music (Shambala, London, 1996) and Victor A Vicente, Dancing to Rumi: The Cultural, Spritiual and Kinetic Dimensions of the Global Sufi Music (Lap Lambert Publishing, 2013).

My Punk Days by Hassan Mahamdallie

This essay is adapted from a series of blogs first published on the Dream Deferred website dreamdeferred.org.uk Thanks to Martin Smith and Tash Shifren. A good book to start with on punk rock and the seventies is Jon Savage's *England's Dreaming*. Faber & Faber, London, 2005. For more on the National Front and Rock Against Racism see my chapter and others in *Reminiscences of RAR*, edited by Roger Huddle and Red Saunders, Redwords, London, 2016.

Aziz Balouch by Stefan Williamson Fa

Aziz Balouch's books include, *Spanish Cante Jondo and its Origin in Sindhi Music* (Mehran Arts Council, Hyderabad, 1968) and *Cante Jondo: Su Origen y Evolución* (Ensayos, Madrisd, 1955). See also: J P Gulrajani, J. P, *Sind and its Sufis* (Theosophical Publishing House, London, 924) and Annemarie Schimmel, *Pearls from the Indus: Studies in Sindhi Culture* (Sindhi Adabi Board, Hyderabad, 1986).

My Pop Star Life by Shanon Shah

I dedicate this essay to the memory of Zaitun (Toni) Mohamed Kasim (1966-2008) and Shiran Mohd Sidik (1971-2019). For a taste of the kind of person Toni was, fellow activist Yeoh Seng Guan's obituary is a good start, although it doesn't quite capture the depth of work she did with the independent arts and theatre scene, which is what made her style of activism so special. It can be found at https://aliran.com/aliran-monthly/2008/2008-5/like-a-star-zaitun-toni-kassim-1966-2008. Toni's quote on the Women's Candidacy Initiative is from https://www.thestar.com.my/news/community/2008/02/19/womens-right-activist-ready-for-the-challenge. My brother was very reclusive and, besides his academic biodata and publications in histopathology, has barely left a digital footprint.

Based on a *fatwa* – technically an Islamic legal opinion, but which carries the force of law in Malaysia – Muslim women are prohibited from entering beauty pageants. For a more detailed reflection from a Malaysian Muslim woman's perspective, read Nadia Mohd Rasidi's excellent contribution, 'Beauty Pageants', in *CM 27: Beauty*.

Amnesty International is still seeking justice and answers from Shell about the execution of Ken Saro-Wiwa. See Hannah Summers, 'Amnesty Calls for Criminal Investigation into Shell over Alleged Complicity in Murder and Torture in Nigeria'. *The Guardian*, 28 November 2017, https://www.theguardian.com/global-development/2017/nov/28/amnesty-seeks-criminal-inquiry-into-shell-over-alleged-complicity-in-murder-and-torture-in-nigeria.

The political context and cultural specificities of Malay humour magazines was studied by the anthropologist Ronald Provencher. I've drawn upon his summary of the history of *Gila-Gila* magazine in his 1990 journal article, 'Covering Malay Humor Magazines: Satire and Parody of Malaysian Political Dilemmas'. *Crossroads: An Interdisciplinary Journal of Southeast Asian Studies* 5 (2): 1–25.

My reflections on 'African philosophy' and cultural nationalism have been profoundly shaped by Paulin J Hountondji, 1996, *African Philosophy: Myth & Reality*. Second Edition. Indianapolis, Indiana: Indiana University Press.

The Women's Candidacy Initiative series of videos can be found on YouTube. I'm particularly chuffed about my adaptation of Justin Timberlake's 'SexyBack' (retitled 'Democracy Back') at https://www. youtube.com/watch?v=6R0Wsj06jz8&t=13s, Fergie's 'Fergalicious' (retitled 'Bedahlicious') at https://www.youtube.com/ watch?v=jONyhlOHZmA, and the Pussycat Dolls' 'Dontcha' (which didn't need retitling) at https://www.youtube.com/ watch?v=0pFFxTAtIVY&t=1s.

My albums, *Dilanda Cinta* (2005) and *Suara Yang Ku Dengar* (2010), were released by InterGlobal Music (Malaysia). A high definition music video of my first single 'Dilanda Cinta' can be found on YouTube.

Sufi Sounds of Senegal by Estrella Sendra

For more on Senegalise music see: Eric Charry, *Mande music: traditional and modern music of the Maninka and the Mandinka of Western Africa* (Chicago: Chicago University Press, 2000); Papis Samba, *Musique sénégalaise: Itinérances et vibrations.*(Vives Voix, Dakar, 2014); Lucy Durán, 'Cheikh Lô' *Folk Roots* 161, 1996: 42-47; Fiona McLaughlin, 'Islam and Popular Music in Senegal: The emergence of a "new tradition".' *Africa*, 67: 4. Edinburgh: Edinburgh University Press, 1997: 560-581; Music in Africa. 'Sénégal: Maïna laureate du programme Visa pour la creation 2019.' *Music in Africa*, 20.08.2019.

On music festivals see, Estrella Sendra, 'Contemporary Festivals in Senegal: Navigating the Local and the International' in Royal African Society, *Contemporary African Arts: Mapping Perceptions, Insights and UK-Africa Collaborations* (British Council, London, 2019).

See also: Khadim Mbacké, *Sufism and Religious Brotherhoods in Senegal* (Markus Winer, Princeton: N. J., 2005)

CRITICAL MUSLIM

Led Zeppelin and Me by Hafeez Burhan Khan

For the best music journalism on Led Zeppelin, read MOJO magazine's interviews with Robert Plant and Jimmy Page from the 1990s and Classic Rock from the 2000s. To find out everything you ever wanted to know about the band read Ritchie Yorke's Led Zeppelin: The Definitive Biography: From Early Days to Page and Plant (Virgin Books, 1999). Also see Paul Rees, Robert Plant: A Life: The Biography (HarperCollins, 2014) to learn about the influence of Arab and Indian traditions on his music.

Meena Kumari by Leyla Jagiella

On the life of Meena Kumari, see Vinod Mehta, Meena Kumari: The Classic Biography (HarperCollins, Delhi, 2013); and Noorul Hasan, Meena Kumari: The Poet (A Life Beyond Cinema) (Roli Books, Delhi, 2014). On Pakeezah see Meghnad Desai, Pakeezah: An Ode to a Bygone Age (HarperCollings, Delhi, 2013). Songs from Meena Kumari's films are widely available on YouTube as are many of her fims. Ziauddin Sardar's A Person of Pakistani Origins is published by Hurst, 2018.

Raving Iran interview with Rim Jasmin Irscheid

Susanne Regina Meures documentary, Raving Iran is available on Dvd, Klagenfurt am Wörthersee: SchröderMedia HandelsgmbH, 2016; see also: 'How a German Filmmaker Secretly Captured Iran's Illegal Techno Scene', Deutsche Welle [DW]. 22 September 2016: http://www.dw.com/en/how-a-german-filmmaker-secretly-captured-irans-illegaltechno-scene/a-19563632.http://www.factmag.com/2017/09/03/sote-iran-ata-ebtekar-interview/.

On Iranian underground music culture, see: Parmis Mozafari, 'Dance and the Borders of Public and Private Life in Post Revolution Iran', in Cultural Revolution in Iran. Contemporary Popular Culture in the Islamic Republic, edited by Annabelle Sreberny and Massoumeh Torfeh (I.B. Tauris, London, 2013); Kaveh Basmenji, Tehran Blubes: Youth Cultures in Iran (Saqi, London, 2005); Laudan Nooshin, 'Underground, Overground: Rock Music and Youth

Discourses in Iran', *Iranian Studies* 38(3):463-494 2005; Ameneh Youssefzadeh, 'The Situation of Music in Iran since the Revolution: The Role of Official Organisations' *British Journal of Ethnomusicology* 9(2):35-61 2000; Mollie Zhang, 'Underground Tehran: Techno & Experimental Electronic Music in Iran' *The Quietus* 12 September 12, 2016: http://thequietus.com/articles/20902-techno-electronic-music-tehran-iran-ash-kooshasote-siavash-amini; Nahid Fallahi, 'Culture in Iran: Music in Rouhani's Iran: A change in tune?' *Qantara* 2017: . https://en.qantara.de/content/culture-in-iran-music-in-rouhanisiran-a-change-in-tune; and Tristan Bath, 'A Guide to Iran's Electronic Underground', *Bandcamp Daily* April 6, 2017: https://daily.bandcamp.com/2017/04/06/iran-electronicmusic/.

On rave culture, see Simon Reynolds, 'Rave Culture: Living Dream or Living Death' in *The Clubcultures Reader: Readings in Popular Cultural Studies*, edited by Steve Redhead, Derek Wynne and Justin O'Connor (Blackwell, Oxford, 1997); and Simon Reynold, *Generation Ecstasy: Into the World of Techno and Rave Culture* (Little Brown, London, 1998).

See also: Howard Backer, Outsiders (Free Press, New York 1973); Orlando Crowcroft, *Rock in a Hard Place: Music and Mayhem in the Middle East* (Zed Books, London, 2017); and Peter Johnson, 'Some reflections on the relationship between utopia and heterotopia', *Heterotopian Studies*, May 2012. http://www.heterotopiastudies.com/wp-content/uploads/2012/05/Reflections-on-therelationship-between-utopia-and-heterotopia.pdf.

Last Word On Recycled Music by C Scott Jordan

On Ear Worms and INMI, see Ashley Welch (2016), "Psychologists identify why certain songs get stuck in your head," *CBS News* 3 November. For more information on repetition and trends in music, especially the return of themes from the 1980s into contemporary Western music, see Estelle Caswell's video reports titled "Earworm" for Vox. The episodes "Why pop songs should end with a fade out", "Why we really really really like repetition in music", "How a recording-studio mishap shaped '80s music" and "the secret rhythm behind Radiohead's "Videotape"" reference in this work. All can be found at https://www.youtube.com/playlist?list =PLJ8cMiYb3G5fyqfIwGjH2fYC5fFLfdwW4. For more on the hidden reality of K-Pop see Jeremy Mersereau (2017) "A brief history of K Pop," The A Side, 14 June, https://ontheaside.com/ music/a-brief-history-of-k-pop/; Justin Heifetz (2016) "Inside the Intense Training Centres Where Young Girls Compete to be K-Pop Stars" *Vice*, 5 October, https://www.vice.com/en_us/article/6vg3n8/primary-and-suran-mannequin-south-korea-interview ; Helienne Lindvall (2013) "How K-Pop and J-Pop Are Saving Physical Music Sales..." *Digital Music News*, 10 April, https://www.digitalmusicnews.com/2013/04/10/kpopjpop/ ; Ben Sit (2018) "Inside the K-pop hit machine: how South Korea's music industry has gone global," *South China Morning Post*, 2 April, https:// w w w . s c m p . c o m / c u l t u r e / m u s i c / a r t i c l e / 2 1 3 9 8 6 4 / inside-k-pop-hit-machine-how-south-koreas-music-industry-has-gone.

CONTRIBUTORS

Mohammad Shahid Alam, a Pakistani economist and social scientist, is professor of Economics at Northeastern University, Illinois ● **Shaizir Aly**, a GP based in Kent, has seen Bruce Springsteen live in concert five times ● **Nadira Babayev** lives in the shadows of her post-communist, sci-fi past ● **Elma Berisha** is working on a book on semiotics ● **Zia Chaudhry**, a barrister, is director of the Foundation for Citizenship at Liverpool John Moores University, Liverpool ● **Wasi Daniju**, a photographer, counsellor and singer, has a penchant for hanging out in libraries and bringing disparate groups of people together ● **Stefan Williamson Fa**, an anthropologist, is co-founder of Mountains of Tongues, a project promoting musical diversity in the Caucasus ● **Ari Haque**, a Bengali British writer, mainly writes personal essays on cultural identity and mental health ● **Jeremy Henzell-Thomas** is a Research Associate and former Visiting Fellow at the Centre of Islamic Studies, University of Cambridge ● **Rim Jasmin Irscheid** graduated in Psychology and Musicology from the University of Heidelberg and continued her graduate studies in ethnomusicology at the University of Oxford ● **Leyla Jagiella** is a cultural anthropologist exploring orthodoxy and heterodoxy in South Asian Islam ● **Azeezat Johnson** is a postdoctoral Fellow at QMUL researching Black feminism and Black Muslim women ● **C Scott Jordan** is Executive Assistant Director of the Centre for Postnormal Policy and Futures Studies and Deputy Editor of Critical Muslim ● **Hafeez Burhan Khan** got 19 out of 20 in a Led Zeppelin Mastermind special, a testament to his encyclopaedic knowledge of all things Zep ● **Hassan Mahamdallie**, a playwright, writer and senior editor of *Critical Muslim* has put his punk days behind him ● **Latifa Nur** is a poet ● **Irna Qureshi** is an oral historian and storyteller who writes about British Asian culture ● **Samia Rahman** is director of the Muslim Institute ● **Katharina Schmoll** is a Lecturer in Media and Communication at the University of Leeds ● **Estrella Sendra** is currently working as Senior Teaching Fellow in Film and Screen Studies at SOAS, University of London ● **Shanon Shah** gave up being a struggling musician to become a struggling academic ● **Paul Abdul Wadud Sutherland**, writer and poet, is founding editor of *Dream Catcher*, the international journal of poetry and prose.